2030

2030

HOW TODAY'S BIGGEST TRENDS WILL COLLIDE AND RESHAPE THE FUTURE OF EVERYTHING

MAURO F. GUILLÉN

ST. MARTIN'S PRESS ≋ NEW YORK

First published in the United States by St. Martin's Press,
an imprint of St. Martin's Publishing Group

Figure 5, page 76, © Homi Kharas, The Brookings Institution

Figure 7, page 115, from United Nations, World Population Prospects 2019 Revision

Figure 8, page 128, from NASA

Lyrics page 178, "Imagine," Words and Music by John Lennon © 1971 (Renewed)
LENONO MUSIC. All Rights Administered by DOWNTOWN DMP SONGS/
DOWNTOWN MUSIC PUBLISHING LLC. All Rights Reserved.
Used by Permission. *Reprinted by Permission of Hal Leonard LLC.*

Figure 9, page 205, Dalí, Salvador (1904–1989) © ARS, NY. "Assumption of the Virgin". Oil
on canvas. 20.1 x 14. © Artists Rights Society, New York. Private Collection.
Photo Credit: Visual Arts Library / Arts Resource, NY.

www.stmartins.com

Book design by Richard Oriolo

Library of Congress Cataloging-in-Publication Data is available upon request

ISBN 9781250268174 (hardcover)

ISBN 9781250268181 (ebook)

Our books may be purchased in bulk for promotional, educational, or business use.
Please contact your local bookseller or the Macmillan Corporate and Premium Sales
Department at 1-800-221-7945, extension 5442, or by email
at MacmillanSpecialMarkets@macmillan.com.

First published in the United States by St. Martin's Press

First Edition: 2020

10 9 8 7 6 5 4 3 2 1

CONTENTS

SOME FACTS AND FIGURES

Birthplace of the next industrial revolution: sub-Saharan Africa
The reason: 500 million acres of fertile yet undeveloped agricultural land
The size of Mexico: 500 million acres

Percentage of the world's wealth owned by women in 2000: 15
Percentage of the world's wealth owned by women in 2030: 55
If Lehman Brothers had been Lehman *Sisters*: global financial crisis averted

Worldwide, the number of people who went hungry in 2017: 821 million
Worldwide, the number of people who will go hungry in 2030: 200 million
Worldwide, the number of people who were obese in 2017: 650 million
Worldwide, the number of people who will be obese in 2030: 1.1 billion
Percentage of Americans projected to be obese in 2030: 50

Percentage of the world's land occupied by cities in 2030: 1.1
Percentage of the world's population living in cities in 2030: 60
Percentage of worldwide carbon emissions produced by cities in 2030: 87
Percentage of world's urban population exposed to rising sea levels in
    2030: 80

The largest middle-class consumer market today: United States and
    Western Europe
The largest middle-class consumer market in 2030: China
By 2030, the number of people entering the middle class in emerging
    markets: 1 billion
The number of people currently in the middle class in the United States:
    223 million
The number of people in the middle class in the United States in 2030:
    209 million

2030

Introduction:
The Clock Is Ticking

People generally see what they look for,

and hear what they listen for.

—JUDGE TAYLOR IN HARPER LEE'S *TO KILL A MOCKINGBIRD*

The year is 2030.

From Paris to Berlin, Western Europe is unusually warm, with no end in sight to the summer's record temperatures, a fact the international press reports with increasing alarm. Rehema has just landed in her native Nairobi on a return flight from London, where she spent a couple of weeks with some distant relatives. She was disappointed to see fewer stores open than during her previous trip, perhaps because so many people had become used to buying online during the pandemic. Seeing Britain through the eyes of immigrants afforded her great insight into the diversity of the world around her. Walking through the Nairobi airport, she reflects on how her homeland differs from Britain, which she found to be behind Kenya in areas like tele-medicine and mobile payments. Later, she jokes with her cousin on the trip home at how strangely the British reacted when she told them she had been "attending" an online school since she was six, along with most of her neighborhood friends.

Thousands of miles away, Angel is waiting to clear customs at JFK Airport in New York City. In two weeks' time, she will begin a two-year master of science program at New York University. As she waits, she reads the day's *New York Times,* which opens with a report that the United States, for the first time in its history, has more grandparents than grandchildren—a reality in stark contrast to the situation back home in the Philippines. As it turns out, tens of thousands of American senior citizens, under the care of robots for their basic needs, are renting out spare rooms in their homes to make ends meet, especially since their pensions are no longer providing the financial safety net they once expected. Angel turns to a rather reactionary op-ed decrying the fact that American women now outpace men in terms of their share of wealth, a trend the author somehow finds disturbing for the future of the U.S. economy. Angel has time to read most of the newspaper, as the line for foreigners is long and slow-moving. Meanwhile, the line for citizens and permanent residents is moving quite quickly, and she overhears a conversation detailing how Americans can now clear passport control using some fancy blockchain technology, which is a breakthrough with a wide range of benefits: it can assess a sales tax on goods purchased abroad and arrange for the arrival of a self-driving vehicle shortly after you've retrieved your luggage.

·

2020: "China will be number one at everything."

That's a phrase one hears frequently nowadays. Another is that the United States and China will battle for global supremacy for the foreseeable future. There is some truth to these statements, but they hardly reveal the whole picture. In 2014, India stunned the world by successfully placing a space probe in orbit around Mars—the first country to accomplish the feat in its maiden attempt. Since the dawn of the space age, fewer than half of the missions launched by the United States, Russia, and Europe have been successful, making India's accomplishment truly extraordinary. What's more, the Indian Space Research Organisation made history with the mission's low $74 million budget.

Now, exactly how much money should it take to set a satellite orbiting around the red planet? Well, a single space shuttle mission might burn as much as $450 million, and it cost $165 million to produce the movie *Interstellar* and $108 million to bring *The Martian* to a theater near you.

The Indians demonstrated that they too have the "right stuff," as Tom Wolfe once put it. They showed they are a world-class technological power-house and can get things done efficiently and on time. The Mars mission wasn't a fluke. In fact, it was the second time that India had surged ahead of the world's established superpowers. Back in 2009, its maiden mission to the Moon pro-duced the first evidence of the existence of water, "apparently concentrated at the poles and possibly formed by the solar wind," as *The Guardian* reported. It took NASA ten years to independently confirm India's finding.

Most of us grew up in a world in which the exploration of the cosmos was an expensive endeavor conceived by rocket scientists, funded by global super-powers with vast resources, and carried out by heroic astronauts and capable mission specialists. The comparative complexity and cost of space missions (and which countries had the capacity to accomplish them) were taken for granted. But that reality is now part of history.

Once upon a time, not only was the world neatly divided into prosperous and backward economies, but babies were plentiful, workers outnumbered re-tirees, and people yearned to own homes and cars. Companies didn't need to see any farther than Europe and the United States to do well. Printed money was legal tender for all debts, public and private. In school they told us how we were supposed to "play the game," and we grew up thinking that the rules would remain the same as we took our first job, started a family, saw our chil-dren leave the house, and went into retirement.

That familiar world is rapidly vanishing as we encounter a bewildering new reality driven by a new set of rules. Before we know it there will be more grand-parents than grandchildren in most countries; collectively, middle-class mar-kets in Asia will be larger than those in the United States and Europe combined;

women will own more wealth than men; and we will find ourselves in the midst of more industrial robots than manufacturing workers, more computers than human brains, more sensors than human eyes, and more currencies than countries.

That will be the world in 2030.

I have conducted research on the outlook ten years down the road over the last few years. As a professor at the Wharton School, I worry not only about the future state of business but also about how workers and consumers might be affected by the avalanche of change coming our way. I've made countless presentations on the material contained in this book to audiences as diverse as executives, policymakers, middle managers, and college and high school students. I have also reached out to tens of thousands of people through social media and online courses. Invariably, my audiences react with a mix of bewilderment and apprehension to the future I outline to them.

This book offers a road map to navigate the turbulence ahead.

Nobody knows for sure what the future will bring. If you do, please let me know—together we can make truckloads of money. But while predictions are never fully accurate, we can certainly make a series of relatively safe assumptions about what might happen in the decade to come. For example, the majority of people impacted by the forecasts in this book have already been born. We can perhaps describe in general terms what we can expect of them as consumers, given their likely educational attainment or current patterns of social media activity. We can also calculate with reasonable accuracy how many people will live to be eighty or ninety years old. And we may even be in a position to predict with some acceptable degree of confidence that a certain percentage of seniors will need a care provider—whether it's another human or a robot. When it comes to the latter, imagine that these robots speak different languages with a variety of accents, aren't opinionated, don't take days off, and don't abuse their patients financially or otherwise.

The clock is ticking. The year 2030 isn't some remote point in the unforeseeable future. It's right around the corner, and we need to prepare ourselves for both the opportunities and the challenges. Simply put, the world as we know it today will be gone by 2030.

For many of us these trends are not only confusing but profoundly unsettling. Do they spell our downfall? Or might they actually represent more boom than doom? This book provides a guide to help readers grasp the implications of so many moving parts, and it offers a message of optimism about the future while we are managing the anxieties of the present. It presents a tool to help navigate the epochal transformations ahead, suggesting what to do and what not to do under these new and unfamiliar circumstances.

The basic point is this: every finale signifies the dawn of a new reality replete with opportunity—if you dare to dig beneath the surface, anticipate the trends, engage rather than disconnect, and learn how to make effective decisions for yourself, your children, your partner or spouse, your future family, your company, and so forth. Everyone will be impacted.

▪

It's useful to think about epochal transformations as a slow process, with each tiny change bringing us closer to a paradigm shift when, all of a sudden, everything is different. We tend to forget that these small changes are cumulative. Think about it as a slow drip filling up a container, where the *drip-drip-drip* conveys a sense of time passing. When the water suddenly overflows, we're caught by surprise.

Consider that by 2030, South Asia and sub-Saharan Africa will be vying for the title of the world's most populous region. That's a far cry from the final years of the twentieth century, when East Asia—comprising China, South Korea, and Japan, among other countries—was the region that could make that claim. It's true that as time goes on, fewer babies are being born in countries like Kenya and Nigeria, but they're still arriving in far greater numbers compared to most of the world. In addition, people in those regions are seeing their life expectancy lengthen significantly.

You might think that sheer population size doesn't matter much. Well, multiply those additional people by how much money they might have in their pockets in the years to come. You'll see that around 2030 Asian markets, even excluding Japan, will be so large that the center of gravity of global consumption will shift eastward. Companies will have no choice but to follow market trends in that part of the world, with most new products and services reflecting the preferences of Asian consumers.

Pause for a moment and think about that.

Then consider what it means as we add a few more intertwined trends.

Fewer babies in most parts of the world means that we are steadily marching toward a rapidly aging population. Much of that demographic shift is driven by women, who more and more are remaining in school and pursuing careers (not merely jobs) outside of the home—and bearing fewer children. Before you realize it, there will be more female millionaires than male millionaires. Wealth is also becoming more urban: the population of cities is growing at a rate of 1.5 million per week. While cities occupy just 1 percent of the world's land area, they are home to 55 percent of the population and account for 80 percent of energy consumption (and carbon emissions). That's why cities are on the front lines of efforts to combat climate change.

Meanwhile, different generations of people are displaying divergent longings and aspirations. Millennials are spearheading the sharing economy (while eschewing ownership), but they're getting more attention than they deserve. Within a decade, the largest generation will be the population above age sixty, which today owns 80 percent of the wealth in the United States and is giving rise to the "gray market"—the largest consumer bloc of all. Companies large and small should redirect some of their attention to senior citizens if they wish to remain relevant as time goes on.

Look at Figure 1. It depicts a process of concatenated small changes. In isolation, none of them will result in a shift of truly global proportions. You might be perfectly capable of coping with the changes if you keep each of them separate from the others. Humans are great at mental compartmentalization. It's a subconscious psychological defense mechanism. We use it to avoid cognitive dissonance—the discomfort and anxiety caused by conflicting trends, events, perceptions, or emotions. The whole point of mental compartmentalization is to keep things apart so that we are not overwhelmed by the interactions among them.

Population aging is becoming the norm in America and Western Europe. Meanwhile, the younger generations are driving the ascendancy of the middle class in most emerging markets. They are a very different type of consumer from the one the world has seen so far; more aspirational in their habits, for example. As the middle classes expand, more and more women will accumulate wealth like never before, with both genders adopting urban lifestyles and driving the largest influx of migration we've ever witnessed to cities around the world. And cities create a critical mass of inventors and entrepreneurs intent on disrupting the status quo with innovation and technology.

For their part, technologies alter old habits and lifestyles, bringing forth new ways to think about and engage with everything from homes and offices to cars and personal items. This, in turn, will lead to alternative conceptions of money that are more distributed, more decentralized, and easier to use. Some of these trends are already under way, but they will not reach critical mass until around 2030. (All of these trends, however, accelerate and intensify when an epochal event occurs, like the COVID-19 pandemic, which I explore in detail in the Postscript.)

Such a *linear* representation of the changes taking place around us provides for a neat and convenient sequence of chapters for this book. But that's not how the world really works.

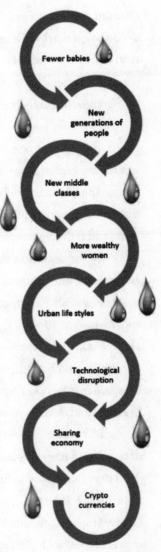

Figure 1

Anthropologists and sociologists have long established that we reduce the complexity of the world by breaking it into categories, which enables us to sort things out, develop strategies, make decisions, and carry on with our lives. Those categories serve as frames of reference, helping us navigate the often ambiguous nature of our surrounding landscapes. They reassure us that we remain in control.

Companies and organizations also think this way. They compartmentalize everything. They put customers into little boxes such as "lead users," "early adopters," or "laggards." They classify products as "stars," "cash cows," "dogs," or "question marks," depending on their present market share and future potential growth. And they consider employees to be "team players" or "ladder-climbers," depending on their attitudes, behavior, and potential.

Compartmentalizing, however, blinds you to new possibilities.

Let me offer you an example. In addition to the electric lightbulb, the telephone, and the car, one of the great inventions of the late nineteenth century was the concept of retirement: a period dedicated to our hobbies and our families, and our chance to reflect on all that we've accomplished. We inherited from that century a concept of life as a progression of distinct stages—childhood, work, and retirement—that we, hopefully, enjoy along the way.

With the decline in the number of babies and the new dynamics between generations, our future society may well have to rethink quite a few assumptions of how we have traditionally lived. Senior citizens are also consumers, with distinctive lifestyles, and they can be technological early adopters as much as millennials, if not more so. Think about virtual reality, artificial intelligence, or robotics and how these technologies will revolutionize the tail end of our lives. We may have to dispel the old order. Unlike in the past, we may re-enroll in school and develop new skills many times over before we're done. Consider this headline that ran in the *New York Times* in 2019: "Running Out of Children, a South Korean School Enrolls Illiterate Grandmothers."

I urge that we avoid linear thinking, sometimes called "vertical" thinking, as in Figure 1. Instead, I suggest we approach change laterally. Developed by inventor and consultant Edward de Bono, the concept of lateral thinking "is concerned not with playing with the existing pieces but with seeking to change those very pieces." It essentially involves reframing questions and attacking problems sideways. Breakthroughs occur not when someone works within the established paradigm but when assumptions are abandoned, rules are ignored, and creativity runs amok. The artists Picasso and Braque pioneered Cubism by departing from accepted assumptions and rules about proportion and perspective. Le Corbusier launched modernist architecture by eliminating walls to create large open spaces, letting windows run the full length of a building's façade, and exposing the intrinsic elegance of steel, glass, and cement without

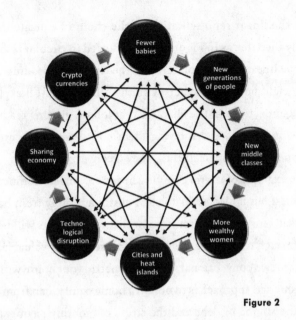

Figure 2

attempting to hide it behind superfluous ornaments. "The real voyage of discovery consists not in seeking new landscapes," Marcel Proust once wrote, "but in having new eyes."

Indeed, lateral thinking can be further augmented through "peripheral vision," a concept developed by my Wharton colleagues George Day and Paul Schoemaker. Very much as with human vision, companies and other types of organizations cannot be effective if they do not sense, interpret, and act on the weak signals coming from the periphery of their immediate area of focus.

For example, Kodak, founded in 1888, made massive profits selling photographic film and other related products throughout the twentieth century. In the early 1990s, its engineers became aware of the possibilities of digital photography, but top management was more focused on the short term, believing that people would continue to prefer printed pictures. The result? In 2012, Kodak filed for bankruptcy. They were a victim of a phenomenon well expressed by Judge Taylor in Harper Lee's *To Kill a Mockingbird*: "People generally see what they look for, and hear what they listen for"—they're blind to the unexpected, the unusual, the periphery.

Consider Figure 2, above, an alternative graphical representation of what's going on in the world.

The thicker block arrows pointing clockwise around the rim of the chart depict the linear representation of the chain of concatenated trends; it's essentially the same as in Figure 1, but arranged in circular fashion. Focusing only on the linear connections around the chart is misleading. Each of the trends in the eight bubbles interacts with the other seven. I'll explore each of those lateral connections in the chapters that follow, guiding readers through these intertwined trends and showing them how these trends are occurring around the globe—and especially how they'll converge in 2030.

Here's an example of lateral thinking in action. Airbnb competes for business with hotels, but it also seeks to steal customers away from banks. How? Many senior citizens realize at some point that their savings will not suffice to carry them through retirement. But they do possess a very valuable asset: their home. There are two conventional ways to monetize your house without selling it. The old-fashioned approach is to obtain a home equity loan from a bank, but that carries the stigma of debt and the stress of monthly payments. Another possibility is to obtain a reverse mortgage (relinquish equity), but then the children won't inherit the family home.

Enter Airbnb. Empty-nesters can rent the extra rooms they don't use to travelers who will be in the area for a short while, an arrangement that gives both parties more flexibility. Or, if the empty-nesters travel or visit their children a lot and frequently aren't home, they can choose to rent the whole house for short-term stays. Either way, they're getting money *and* keeping their home. Airbnb wouldn't be so successful if it weren't for a number of converging trends: declining fertility, longer life expectancy, doubts about the future viability of public pensions, expanded use of smartphones and apps, and a growing interest in sharing rather than owning. I will guide you through these interrelated developments, showing how they unfold, and how they will all reach critical mass by 2030. This new world presents opportunities and threats; individuals, companies, and organizations will each have their own strengths and weaknesses in confronting them. Yet, as I show in the conclusion, all of us will need to approach this new world differently than we have approached things in the past. The closing pages offer principles and approaches we can use to make sense of this new reality—and prosper from the opportunities it creates.

Remember, it's all unfolding in our lifetime, and it's right around the corner.

1.

Follow the Babies

POPULATION DROUGHT, THE AFRICAN BABY
BOOM, AND THE NEXT INDUSTRIAL REVOLUTION

A baby comes to the world not only with a mouth and
a stomach, but also with a pair of hands.

—EDWIN CANNAN, BRITISH ECONOMIST AND DEMOGRAPHER

The pace of population growth seems terrifying. In 1820 there were a billion people on Earth. A century later, there were more than 2 billion. After a brief hiatus resulting from the Great Depression and World War II, the rate of growth gathered breathtaking speed: 3 billion by 1960, 4 billion by 1975, 5 billion by 1987, 6 billion by 2000, and 7 billion by 2010. "Population control or race to oblivion?" was a tagline on the cover of Stanford University professors Paul and Anne Ehrlich's highly influential book *The Population Bomb,* published in 1968. Since then, governments around the world and large segments of the public have been seriously alarmed by what they think is inevitable: we'll overrun the planet and destroy ourselves (and millions of plant and animal species) in the process.

The reality is that by 2030 we will be facing a baby *drought*.

Over the next few decades, the world's population will grow less than half as swiftly as it did between 1960 and 1990. In some countries, the population will actually decrease in size (absent very high rates of immigration). For instance, since the early 1970s, American women have on average had fewer than two babies each over their reproductive lifetime—a rate insufficient to ensure generational replacement. The same is also true in many other places around the world. People in countries as diverse as Brazil, Canada, Sweden, China, and Japan are starting to wonder who will take care of the elderly and pay their pensions.

As birth rates decline in East Asia, Europe, and the Americas, combined with a much slower decline in Africa, the Middle East, and South Asia, the global balance of economic and geopolitical power shifts. Consider: For every baby born nowadays in developed countries, more than nine are being born in the emerging markets and the developing world. Told another way, for every baby born in the United States, 4.4 are being born in China, 6.5 in India, and 10.2 in Africa. Moreover, improvements in nutrition and disease prevention in the poorest parts of the world have made it possible for an increasing number of babies to reach adulthood and become parents themselves. Half a century ago one in four children under the age of fourteen in African countries such as Kenya and Ghana died, whereas today it's fewer than one in ten.

These swift changes in the relative populations of various parts of the world are being driven not only by who's having more babies but also by whose life expectancy is increasing more rapidly. For instance, back in the 1950s people born in the least developed parts of the world were expected to live an average of thirty *fewer* years than those born in the most developed. Nowadays the difference is seventeen years. Between 1950 and 2015, mortality rates dropped by just 3 percent in Europe but by a whopping 65 percent in Africa. The poorer countries are catching up in life expectancy thanks to lower mortality across all age groups.

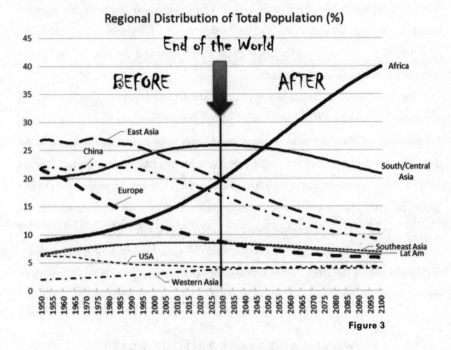

Figure 3

To assess the worldwide impact of these demographic shifts, look at Figure 3. It shows the percentage of the world's total population in different regions between 1950 and 2017, with forecasts to the year 2100 as calculated by the United Nations.

Focus your attention on 2030. By that year, South Asia (including India) will consolidate its position as the number-one region in terms of population size. Africa will become the second-largest region, while East Asia (including China) will be relegated to third place. Europe, which in 1950 was the second largest, will fall to sixth place, behind Southeast Asia (which includes Cambodia, Indonesia, the Philippines, and Thailand, among other countries) and Latin America.

International migration might partially mitigate these epochal changes by redistributing people from parts of the world with a surplus of babies toward others with a deficit. In fact, that has happened repeatedly throughout history, as when many Southern Europeans migrated to Northern Europe during the 1950s and 1960s. This time around, however, migration won't offset the population trends (see data in figure 3). I say this because too many govern-ments seem intent on building walls, whether the old-fashioned way (with brick and mortar), by leveraging technology such as lasers and chemical detectors to monitor border crossings, or both.

But even if the walls are never built or something renders them ineffective, my forecasts indicate that the impact of migration may not have a big impact on these population trends. Given present levels of migration and population growth, sub-Saharan Africa—the fifty African countries that do not border on the Mediterranean Sea—will become the second-most populous part of the globe by 2030. Let's assume for a moment that migration doubles in volume over the next twenty years. But twice as much migration will merely delay that reckoning until the year 2033. It won't derail the main population trends lead-ing to the end of the world as we know it, but merely postpone them by approxi-mately three years.

WOMEN AND BABIES RULE THE WORLD

So what's behind the global fertility slowdown? This is a tricky question to an-swer. After all, conceiving babies involves a widely known method that's easy to use and exceedingly popular. Let me begin answering the question by telling you about my own family tree. One of my great-great-grandmothers in Spain went through twenty-one pregnancies, giving birth to nineteen babies. Her first was born when she was twenty-one, and her last when she was forty-two. As the country developed and women gained better access to education, fami-lies became smaller, all the way down to one or two children per woman.

What's important to grasp is that in other parts of the world, including Africa, the Middle East, and South Asia, there are millions of women today who give birth to five, ten, or even more babies over their lifetime. On aver-age, however, the number of babies per woman is also falling in the developing countries as time goes by, and for the same reasons it began to plummet in the developed world two generations ago. Women now enjoy more opportunities outside the household. To seize those opportunities, they remain in school and, in many cases, pursue higher education. This, in turn, means that they postpone childbearing. The change in women's roles in the economy and in society more generally is the single most important factor behind the decline in fertility worldwide. Women are increasingly determining what happens around the world.

Consider the case of the United States, where women's priorities have shifted rapidly. In the 1950s, American women married on average at the age of twenty; men, on average, married at twenty-two. Nowadays it's twenty-seven and twenty-nine, respectively. The average age of first-time mothers has also climbed, to twenty-eight. Much of this change has been driven by longer schooling. More women now graduate from high school, and more of them go on to get a college education. Back in the fifties about 7 percent of women between the ages of twenty-five and twenty-nine had a college degree, half the rate of men. Nowadays, the proportion of women with a college degree is nearly 40 percent, while for men the figure is only 32 percent.

OUR DECLINING INTEREST IN SEX

The evolution of human populations tends to be messy. For millennia, population growth was shaped by the availability of food, the occurrence of wars, the spread of disease, and the impact of natural disasters. Philosophers, theologians, and scientists have wrestled for centuries with the question of how many human beings can be supported by Earth's resources. In 1798, the Reverend Thomas Robert Malthus, a British economist and demographer, warned about what would later become known as the "Malthusian trap," or our tendency to overbreed and deplete our sources of sustenance. During Malthus's lifetime, the world's population was below 1 billion (compared to today's 7.5 billion). He thought that humans are their own worst enemies because of their unfettered sexual impulses. In his view, runaway population growth would result in famine and disease because the food supply could not keep pace with the population. Malthus and many of his contemporaries feared that the human species was at risk of extinction due to overbreeding. "The power of population," he wrote, "is so superior to the power in the earth to produce subsistence for man, that premature death must in some shape or other visit the human race."

With the benefit of hindsight, we can say today that Malthus underestimated the potential of invention and innovation, which has led to phenomenal improvements in agricultural yields. He also downplayed the immense possibilities for expanding the food supply through international trade thanks to faster and cheaper transoceanic transportation. He was correct, however, in emphasizing that population and food are two sides of the same coin.

If Malthus underestimated the potential impact of innovation on food production and distribution, he completely missed how modern technology might reduce our appetite for sex. The connection between the two is disarmingly simple. The greater the number of alternative forms of entertainment that become available to us, the less frequently we engage in sex. Modern society offers a panoply of entertainment options, from radio and TV to video games and social media. In some developed countries, including the United States, rates of sexual activity have been declining over the last few decades. A comprehensive study published in the *Archives of Sexual Behavior* found that "American adults had sex about nine fewer times per year in the early 2010s compared to the late 1990s," a decline mostly felt among married Americans and those with a steady partner. Adjusting for age, "those born in the 1930s (Silent generation) had sex the most often, whereas those born in the 1990s (Millennials and iGen) had sex the least often." The study concluded that "Americans are having sex less frequently due to . . . an increasing number of individuals without a steady or marital partner and a decline in sexual frequency among those with partners."

One amusing example demonstrating the effect of alternative forms of entertainment on our sexual appetite involves a blackout. In 2008, on the island of Zanzibar, off the coast of East Africa, one particularly nasty power outage lasted an entire month. It only affected the part of the island where homes were connected to the grid; the rest of the population continued to use their diesel generators. This situation provided researchers with a unique "natural experiment" to study the effect of the blackout on people's fertility behavior because the "treatment group" of utility grid customers went without electricity for a month, while the "control group" using diesel generators did not. Nine months later, about 20 percent more babies than usual were born in the treatment group, but no such increase took place in the control group.

MONEY MAKES THE WORLD GO ROUND

Money, unsurprisingly, also plays a big factor in our fertility decisions. In 2018, the *New York Times* commissioned a survey to discover why Americans are having fewer children or no children at all. Four of the top five reasons had to do with money. "Wages are not growing in proportion to the cost of living, and with student loans on top of that, it's just really hard to get your financial footing—even if you've gone to college, work in a corporate job and have dual incomes," observed David Carlson, a twenty-nine-year-old married man whose wife also works. Young people from lower-income families are also fearful about having children, forced to choose between starting a family or spending money on other valuable things. For example, Brittany Butler, a native of Baton Rouge, Louisiana, is the first in her family to graduate from college. At age twenty-two, her priorities are getting a graduate degree in social work, paying down her student loans, and living in a safe neighborhood. Babies can wait.

Back in the 1960s, the University of Chicago economist Gary Becker proposed a pathbreaking way of thinking about people's fertility decisions: parents make trade-off calculations between the *quantity* and the *quality* of children they desire to have. For example, as family incomes rise, people may buy a second or third automobile, but they don't purchase a dozen or two dozen of them if their finances continue to improve indefinitely. They don't buy a dozen refrigerators or washing machines either. Becker reasoned that instead of increasing quantity, rising incomes lead people to focus on quality; that is, they replace their clunkers with newer, larger, or more luxurious sedans or SUVs. In the case of children, this translates into paying more attention and devoting more resources to a smaller number of children. "The interaction between quantity and quality of children," he wrote, "is the most important reason why the effective price of children rises with income," meaning that as parents see their earnings rise, they prefer to invest more in each child, giving them better opportunities in life.

Becker's insights about human behavior earned him the 1992 Nobel Memorial Prize in Economic Sciences, and though his treatment of such a complex subject as fertility neglected the role of preferences and cultural norms and values, he did put his finger on an important societal trend. Many parents nowadays would much rather invest more of their time and resources in a smaller number of children and provide them with the best possible chance to succeed, whether that means starting a college savings plan or paying for extracurricular activities. As Philip Cohen, a sociologist at the University of Maryland, explains, "We want to invest more in each child to give them the best opportunities to compete in an increasingly unequal environment." From this perspective, children are investment projects, with net present values and rates of return.

To understand how parents make decisions about the number of children they'd like to have, it is instructive to calculate how much they spend on each of them. In 2015, the federal government calculated that the average American family would spend the staggering sum of $233,610 to raise a child until age seventeen. That amount can easily double if one includes paying for college. On my laptop, I have a spreadsheet in which one can list family income and expenses for each year. It is striking to note that the average American family may end up spending well in excess of half a million dollars on each of their children, assuming they graduate from an expensive college. I created a second spreadsheet with the same information except that it excludes the children and their expenses. At the bottom of that second spreadsheet, instead of a highly educated child, people would have a luxury car or a vacation home on the shore.

CAN GOVERNMENT "BIG BROTHERS"
INFLUENCE OUR FERTILITY DECISIONS?

A few years ago, the Singaporean government tried to put this question to the test. It was concerned that couples in this tiny but affluent island nation where three-quarters of the population are ethnic Chinese were forgoing having babies in favor of the "five C's"—cash, car, credit card, condominium, and country club. Officials wrote a letter to a sample of childless married couples arguing that it was necessary for the country to have a young population in order to sustain the growth of its burgeoning economy. The missive included an unusual offer: a free vacation in Bali, which the government thought would help couples get in the mood. The couples, eager for a chance to spend some time on a beautiful beach, jumped at the opportunity. They took the vacation, but did not uphold their end of the bargain—no babies were born, at least not enough to satisfy government officials. The pilot program was discontinued after nine months.

The People's Republic of China also tried to change population trends, with its draconian one-child policy. In the late 1970s, faced with a backward and disorganized collectivistic economy, Chinese reformers, led by the visionary Deng Xiaoping, concluded that the county's rapid population growth could only lead to continued poverty. They had studied Chinese history carefully: Their country's population grew at roughly the same pace as Western Europe's between 1500 and 1700, but much faster during the 1700s, a long period of peace and prosperity that enabled agricultural output to expand in an unprecedented way. During that time yields in rice and wheat fields increased two- and even threefold, and new crops transplanted from the Americas such as maize and sweet potatoes helped boost productivity. This increased the standard of living in parts of China even sooner than in England, the birthplace of the first industrial revolution. Between 1800 and 1950, population growth actually *slowed* in the lower Yangtze River watershed. Much of this was also due to overfarming, political turmoil, civil wars, and foreign interventions and invasions.

But then, in spite of the awful famine caused by the Great Leap Forward of the 1950s and the dislocation of the Cultural Revolution of the 1960s, the People's Republic of China added between 120 and 150 million people during each of the three decades between 1950 and 1979. China was then close to becoming the first country to have a population in excess of 1 billion. Deng and his fellow reformers concluded that if something wasn't done about this, the country would face economic ruin. In 1979, the coercive one-child policy was launched.

But it turned out that the policymakers were unaware of the reality that fertility in China had been dropping precipitously since the 1960s, with most of the decrease driven by the same factors as in other parts of the world: urbanization, women's education and labor force participation, and the growing preference for giving children greater opportunities in life as opposed to having a large number of them. The policymakers did not think laterally about the problem. Consider the following figures: Back in 1965, the fertility rate in urban China was about 6 children per woman. By 1979, when the one-child policy came into effect, it had already declined all the way down to about 1.3 children per woman, well below the replacement level of at least 2 children per woman. Meanwhile, in rural China, fertility hovered around 7 children per woman in the mid-1960s, a number that decreased to about 3 by 1979. During the one-child policy period, the urban rate came down from 1.3 to 1.0, while the rural rate decreased from 3 to 1.5. As demographers writing in the *China Journal* have pointed out, "Most of China's fertility decline cannot be attributed to the one-child policy." The slowdown was driven by people's decisions under changing circumstances, not by government bureaucrats. "The one-child campaign was based on politics and pseudo-science, rather than on necessity, much less on good demography," the experts concluded.

In 2015, China eliminated the policy altogether. Will population growth now resume in the world's second-largest economy? Nobel laureate and economist Amartya Sen notes that "women's progress outdid China's one-child policy." Access to education and job opportunities continues to expand for Chinese women, which means an increase in children is unlikely. As a point of comparison, in neighboring Taiwan and South Korea—where such a policy never existed—the fertility rate hovers around 1.1 children per woman, well below China's current level of 1.6. In the end, the popular slogan "Economic development is the best contraceptive" proved to be as true in China as elsewhere in the world.

Ironically, the largest impact of the one-child policy will be generational. By 2030 China will have 90 million *fewer* people between the ages of fifteen and thirty-five and 150 million *more* people above the age of sixty. The country is experiencing the largest and fastest process of population aging in the world. We will analyze the implications of these whopping generational changes in Chapter 2.

THE SURPRISING BENEFICIARY OF CHINA'S ONE-CHILD POLICY

These days the news is full of stories about trade deficits, stolen technology, and Chinese spies masquerading as businesspeople. "One in Five Companies Say China Has Stolen Their Intellectual Property," read a 2019 headline in *Fortune* magazine. It would seem, according to many, that China is out to get the United States and other Western countries, that the upcoming global giant is on the path to overtake us by hook or by crook.

Few politicians or journalists consider that China's one-child policy has represented a formidable windfall for the American consumer. In a fascinating example of lateral thinking, economists found an improbable connection between fertility and savings. While it was the law, the one-child policy created a gender imbalance of about 20 percent more young men than women, driven by the cultural preference for boys. "A Distorted Sex Ratio Is Playing Havoc with Marriage in China," read a 2017 headline in the *Economist*. "In China," the *New York Times* echoed, "A Lonely Valentine's Day for Millions of Men." Parents decided to take matters into their own hands. "Due to intensified competition in the marriage market, households with a son ratchet up their savings rates, in hopes of improving their son's odds of finding a wife," concluded economists Shang-Jin Wei and Xiaobo Zhang after exhaustively analyzing a wealth of data. "The increase in the sex ratio from 1990 to 2007 can explain about 60 percent of the actual increase in the household savings rate during this period." This phenomenon has been so widespread that China exported not only a variety of manufactured goods but also its excessive savings. Americans' voracious consumption was mostly funded through the savings of families. Without the Chinese gender imbalance and its associated high level of savings, Americans would have had to pay higher interest rates on their mortgages and consumer loans over the last two decades. For instance, had interest rates for a fixed thirty-year mortgage loan been on average 6 percent over the last twenty years as opposed to 5 percent, the monthly payment would have been about 25 percent higher, leaving much less money for other purchases. Thus the cost of buying a home in San Francisco has indeed something to do with the price of tea in China, as the old saying goes.

The Chinese gender imbalance has also affected consumption in the new digital economy. Consider how much money people spend on digital dating services of various kinds. Dating platforms now have hundreds of millions of customers worldwide who spend a total of about $5 billion annually. People are flocking to them in search of potential marriage partners, romantic relationships, or one-night stands. But the differences in spending patterns by nation are revealing. In China, just 2 percent of total partner-search spending goes toward casual dating apps, whereas in Europe and the United States, 21 percent of spending goes to platforms that offer just that, such as Ashley Madison, C-Date, First Affair, Victoria Milan, and Tinder. By contrast, 85 percent of spending in China goes to matchmaking services such as Baihe and Jiayuan, compared to only 40 percent in Europe and the United States. This disparity is easily explained. For Chinese men, finding a long-term partner (as opposed to a one-night stand) is more important, as the gender imbalance has created somewhat of a national crisis. It should also be no surprise that Chinese women have become much more selective. In an experiment involving artificial profiles of men and women on one of China's largest dating platforms, "men of all income levels visited our female profiles of different income levels at roughly equal rates," the authors found. "In contrast, women of all income levels visited our male profiles with higher incomes at higher rates. . . . Our male profiles with the highest level of income received 10 times more visits than the lowest."

Curiously enough, in other countries the gender imbalance goes in the opposite direction. In Russia there is a deficit of young men because so many of them die prematurely, mostly from excessive drinking. The problem appears to be so bad that in some parts of Siberia the scarcity of men of marriageable age has led women to lobby the government to legalize polygamy. According to Caroline Humphrey, an anthropologist at Cambridge University, Siberian women have increasingly become persuaded that "half a good man is better than none at all." They argue that "the legalization of polygamy would be a godsend: it would give them rights to a man's financial and physical support, legitimacy for their children, and rights to state benefits." It goes without saying that the ideal solution would be for China and Russia to trade with each other, given that China has more men and Russia more women. Unfortunately, the Chinese gender imbalance is seven times greater than the Russian gender gap because the Chinese population is so much bigger. Matchmaking apps it is.

THE NEW KIDS ON THE BLOCK:
THE AFRICAN BABY BOOM

While populations are not replacing themselves in Europe, the Americas, and East Asia, they are growing in sub-Saharan Africa, albeit much more slowly than in the past. Even so, its population is projected to grow from 1.3 billion today to 2 billion by 2038 and 3 billion by 2061. Some people predict that a big war or a devastating epidemic might derail Africa's demographic momentum. The armed conflict that resulted in the largest death toll in history was World War II, claiming 50 million to 80 million lives, but it affected Africa only tangentially. The global AIDS epidemic has so far resulted in 36 million deaths, of which two-thirds occurred in Africa, with South Africa, Nigeria, Tanzania, Ethiopia, Kenya, Mozambique, Uganda, and Zimbabwe suffering the most. And yet Figure 3, depicting the regional distribution of population, shows that during the 1980s and 1990s, when the epidemic was at its most lethal, the population curve for Africa barely shifted. Thus, only a massive war or epidemic claiming hundreds of millions of lives would significantly alter the continent's demographic growth relative to other parts of the world.

You might be thinking that Africa cannot possibly accommodate its projected population growth. Consider, however, how big Africa *actually is*. Cartographical representations of the continent in our school textbooks greatly

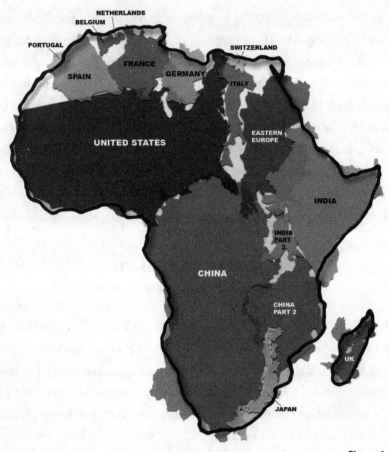

Figure 4

underestimate its true size relative to the Northern Hemisphere. Figure 4 shows that Africa's landmass is just about as big as that of China, India, Western and Eastern Europe, the United States, and Japan combined.

To be sure, there are big, largely uninhabitable deserts in Africa. But that's equally true of each of those other countries on the map (except Japan). Even Europe has deserts—the famous movie *Lawrence of Arabia* was filmed not on the Arabian Peninsula but mostly in southern Spain. Even taking into consideration the vastness of the African deserts, the continent contains the most undeveloped yet fertile land for agricultural development on the planet. Given Africa's size, overpopulation seems unlikely. The continent currently has 1.3 billion people; the other countries on this map have populations that exceed 3.5 billion. Today the density of the population per square mile is more than three times higher in Asia than in Africa, and four times in Europe.

Africa's population growth creates some thorny problems. The continent is home to some of the world's most intractable hotspots of religious and ethnic conflict. Decades of intermittent civil wars fueled by the Cold War wreaked havoc on the continent's infrastructure. In particular, political and social institutions—from governmental structures to the judiciary and civil society—suffered immensely or never developed, resulting in the largest concentration of "failed states." About half of Africa's fifty-four sovereign states are beset by political chaos, anarchy, and lawlessness. Much of the migration from rural areas to cities, and from those to international destinations, mostly in Europe, is due to conflict and violence, which endanger not only personal safety but also economic development.

Thus Africa is not risk-free, but the potential returns to its own growing population are huge. Because of its increasingly large population, Africa can no longer be ignored. For better or worse, its fortunes will matter globally. If things go well, Africa will be a vibrant source of dynamism to the benefit of the entire world. If things take a turn for the worse, the negative consequences will be felt globally. Demography is not destiny, but it does shape people's lives.

FEEDING AFRICA'S POPULATION
AS A HUGE OPPORTUNITY

Most people believe that the largest business opportunities lie in the service sector and can be pursued through technological platforms or apps. Let's think laterally about Africa's population growth. According to the World Bank, African agriculture will become a trillion-dollar sector by 2030. It is a veritable goldmine in the making, one that might well transform the entire global economy. The future of Africa's babies, most of them born in rural areas, hinges on the transformation of its agricultural sector. Despite its enormous landmass and abundant water, the continent is currently a net importer of food. And while extractive industries such as cocoa, mining, and oil have been fundamental to national economies for the longest time, most African growth in the near future will result from the expansion of agriculture and of the associated manufacturing and services catering to the continent's expanding population. The agricultural challenge is dual: bringing into cultivation up to 500 million acres of land—about the area of Mexico—*and* vastly improving productivity.

Africa is about to witness a dual agricultural and industrial revolution akin to what happened in Europe, the Americas, and East Asia in centuries past. Consider the benefits of creating a virtuous dynamic around an expanding agricultural sector. A farmer needs better inputs like seeds and fertilizers to increase productivity and enjoy a better standard of living. Her success in turn spurs the creation of jobs in the village in support of farming, including those to repair tractors and other machinery. As subsistence farming evolves into high-yield agriculture, surpluses are transported to the growing cities, thus reducing the amount of imported food. The transformation of the basic foodstuffs into baked goods, canned fruits, or prepared dishes creates even more jobs— perhaps tens of millions of them all throughout the continent, giving rise to both a thriving manufacturing economy and a burgeoning service sector that distributes and sells the processed goods among the urban population. That's the coming African agricultural-industrial revolution in a nutshell.

In order to realize this potential, many different kinds of organizations and companies are bringing new ideas and new practices to African agriculture. For instance, the African Agricultural Technology Foundation has introduced subsistence farmers to soil testing and seed selection techniques. According to the foundation's field personnel, "Some farmers just laughed off a suggestion that if they prepared the fields properly, used the right seeds and used fertilizers, their harvest would multiply ten times. It is a language they never heard before." Consider the case of Samuel Owiti Awino. His farm in the Lake Victoria region of Kenya was beset by unreliable rains and the destructive *striga* weed. Desperate, he tried every conceivable gimmick to produce a yield high enough to sustain his family and sell the rest in the local market. "When you are sick and you don't know what ails you, you will take any concoction hoping that one of them will eventually cure you," he says. "In farming that is what I had been doing for quite a long time." Awino, for one, was stunned when his demonstration plot produced twice as much maize as his best plot.

Contrary to the scaremongers who coined the term "population bomb," demographic growth might actually provide the incentive for Africa to improve its agricultural sector, which in turn would create jobs and spur related economic activities, not just in Africa but also in other parts of the world. Improvements in soil management, irrigation, and distribution can deliver huge benefits.

Africa's path toward the future lies in turning subsistence farmers like Awino into sophisticated agriculturalists. One ingenious way to turn the African population boom into an opportunity involves growing, harvesting, and processing a prodigious plant called cassava. This root vegetable, which is native to South America, is remarkably resilient to drought, can be harvested at any time within a flexible eighteen-month window, and requires manual labor to be planted, thus providing locals with a source of income. Throughout the developing world cassava already is the third main source of carbohydrates after rice and maize. At present it's mainly used to produce flour and beer. In sub-Saharan Africa at least 300 million people rely on it for their daily dietary needs. Additionally, cassava is naturally gluten free and has a lower sugar load than wheat, making it a healthy alternative to grains and a better carbohydrate source for diabetics. As the continent improves cassava yields, some portion of its production could also be turned into higher value–added products for export: it's an ingredient in plywood; it's used as a filler for many pharmaceuticals, including pills, tablets, and creams; and it can be turned into a biofuel.

Realizing the immense possibilities of cassava production requires both expertise and equipment. In the heartland of Zambia, Celestina Mumba spends many hours each week showing fellow cassava farmers how to improve yields by simple techniques such as seed selection and plant spacing. She has become an expert at it and now spends most of her time helping other farmers use the best available methods. Two thousand miles away in Nigeria, Pastor Felix Afolabi founded Afolabi Agro Divine Ventures to mentor young cassava farmers and obtain the plows, harrows, boom sprayers, planters, root diggers, tractors, and bulldozers needed to mechanize Nigerian agriculture. Farmer-entrepreneurs like Mumba and Afolabi are the pioneers of the African agricultural-industrial revolution.

While many of the human, technological, and financial resources needed to further develop cassava production throughout sub-Saharan Africa are locally available, foreign companies and nonprofits can also make a crucial contribution. Given its high water content, cassava needs to be processed within twenty-four to forty-eight hours after harvest, so the necessary equipment must be available near plant sites. The Dutch Agricultural Development and Trading Company (DADTCO), a for-profit social enterprise focused on improving the lot of poor communities, offers small African farms processing, refinery, and drying units installed inside truck-mounted containers that move from village to village. Harvesting can begin as soon as this mobile equipment is positioned. In no time, these farmers, or other local entrepreneurs, might use these resources to make foodstuffs themselves.

In the near future, the expansion of cassava production may well provide today's rural babies with the jobs they will need to make a living. And what if Africa became a powerhouse in the global beer industry? Some of the world's largest companies, SABMiller and Diageo among them, are already sourcing from cassava producers the raw material for brewing beer, thus reducing the cost of their final product and Africa's overall dependence on expensive foreign imports. If cassava-based beer proves cost-effective and environmentally sustainable, expect several African beers available at your local pub or bar, at prices you can't ignore. Look out, Anheuser-Busch!

THE SILICON SAVANNA

Beyond the coming agricultural-industrial revolution, Africa has leapfrogged into the twenty-first century faster than anyone else in one area: mobile telecommunications technology. And this transformation is already changing lives across the continent. Consider the story as told in the *Irish Times* of Naomi Wanjiru Nganga, who lives in the Nairobi slum of Korogocho. She is thirty-four and in poor health, and she supports her four children by gathering discarded cardboard boxes and selling them in the local market. Her only technological gadget is a rather basic cellphone, which she uses not only to communicate but also to make and receive payments, including a monthly stipend from an Irish charity. She is a direct beneficiary of the rapid deployment of mobile networks. Kenya stunned the world a decade ago by becoming one of the world's leaders in mobile payments, with three-quarters of its population using them assiduously. Not surprisingly, Nairobi is now dubbed the "Silicon Savannah." That's why I believe that if you'd like to open a window to see what 2030 might look like, you must travel to Africa.

Mobile technology has proved to be especially helpful in the healthcare sector. In Kenya, for example, most of the rural population lives at least an hour away by bus from the closest doctor or medical facility. To solve the issue of access, many mobile services have been launched, from medical hotlines and early-diagnosis tools to education, medicine reminders, and follow-ups. Today, 90 percent of the population has a cellphone. Phone records in Kenya are actually more comprehensive than official censuses. Government agencies use cellphone data rather than payroll or school records to plan for healthcare policy and outreach.

Like many other countries—rich and poor alike—Kenya faces a shortage of qualified healthcare personnel, rising costs, and skyrocketing demand. There are hundreds of e-health projects and programs benefiting an increasing number of rural residents. The model of using mobile telecommunications technology in healthcare, as seen in Kenya, may offer a technological solution to healthcare access that is both efficient and inclusive, something that other nations can emulate—even a country like the United States, where healthcare has been a perennial political talking point and the costs of care seem to increase year after year.

ANXIETY AND ANGER OVER IMMIGRATION

By 2030 the human population will be distributed across the globe in very different ways than it is now, with much greater numbers of people in Africa and South Asia than in other parts of the world. And although the number of people who will be migrating from one country to another will change, the causes will not: migration tends to become a prominent phenomenon whenever babies are plentiful in one part of the world but scarce in another, or in the wake of crises such as civil wars, political unrest, famines, economic emergencies, or natural disasters. Lately, international migration is considered to be a "flood" in need of containment. Political leaders are calling for walls. Countries are exiting trade agreements and political/economic organizations such as the European Union. Citizens are marching in the streets with signs declaring that immigrants aren't wanted. But what if the fear that immigrants take away jobs and are a drain on government resources is all wrong and shortsighted?

The conventional wisdom is that migrants displace blue-collar workers and steal good manufacturing jobs. In reality, most immigrants do not compete for jobs with locals, as the U.S. National Academies of Sciences, Engineering, and Medicine have concluded in a number of landmark reports. The reason is that most immigrants are people who have either few skills or very high-level skills and, as a result, do not have good employment prospects in their home countries. By contrast, their compatriots with intermediate levels of skills—such as handymen or mechanics—have plenty of job opportunities available in their communities of origin, and thus tend not to migrate. In developed economies like the United States, Japan, and Europe, low-skilled jobs are still plentiful, especially in agriculture and the service sectors, as is the demand for highly skilled workers. Meanwhile, most of the job losses in developed countries have occurred in the manufacturing sector, among workers of intermediate skill, because their jobs are easier and more economical to automate. In rich countries, it makes the most economic sense to deploy technology to replace jobs that require intermediate skill levels, precisely because the wages are high enough to provide an incentive for automation and the tasks are relatively easy to automate (as we shall see in Chapter 6). Thus, the anxiety and anger that job losses generate should be mostly directed at technological change, not immigration. My Wharton colleague Britta Glennon has found that restricting the number of visas available for scientists and engineers actually destroys jobs in the United States because companies move their research and development labs abroad in order to tap into the talent pool. The biggest beneficiaries of the clampdown on immigration? China, India, and Canada—the countries to which those R&D activities are moved.

When we break down the statistics on how many foreign-born people are employed in the United States by level of education, we see that immigrants tend not to steal jobs away from Americans. About 42 percent of all workers who dropped out of high school are immigrants, and among doctoral degree holders 29 percent are foreign-born. By contrast, only 15 percent of those with a high school diploma, 10 percent of those with some college education but without a degree, and 14 percent of bachelor degree holders are immigrants. Meanwhile, the U.S. Bureau of the Census reports that the number of highly skilled managerial and technical jobs has increased, while the number of blue-collar and clerical jobs characterized by intermediate skill levels has declined sharply—due to automation.

If we dive into the data on specific occupations, we find more evidence that most immigrants do not compete for jobs with locals. According to the Urban Institute, the top three occupational groups among immigrants in the United States without high school diplomas are maids and housekeepers, cooks, and agricultural laborers. Meanwhile, native-born workers without a high school diploma are more numerous among cashiers, drivers of trucks and other vehicles, and janitors. Head-to-head competition for jobs between immigrants and natives is rather limited.

Migration will help overcome some of the difficulties associated with the aging of the population. The United Nations calls it "replacement migration." The data from the U.S. Bureau of Labor Statistics suggest that as the baby boom generation goes into retirement, the American economy will need a larger influx of immigrants to cover the demand for dozens of occupations, from nursing assistants and home health aides to construction laborers, cooks, and software developers. By 2030, more than half of these and other jobs in the United States will be occupied by foreign-born workers.

Another way of assessing whether immigration undermines the economic status of locals is to examine earnings. Wages for locals should decrease if immigrants compete for the same jobs. After carefully examining the evidence, the U.S. National Academies of Sciences, Engineering, and Medicine concluded that "the impact of immigration on the overall native wage may be small and close to zero." More importantly, most research has found "larger negative effects for disadvantaged groups [like ethnic minorities] and for prior immigrants than for natives overall." This may explain the paradox of why significant proportions of recent immigrants in Europe and the U.S. vote for candidates who demonize immigration. Tellingly, the native group most exposed to the effects of immigration is high school dropouts, who also tend to favor stiffer immigration controls, a big factor in elections nowadays.

While the evidence suggests that immigrants do not compete for jobs with locals, it is still possible that immigration represents a net loss to the destination country if newcomers disproportionately benefit from government welfare services. In fact, much of the popular anger against immigrants in both Europe and the United States is based on the accusation that they represent a fiscal burden because they take in more as the beneficiaries of social services than they contribute as workers. Once again, the evidence contradicts this conventional wisdom. About 72 percent of all international immigrants in the world are of working age, compared to 58 percent for the total population. According to a study by the prestigious Organisation for Economic Co-operation and Development (OECD), immigrants accounted for 47 percent of the increase in the workforce in the United States and 70 percent in Europe since 1990, and they tend to contribute more in taxes than they receive in benefits from government programs. "At any given age," noted the National Academies report, "adult members of the second generation [of immigrants] typically have had a more positive net fiscal impact for all government levels combined than either first or third-plus generation adults." Between 1994 and 2013 the ratio of taxes to benefits "increased for both the first and second generation groups," indicating that over time immigrants are contributing more fiscally through payroll and income taxes than they are receiving in benefits from government programs. It is worth noting that the fiscal impact of immigrants is more positive at the federal level—given that most of them are of working age—than at the state and local levels, which fund the education of their children. The National Academies concluded that "an immigrant and a native-born person with similar characteristics [e.g., age, education, income] will likely have about the same fiscal impact."

IMMIGRANTS DON'T STEAL JOBS—
THEY *CREATE* JOBS

Google, Intel, eBay, Facebook, LinkedIn, and Tesla have two things in common: they have transformed the American economy, and they were founded or co-founded by immigrants. The global economy would not be the same without them. About 23 percent of all high-tech ventures in the United States are founded by immigrants, and the proportion is significantly higher in certain states—40 percent in California, 42 percent in Massachusetts, and 45 percent in New Jersey, according to the Kauffman Foundation and the Bay Area Council Economic Institute. Immigrants founded forty-four of the eighty-seven American "unicorns"—privately held companies valued at $1 billion or more—as of 2016, as reported by the National Foundation for American Policy, a nonpartisan think tank. Twenty-three of the entrepreneurs who founded those forty-four ventures initially came to the United States to pursue undergraduate or graduate education, with the largest numbers hailing from India, Canada, the United Kingdom, Germany, and Israel. David Hindawi, for instance, was born in Baghdad in 1944 to an Iraqi Jewish family. His parents took him to Israel in 1951, where he served in the Israeli air force. In 1970 he came to the United States to pursue a doctoral degree at the University of California at Berkeley. In 2007 David joined forces with his son Orion to found Tanium, a cybersecurity firm that eventually grew to employ five hundred people.

Immigrants are a boon to the economy because they're more inclined to become entrepreneurs. A comprehensive report from the National Academies found that "immigrants are more innovative than natives," as measured by patenting, for instance. "Immigrants appear to innovate more than natives not because of greater inherent ability but due to their concentration in science and engineering fields," the study concluded. "Immigration is pure entrepreneurship," LinkedIn co-founder Reid Hoffman wrote in a 2013 op-ed in the *Washington Post*. "You leave behind everything familiar to start somewhere new. To succeed, you need to develop alliances. You must acquire skills. You will have to improvise on occasions. It's a bold proposition."

Besides entrepreneurship, consider the contribution of immigrants to the American healthcare sector. According to a 2016 study by George Mason University, immigrants represent about 13 percent of the total population of the United States but are 28 percent of physicians and surgeons; 22 percent of nursing, psychiatric, and home health aides; and 15 percent of registered nurses. They are more than half of medical scientists employed in biotechnology. The key factor behind these percentages is that most of these immigrants were trained as healthcare providers in their countries of origin. While some of those holding foreign degrees need to acquire more advanced skills before working in the United States owing to our higher occupational training standards, it is still the case that the United States simply does not produce enough advanced-degree healthcare workers. Clearly, immigrant healthcare workers are not competing with Americans for jobs.

Another useful indicator is Nobel laureates in the sciences. Among the eighty-five American citizens who won the prizes for chemistry, physics, and physiology or medicine since the year 2000, thirty-three, or nearly 40 percent, were foreign-born. If America is to retain its status as the world's most innovative country, immigration must play a role, especially as the knowledge-based economy continues to grow.

The National Academies had already concluded in a 1997 report that the net effect of immigration on the American economy was positive. In their 2017 report they observed that without immigration to the United States, "clearly GDP would be much smaller, and perhaps per capita GDP would be as well—in no small part because the United States would have an older population with a considerably lower percentage of individuals active in the workforce." The arrival of immigrants tends to reduce prices for "child care, food preparation, house cleaning and repair, and construction." The report also noted that, given the importance of the real estate market to the U.S. economy, immigrant arrivals and their descendants provide welcome additional demand for housing. It is also hard to imagine how many American middle-class families with two working parents would be able to function without immigrants helping to raise their children. By 2030 the U.S. economy will be even more driven by the creative dynamism of immigration than today—unless the wall-builders have their way.

OUR COGNITIVE BIASES AGAINST IMMIGRATION

Immigration is so controversial because we tend to focus more on the downside than the upside. The psychologists Amos Tversky and Daniel Kahneman proposed that in many areas of life we make bad decisions because our thinking is clouded by the "loss aversion bias." After conducting many experiments, they concluded that people have a tendency to prefer avoiding losses rather than locking in equivalent gains. As surprising as it may seem, most people find it more attractive to avoid losing $10 than to win $10.

For her master's thesis at the University of Bergen, Norwegian behavioral economist Thea Wiig conducted an experiment presenting some people with statistics about the employment of immigrants (showing the potential societal gains from immigration) and about the impact of immigration on welfare programs (showing the potential losses). She found that "losses loom larger than gains" in people's minds, which contributed to a negative attitude toward immigration. "People are susceptible to negative framing emphasizing the costs of immigration," she wrote. Specifically, "behavioral information about the employment rate of immigrants in Norway, which is 60 percent, causes individuals to rate their preferences for immigration policy more strictly." The implication of this research is that preferences about immigration, and hence the range of plausible policies, can be shaped and even manipulated once we note that "people are more willing to forgo the benefits of immigration than to bear the costs of it." As we approach 2030, it's important to recognize how adept—and influential—the negative framing of immigration has been, and how effectively it has overpowered those who have promoted its benefits. Writing in *The New Yorker*, journalist James Surowiecki argues that the rhetoric of "we're losing our country" is so convincing because it appeals to our loss aversion bias, which has given an electoral edge to anti-immigration candidates.

Other research exploring the loss aversion bias sheds light on the behavior of immigrants themselves. In analyzing the behavioral differences between natives, foreign-born individuals who decide to immigrate, and foreigners who stay put in their home country, one study found that of those three groups, migrants have the highest tolerance for risk. It may explain why so many immigrants become entrepreneurs. But it is also important to note that potential immigrants respond more strongly to bad news regarding future economic conditions than to good news just like everyone else. Moreover, immigration is driven more strongly by economic difficulty in the country of origin than by the opportunities in the destination country, notes Mathias Czaika in another study. This finding shows that most immigrants are not merely trying to improve upon the standard of living they had in their home country; they are escaping from inhospitable, even desperate, economic conditions.

Property (or lack thereof) is also a key factor in immigration because it affects attitudes toward risk. In a study published in the *Proceedings of the National Academy of Sciences*, William Clark and William Lisowski found that immigrants carefully ponder the gains and the losses from the decision to move to a different country. People who own a home or have other types of property are less likely to move within or across countries. That's why land redistribution in poor countries would reduce rates of migration more effectively than border walls.

The reality is that there are plenty of reasons to focus on the upside of immigration. A 2018 report from the trustees of the Social Security Administration warned that by 2030 the minimum level for "short-term financial adequacy" of the trust fund would not be met because the government is using it to continue paying out benefits as opposed to ensuring the long-term viability of the system. *USA Today* greeted the report with the headline "Social Security and Medicare Are Slowly Dying, But No One in Washington Will Lift a Finger."

It turns out that immigration represents not a threat but a lateral opportunity to ensure the future viability of pension systems. Immigrants pay billions of dollars each year in Social Security payroll taxes, even if they are undocumented and use fake Social Security numbers. The think tank New American Economy estimates that though 8 million undocumented workers contributed about $13 billion in payroll taxes in 2016, they generally cannot claim Social Security benefits. And it is low-wage immigrants who contribute the most because the 6.2 percent Social Security tax applies only to the first $128,400 in income. "Deporting undocumented immigrants would have a negative impact, short and long term, on the Social Security funds, which are directly linked to population growth," says Monique Morrissey, an economist at the Economic Policy Institute. In their report, the Social Security Administration's trustees observed why a rising immigration wave can be potentially advantageous: "The cost rate decreases with an increase in total net immigration because immigration occurs at relatively young ages, thereby increasing the numbers of covered workers earlier than the numbers of beneficiaries."

The bottom line is that framing matters. If you think laterally, you can turn a problem into a huge opportunity. The more we refocus on opportunities, the greater our chances of adapting successfully to the challenges of 2030.

IS BRAIN DRAIN A MYTH?

Even the staunchest opponents of immigration agree that highly skilled foreigners are needed to fill in gaps in the American economy. But does that mean that we're taking advantage of poorer countries as they lose some of their best talent to us? Back in the 1950s, the British coined the term "brain drain" to decry the loss of their human capital to the United States and Canada, where physicians, engineers, and other highly qualified people were finding better-paying jobs than in their homeland. Over the last three or four decades, a similar process of talent migration has deprived developing countries including Bangladesh, Nigeria, and the Philippines of some of their most precious human capital. According to AnnaLee Saxenian, a geographer and political scientist at the University of California at Berkeley, the impoverishing cycle caused by the brain drain can be turned into a virtuous circle of "brain circulation," to the benefit of both the origin and destination countries.

Miin Wu, for example, came to the United States from his native Taiwan to pursue a doctorate in electrical engineering at Stanford University. After graduating in 1976, he went to work for legendary firms Siliconix and Intel. Ten years later he co-founded VLSI Technology in Silicon Valley, a company dedicated to the design and manufacturing of integrated circuits. By the late 1980s, Taiwan had become a magnet for chip manufacturing, so he decided to use his American connections to start Macronix, one of the country's first semiconductor companies and the first Taiwanese company to be listed on Nasdaq. His life became a permanent commute across the Pacific. Wu's entrepreneurship draws on, and benefits, both his birth country and his adopted one.

James Joo-Jin Kim left South Korea for the United States in the 1960s in search of an education. When he arrived at the Wharton School, "both parts of the Korean peninsula had been ravaged by the war, and you cannot begin to imagine how grim the outlook was for all Koreans. We were desperately poor, and our nation was in shambles." In 1969, after getting a doctoral degree and working as a college professor, he founded Amkor Technology, a semiconductor packaging and test services provider, which in 2018 reported $4.2 billion in sales. Additionally, Amkor employs nearly thirty thousand people in factories throughout East Asia and Portugal plus a number of facilities in the United States. The company's name says it all: it's a portmanteau of "America" and "Korea." Amkor has helped South Korea become the technological powerhouse that it is today. "We survived, we persevered, and then we prospered," Kim says.

Visionary entrepreneurs like Wu and Kim demonstrate the power of immigration to have an impact on many nations. Thanks to lower transportation costs and easier communication through digital means, an entrepreneur can now operate a business straddling a pair of distant countries such as India and the United States, or China and the United States, exploiting the complementary resources to be found in each. Real-time collaboration on both routine and complex tasks is now possible across continents. As a result, jobs are created both in the immigrants' country of origin and their destination country. And while until recently the market for such collaborations was primarily the United States, the future growth of the Chinese and Indian consumer markets will create huge opportunities for this type of transnational entrepreneur or firm going forward.

Still, the benefits of this brain circulation across the world, described by

Saxenian, are manifold. It attracts highly qualified immigrants to an economy like America's, which frequently faces labor shortages, and it creates jobs for Americans in some of the industries of the future. But most importantly, it creates a bridge between the United States and some of the biggest emerging markets in the world, something that is likely to deliver huge dividends as the center of gravity of economic activity and consumption shifts from the North Atlantic toward Asia and eventually Africa.

The World Bank assessed the enormous scale of international collaboration through the so-called diaspora networks of entrepreneurs and engineers who came to the United States to study. Depending on the country of origin, between half and three-quarters of them returned to their home countries, where many of them launched startup companies. Among those who stayed in the United States, half of them traveled back to their country of origin on business at least once per year. The beneficial effects of diaspora networks of highly skilled migrants have been greatest in Israel, Taiwan, and India. Information technology is the sector of the economy that best lends itself to this type of transnational development, perhaps because of its low capital requirements.

While the opportunities embedded in immigration are huge, so are the potential pitfalls if natives perceive that they are losing out. There's a great need for a calm debate about the best policies to determine the volume, timing, and composition of immigration so as to maximize the opportunities for both the origin and the destination countries and so that globalization does not leave millions of people behind as they lose jobs and their communities decline. Research shows that quota-based systems do not seem to be the best way to achieve those goals, while systems based on labor demand and qualifications have a better chance of succeeding. Canada provides perhaps the best example: it has successfully attracted highly skilled immigrants by offering foreign university students a path to obtaining a work visa upon graduation. The Conference Board of Canada, an employers' association, estimated in 2018 that the economic growth rate over the next two decades would slow down by a third if immigration were curtailed: "If it stopped immigration, Canada would experience a shrinking labor force, weak economic growth, and greater challenges funding social services such as health care." The most vibrant economies in 2030 will be those that manage to take advantage of the dynamic contributions of immigrants while at the same time taking care of those who are hurt by the constant transformation of the economy.

BABIES, MIGRATION, AND OPPORTUNITY

By following the babies, this chapter has dwelled on what 2030 will look like. The young consumers of the near future have already been born, and some measure of migration will compensate for the rapidly aging populations in certain parts of the world. Meanwhile, apprehension and even anger will grow as the cost of adjusting to the new reality mounts for the people who fall behind. The outcome of these contradictory forces will depend on how we shift from the anxieties of the present to the opportunities of the future.

For many countries around the world, including the United States, the solution will lie in balancing the needs and aspirations of different generational groups. Younger and older population segments see the challenges ahead in sharply different ways, as might be expected. Where one sees value, the other tends to see a loss. Chapter 2 shows how the opportunities embedded in large-scale population changes can be seized.

2.

Gray Is the New Black

**TECH-SAVVY SENIOR CITIZENS, POSTPONING
RETIREMENT, AND RETHINKING "OLD" AND "YOUNG"**

*My generation, faced as it grew with a choice
between religious belief and existential despair, chose
marijuana. Now we are in our Cabernet stage.*

—PEGGY NOONAN, JOURNALIST AND AUTHOR

Today, the world's 2.3 billion millennials—those born between 1980 and
2000—are the focus of the world's attention. Their minds, wallets, and votes—
companies and politicians want them all. According to Morgan Stanley,
millennials are currently "the most important age range for economic activity,"
because they'll start families, have babies, and spend money to settle down in
life.

This is a misconception.

For starters, millennials are no different from previous generations in their
heterogeneity. People in this age range come in many different shapes and sizes.

Some are highly educated; others are not. Some are rich; others struggle to make ends meet. Some are consumer narcissists; others abhor commercialism. The media loves to generalize their attitudes or behavior, often in sensationalist ways:

> "Millennials are killing the dinner date."
> "Millennials have officially ruined brunch."
> "Millennials are killing the beer industry with their rosé obsession."
> "Millennials are killing the napkin industry."
> "Millennials are killing the movie business."
> "Will millennials kill home ownership?"
> "Why aren't millennials having sex?"

But there's another, far more fundamental reason that the fuss around millennials is overblown. Contrary to conventional wisdom, millennials are *not* the fastest-growing market segment in the world. In fact, the fastest-growing segment, by age, may surprise you. They've often been neglected by companies, but they are courted by politicians (because they are more likely to vote), and they happen to own at least half of the net worth globally—around 80 percent in the United States. They're the population above the age of sixty, and by 2030 the world will have 400 million more of them, mostly in Europe, North America, and China. In the United States, this age group includes both the baby boomers and the Silent Generation (those who grew up during the Depression and either lived through or fought during World War II; Tom Brokaw called them the "Greatest Generation"). The American historian Neil Howe, writing in *Forbes*, notes that "the relative affluence of today's elderly is historically unprecedented." Howe knows a thing or two about the topic: he coined the term "millennial."

Federal Reserve data indicate that members of "the Silent [Generation] hold roughly 1.3 times the amount of wealth as Boomers, more than twice that of [Gen] Xers, and 23 times that of Millennials." According to Howe, "Marketers are attracted to [Boomers'] newfound spending power and are pouring ad dollars into drawing older consumers in their 60s and 70s." The industry's magazine of record, *Advertising Age*, "even spotlighted a string of campaigns featuring octogenarians from global brands like Nike and Poland Spring." And it's a myth that healthcare costs associated with the senior population in the United States are soaring. In fact, most of the increase in healthcare spending since 2002 has occurred in the population between eighteen and sixty-four years of age.

HOW TO THINK ABOUT GENERATIONS

We're at an unprecedented juncture in history: several generations of relatively similar size are sharing the stage and competing for influence. Generations matter because they behave in specific ways related both to when they came of age and to their situation at the current moment. "The creation of a world view is the work of a generation rather than of an individual," wrote novelist John Dos Passos. "But we each of us, for better or for worse, add our brick to the edifice."

These days, companies face a two-tiered issue: they are puzzled by millennial consumer behavior *and* uncertain of how to approach an older generation living and spending longer than any other to date (the notion of a comfortable retirement beginning at sixty-five, a familiar benchmark, may no longer be as relevant). To further complicate the issue, is there any common ground between these generational groups? "Boomer bashing is in fashion," wrote Linda Bernstein in a 2016 article in *Forbes*. Many young people are angry with baby boomers, blaming them for everything from the financial crisis and climate change to an unpredictable economy. There's also a rift politically. While, on average, young people tend to be more progressive, they see among their parents and grandparents widespread support for populist politicians, new forms of nationalism, and walls to keep out the unwanted. Furthermore, the 2008 financial crisis made people question the old idea that each successive generation was poised to do better financially than their parents. But the finger-pointing goes both ways, as generations exchange accusations of self-dealing and narcissism.

What's fundamentally new about these intergenerational dynamics is that as 2030 approaches, conventional definitions of "young" and "old" will become obsolete. We can no longer assume that dynamism is a synonym for youth and decline is associated exclusively with old age. New technological developments will completely transform how we deal with retirement and geriatric care. Pause for a moment to visualize a world in which our parents and grandparents are among the most active and productive people on the planet. Imagine millennials, raised in a high-tech world, starting businesses consciously intended to benefit a population over sixty. Consider the possibility of a world where age is less of a factor in hiring—where a seventy-year-old new hire, for example, might not be unusual. How will the spending power of this over-sixty group, which is estimated to reach $15 trillion a year, materialize?

Is gray the new black?

The German sociologist Karl Mannheim was the first to point out the importance of generations. Writing a century ago, he defined generations as groups of people united by time and space who behave in unique ways *that last over their entire life span*, forming a kind of collective meaning attached to certain experiences: the Depression, World War II, the civil rights movement, the Internet, or social media, for example. This is different from an "age cohort," which simply denotes being born within an arbitrary time period, like a decade, with no unifying trait ascribed to it.

Members of a particular generation develop a shared consciousness, despite differences in, say, socioeconomic status or cultural values. Mannheim referred to such subgroups as a "generational unit." For instance, consider the differences within the American "Civil Rights Generation" in terms of their views about society, their proximate relationship to the cause, and their level of political engagement.

But there's another side to generations that was first conceptualized in the 1970s by French anthropologist and sociologist Pierre Bourdieu. Rather than identifying a historical event, Bourdieu focused on "predispositions." In his view, each generation develops "natural and reasonable practices or aspirations which another [generation] finds unthinkable or scandalous." In other words, an element of acquired routine (what he called "habitus") and socialization sets each generation apart.

This element of identity is essential to understanding the impact of generations on the economy, especially in terms of savings and consumption.

Consider the implications of different generations vying to advance their own economic and political agendas. Then consider that within each of these generations are diverse subsets with their own preoccupations and needs.

Let's also ponder how aging within a specific generation impacts attitudes or behavior over time. Whatever their differences at birth, do people in a generation converge on a set of values as they get older?

DON'T WASTE PUFFERY ON THE GRAY CONSUMER

"I'm anticipating the crisis to kick in, the hair to go gray, the physical slowdown to start," writes British journalist and editor Stefano Hatfield. "I'm also waiting for advertisers to talk to me; target me in a look and tone that is aspirational." Survey research indicates that a whopping 96 percent of Britons over the age of fifty feel ignored by advertisers. "Boomers have the bucks, but advertisers don't seem to care," read a recent article published by AARP. If that's how people who turn fifty feel, imagine what it's like for those above sixty or seventy. While the population growth of young people ebbs and flows, the population of people above sixty is growing all around the world.

Let's do the numbers.

In China, roughly 54,000 people celebrate their sixtieth birthday *each day*. In the United States the figure is about 12,000. Around the world, it's an astounding 210,000. Those are numbers few entrepreneurs and companies can resist. By 2030, the number of people in this age group worldwide will be about 1.4 billion, up from 1 billion today—the United States will have 14 million more (for a total of 90 million), Mexico 6 million more, the United Kingdom 3 million more, India 50 million more, and China a whopping 113 million more. Even underdeveloped countries will witness huge increases, especially in relative terms. For instance, Bangladesh will jump from 13 million to 21 million people above the age of sixty.

The key statistic for those in the business of analyzing the social consequences of demographic change is the proportion of the total population this group will represent. By 2030, it will reach 38 percent in Japan, 34 percent in Germany, 28 percent in the United Kingdom, 26 percent in the United

States, and 25 percent in China. Will pension and healthcare systems be able to cope?

That's a fair question to ask, but look at those same figures laterally through the lens of opportunity. In 2018, *Forbes* dubbed population aging "a blessing for business." For its part, the *Economist* recently argued that "older consumers will reshape the business landscape." We are at the dawn of the age of the "gray market," one that is growing in spending power, especially in the emerging economies. Yet the Boston Consulting Group estimates that only one in seven companies is prepared. It is no secret that most technology, marketing, and sales departments at both established companies and startups are populated by young people, who, unsurprisingly, have blind spots when it comes to identifying opportunities in the gray market. But this is a mistake. Not only is the gray market healthier now than it was in generations past, but some estimates put gray consumers' spending power at $20 trillion by 2030.

Addressing the needs and wants of gray consumers is not easy. As Maria Henke, a senior associate dean at the School of Gerontology at the University of Southern California, points out, "Seniors are a tough crowd. Puffery is wasted on them. They've seen it all when it comes to advertising." After all, if you're a baby boomer, born between 1944 and 1964, imagine all the revolutions in advertising you've witnessed, from radio jingles to viral marketing. Fatigue sets in: "Do I really need this?"

But the challenge goes well beyond finding the right communication and advertising strategy. Some people age faster than others. Their needs and preferences evolve differently—and they do not necessarily feel or think "old." Hatfield shrewdly observes that "most of the advertising industry, in particular, and the media generally have failed to notice that today's 50 is not our parents' 50." The problem lies in assuming that people fall into compartmentalized categories defined by age. Coco Chanel famously said that "after forty nobody is young, but one can be irresistible at any age." Yet "ads geared toward older consumers tend to be condescending at best, offensive at worst," notes Jeff Beer in *Fast Company*. Sarah Rabia, global director of cultural strategy at TBWA, an advertising agency, aptly sums up the conundrum: "Either you go more inclusive, don't define by age, but look at values and similarities between your audience, because there are plenty of things a boomer and a millennial have in common, or you get laser-focused on this audience, but with a tone that's upbeat, modern, and progressive."

In one comprehensive study, "the vast majority of people said aging well means spending time with people who are both younger and older than you," notes Nadia Tuma, senior vice president for research at McGann, the global ad agency. "It's about intergenerational connections, something much more powerful than just finding a good moisturizer." Here's the important point: the categories inherited from the past will no longer be useful by 2030. "It's almost like the demographics that we've created are a barrier to us understanding people at a deeper level," Tuma concludes.

Let me offer another example illustrating the difficulty of understanding the gray consumer. Durable consumer goods—such as appliances, tools, and cars—pose a unique challenge. By definition, they are designed and manufactured, ideally, to last for five, ten, or even twenty years. During that time, the needs and the abilities of the aging user may shift in ways that actually make the product obsolete *for that type of user.* Let's not forget that gray consumers prefer not to replace durable goods as frequently as younger people, especially if they need to ensure that their savings will last through retirement. Consider what the ideal washing machine may be for a sixty-year-old. Front-loaders will still be easy to use, and they require less energy than other types. But by age seventy or eighty, a person might find a top-loader more convenient (though the electricity bill will be a bit more onerous). Knobs should be easier to grip, and icons and text displays more legible. "An easy-to-grip lip [on a top-loading washer's lid] is key for anyone who has trouble with their hands," notes an article on gray-friendly washing machines. "Plus, the deeper and wider the lip is, the easier it will be to see and locate for those with vision problems."

There are two possible avenues to reassure seniors that products are being tailored to their needs. The first approach is to offer leasing (as opposed to buying) options, which enables consumers to switch to a new product every few years, and will be more financially attractive to people who may not survive the useful life of the product. The second involves functionally designing products that anticipate declines in health, physical skills, or cognitive abilities in the people who use them. In the case of washing machines, it's entirely possible to accommodate some variation in user preferences across generations with multiple types of digital displays and controls, for example.

GRAY PRIORITIES

The opportunities to launch new products and services for the gray market are formidably large. The key is understanding how older people will spend their money. Quality of life, unsurprisingly, is a high priority. According to AARP, most seniors are optimistic about their overall quality of life, including financial well-being, mental and physical health, recreation and leisure time, and family life. Nearly three in four expect their quality of life to improve or remain the same (though the optimism starts to wane after seventy). Increasingly, it's defined as independence, autonomy, mobility, and connectivity. And it's not just about dealing with the consequences of physical and cognitive decline; it's also about fighting loneliness and finding a continued sense of joy in life. Perhaps the Swedish film director Ingmar Bergman captured these challenges best in *Wild Strawberries* (1957), in which a grouchy seventy-eight-year-old physician embarks on a four-hundred-mile car ride to receive a lifetime recognition award. He encounters people along the way who remind him of troubling incidents and ongoing frustrations, with some joining him on his journey of reevaluation and self-discovery. The odyssey revealed the extent of his loneliness.

As the gray market emerges, healthcare, home care, assisted living, and other similar service industries will be poised to thrive in 2030. Leisure and entertainment will also be big. But perhaps the most exciting opportunities lie within the quality-of-life space, which will benefit from creative and innovative solutions.

Consider shoes. There are so many options in terms of design, quality, and price, not to mention taste and preferences. The industry is full of thousands of companies and brands, and none except for Nike have any significant market share. Now add the needs of the gray market. Shoes that ameliorate knee and hip pain are already in high demand. Designing shoes that are both stylish and easy to use is essential. Able-bodied consumers may not think about this, but there is also a demand for modifying the left and right shoes differently according to need. These kinds of consumer-focused details can swing millions of potential customers toward companies willing to accommodate emerging demographic shifts in their brand strategy. What about in-store experiences? Here are examples of things retailers could do: open stores earlier, since seniors tend to be early risers, and offer discounts during early hours; add a loyalty program; make sure there are plenty of places to sit; and hire staff who are trained to understand the needs and concerns of the gray market.

Another opportunity lies in the health and fitness sector. Gyms and yoga studios have mushroomed in locations close to where (young) people work. For example, the International Council on Active Aging's online locator for age-friendly fitness centers—places that are accessible, inside and out, for an active yet aging demographic—shows only five such gyms within the 77494 zip code in Katy, Texas, for some 105,000 residents; two within my zip code in downtown Philadelphia, where 20,000 people live; and just one in Lexington, Virginia, one of the zip codes with the youngest populations in the United States. In Sumter County, Florida, which has the population with the highest median age, there are just seven age-friendly gyms for 125,000 residents. It's now time to think about opening more of them in areas where seniors live (or would like to live).

And how about online shopping? There's a big debate as to whether seniors will turn to e-commerce sites as a more convenient way to shop, especially as they lose their motor function and mobility. According to eMarketer, Americans sixty and above are just a few percentage points behind other generations when it comes to using Amazon Prime, researching a product digitally before purchasing in-store, or purchasing via an online marketplace. They are, however, much less likely to use a smartphone to conclude a purchase or hear about a product through social media. Although they're not digital laggards by any means, gray consumers show some signs of preferring proximity shopping— small-format, local shops where they can find the personalized assistance they tend to like. Data from the consultancy Nielsen shows that seniors visit all kinds of stores, especially grocery stores, much more frequently than other age groups. But one channel does not preclude the other. In fact, e-commerce and bricks-and-mortar shopping might actually be complementary, though we should keep in mind that a large segment of seniors becomes price sensitive in order to ensure that their savings will last.

Discretionary spending, or spending on things other than the necessities of housing, food, utilities, healthcare, transportation, and education, is another growth area for gray consumption. In the United States, discretionary spending peaks for people in their mid-thirties to mid-fifties, at around 40 percent of total spending. Seniors reduce their non-essential spending gradually because of decreased mobility and a greater need for care services. For those above the age of seventy-five, it drops to less than 33 percent.

If you're thinking globally about discretionary spending by seniors, there's a catch. In Europe, Canada, and Japan the proportion of discretionary spending is up to twelve percentage points higher than in the United States due to lower out-of-pocket healthcare costs. In other words, healthcare coverage impacts non-essential spending. For instance, the average senior above age sixty-five in the United States allocates 14 percent of spending to healthcare, while in the United Kingdom it's less than 3 percent. That enables British seniors to spend twice as much proportionally on things such as apparel, restaurants, and travel.

When it comes to leisure, a common misconception is that seniors spend more than other age groups because they have more time on their hands. In reality, gray consumers are not necessarily bigger spenders than other age groups on travel and entertainment, and the longer they feel healthier and fit the more they engage in other activities such as working (at least part-time), pursuing opportunities in the gig economy, or volunteering. Moreover, the "leisure" category is so heterogeneous that it actually conceals certain important trends. Let's start by thinking about what people do with their leisure time. Seniors spend more of it watching TV, reading, and relaxing or thinking than people in their forties and fifties. When it comes to paid-for leisure, today's seniors are more willing to spend their money on travel than previous generations because they are healthier and in better physical shape. Overall spending on tourism by seniors is higher in Europe, China, and Japan than in the United States, which means that there's more potential for future growth in America than elsewhere, assuming healthcare costs do not rise. And given that many seniors prefer traveling shorter distances, gray demand for tourism will primarily create jobs within their country of residence.

FORTUNE AT THE TOP OF THE AGE PYRAMID

Many companies have found the recipe for success by focusing on the gray market, and some on the decline have averted liquidation by reinventing themselves in its image. Consider Philips, one of the oldest, largest, and most storied multinational companies in the world. Gerard Philips co-founded the company with his father, Frederick, in the Netherlands in 1891. By 1895, it was teetering on the verge of bankruptcy. So Gerard brought in his brother, Anton, who had a degree in engineering. The company then shifted focus, bringing a scientific rigor to its product design. The spirit of innovation was on their side, as the Dutch had pioneered the scientific revolution in the 1600s. A series of groundbreaking inventions followed: the tungsten-filament lightbulb (1907), the electric razor (1939), the compact audiocassette (1963), the VCR (1972), the compact disc (1983), the GSM system for mobile telecommunications (also in 1983), and the DVD player (1998), to name but a few.

However, Philips still ran into trouble during the 1980s and 1990s under pressure from low-cost Japanese, South Korean, and Chinese competitors. A rising multibillion-dollar river of red ink engulfed the company. Top management tried everything they could to return to profitability. They hired some of the best consultants. They restructured their manufacturing plants, adjusted their worldwide logistics. They revamped their marketing. They reorganized the company through the use of dual-reporting structures and cross-functional teams where engineers and marketing people work together to offer the kinds of products that customers really want. Nothing seemed to work.

Philips went through six CEOs in three decades (by comparison, they'd gone through five during their first hundred years). Then Frans Van Houten was appointed CEO in 2011. He was homegrown: he had worked at Philips his entire life, and his father was on the company's board of directors. But he did not replicate his predecessors' mistakes. Rather than swim against the changing currents of global economic and demographic trends, he decided the company should ride them. Lightbulbs and TV sets, the company's bread and butter, were becoming less profitable year in and year out. What was a global brand like Philips to do? Van Houten proposed a different direction: focus on healthcare-related electronics, products that are research-intensive and customized, such as scanners and imaging equipment, for which demand was growing as populations worldwide aged. Nowadays, Philips's medical division accounts for over two-thirds of their corporate revenue, and profits have soared.

REINVENTING "OLD AGE"

"My newly retired mom is a fairly tech-savvy senior," writes Jennifer Jolly, a *USA Today* contributor. "She plays a mean game of Words with Friends, knows how to post photos on Facebook . . . and shoots a decent selfie every now and again," she explains. "Turns out, these seemingly simple digital doses of daily life might soon be just what the doctor orders for both older adults and the people who love them." A study published in the *Journal of Gerontology* led by Sheila Cotten, a professor at Michigan State University, found that American seniors who use the Internet exhibit lower rates of depression. Seniors don't find the results of the research surprising. At age seventy, Annena McCleskey is recovering from hip replacement surgery. "I didn't want to be in a closed situation, where I'd be removed from my buddies and everything," she said. The Internet has "brought my family to me, my friends to me, and my games to me."

The mantra of "technology changes everything" is certainly true when it comes to aging. For starters, breakthroughs in medicine, nutrition, biotechnology, and other fields are helping more people enjoy life for a longer period of time. By 2030, the average seventy-year-old will live like today's average fifty-year-old.

Against the conventional wisdom that virtual reality, artificial intelligence, and nanotechnology, to name a few emerging fields, are being driven by the wants and needs of young people, most of the exciting breakthroughs and developments nowadays are, in fact, being driven by the needs of the population above sixty.

Consider the example of Rendever, a startup focused on developing virtual reality (VR) applications to help seniors overcome their sense of isolation. "Rendever is developing VR experiences specifically for eldercare residents who are no longer able to venture outside and explore the world by themselves," says CEO and co-founder Kyle Rand. "With VR, you put on this headset and you can be anywhere in the world. . . . You play Bingo, do arts and crafts, and all of a sudden you are on top of the Eiffel Tower." Isolation accelerates cognitive decline and increases hypertension, among other health conditions. But the trick is to use VR to create a social situation, a game. "In senior living communities they'll have six residents wearing headsets and experiencing the same thing at the same time," says Rand. "Networking technology allows them to share these group experiences together." They also use "reminiscence therapy" to reduce stress levels. Going "back to a meaningful location experience component of someone's earlier life in a way that is immersive" can be soothing.

Another tantalizing possibility for improving seniors' quality of life is the development of exoskeletons (think Iron Man, but for grandparents) tailored to specific needs like climbing stairs, lifting shopping bags, making beds, or recovering from a broken hip. Remember that seniors are keen on quality of life, autonomy, and self-reliance. Innophys, a Japanese startup, has sold a thousand units of its Exo-Muscle, a robotic back support that helps people lift heavy objects such as a shopping bag or a suitcase, with prices starting at about $6,000. "The key part with exoskeletons is the controlling: the device has to understand when to initiate the movement," says CEO Takashi Fujimoto. Other companies are developing sensors that detect electrical signals from the nervous system in order to track muscle movements.

Japan leads the world in robotics for seniors because it is home to one of the world's largest gray markets in both absolute and relative terms. In Japan, finding affordable caregivers has become a challenge. This is further exacerbated by a lack of immigration. (In most countries, including the United States, about 90 percent of paid senior care is done by immigrants.) By 2025, Japan will need an additional 1 million nurses the country currently doesn't have. Will the Japanese deal with this shortage by turning to robots? Companies like Toyota have developed "human support robot" prototypes, which can retrieve medication, bring a glass of water, or draw the curtains by voice command. Another example is Paro, a robotic seal, which provides comfort to patients confined to bed. Its soothing powers are phenomenal: not only do patients report reductions in anxiety and depression, but for those suffering from dementia, interacting with the robotic seal has discouraged them from wandering away from their monitored areas. It's currently being used in as many as thirty countries. Denmark has Paros in 80 percent of its state-run nursing homes. You may be wondering why design a seal and not, say, a dog or cat. The reasoning, it turns out, is quite human: a dog or cat was the obvious first choice, but the inventor, Dr. Takanori Shibata, noted that the patients compared them to the real thing, and "their expectations were too high." Besides, "dog lovers didn't like the cat robot, and cat lovers didn't like the dog robot." By contrast, most people don't have a point of comparison for a seal.

While the United States lags behind Japan in gray robotics overall, there have been efforts to embrace technological innovation. Brookdale Senior Living, the largest network of senior living communities with over 100,000 residents, is betting big on voice-enabled digital assistants, which are particularly useful to patients with arthritis or macular degeneration. ElliQ , the Brookdale robot, encourages seniors to be active through online games, video chats, TED talks, and other social activities. Seniors who interact with robots appear to be less depressed and more engaged. Brookdale calls its new initiative "robots with open arms."

The Japanese are also pursuing applications of robotic technology for other age groups. The Nao Evolution VS robot interacts with children in long-term hospital care, coaches diabetics to monitor and manage their blood sugar levels, conducts physiotherapy sessions, and tutors students in various academic subjects. Apparently children very much enjoy interacting with the robots, perhaps more so than with human caregivers.

Some people may find a future in which robots will take care of senior citizens and children an aberration. Frankly, we have no alternative, for two reasons: not nearly enough babies are being born today to take all the caregiving tasks that will be required, and there's an effort, pushed by governments around the world, to halt the flow of immigration, which as I've shown has typically provided the workers to fulfill this role in the past.

And seniors are taking to studying and to entrepreneurship. In his sixties, Michael Taylor decided to search for new horizons. "I asked myself, what do I want to do when I grow up?" He pursued bachelor's and master's degrees in interior design and launched his own business. "In 1997, those between ages 55 and 64 constituted only 15 percent of burgeoning entrepreneurs," noted an article in the magazine *Entrepreneur*. "By 2016, that number reached 24 percent, according to the Kauffman Index of Entrepreneurship." Given the future size of the senior population and its longer life expectancy, half of all entrepreneurs may be in that age group by 2030.

THE GRAY WALLET

Besides healthcare, retail, and robotics, among the fastest-changing parts of the global economy in the wake of population aging will be finance. Simply put, people's money-related needs, preferences, and attitudes change as they age. A recent study by two economists at the Federal Reserve Bank of San Francisco illustrates the dynamic. They observed a very high correlation in the U.S. stock market between price-to-earnings (PE) ratios for listed equities and the aging of the population. PE ratios are the price of a share divided by the earnings per share. High PE ratios indicate that investors are willing to pay handsomely to own a portion of the profits that the company is making. That means they are bullish about that stock because they believe the company will do well in the future. The economists found that between the 1950s and the early 2010s average PE ratios for all listed companies in the United States followed a pattern: they fell as the population grew older and rose as it turned younger.

How could that be? What's the relationship between aging and stock prices?

The reasons for the long-term correlation are twofold. From the point of view of investing, people generally become more risk-averse as they age. Young people tend to put their savings into asset classes that offer growth in value, which comes with higher risk. Equities are one such asset class. As people turn fifty or sixty, they start rebalancing their portfolios by purchasing more bonds, which are less risky. Finally, as they approach retirement, they start to cash out or purchase an annuity (a fixed sum of money paid out in intervals).

There's also a correlation between age and consumption. People change their purchasing behavior as they grow older. They no longer replace their cars or household appliances, and they tend not to buy homes. If anything, they actually downsize. Given how investing and purchasing behavior changes over the course of one's life, it is no surprise that stock market valuations reflect demographics. Thinking about 2030, one thing seems likely: as populations age around the world, stock prices relative to company profits will not be as high as they traditionally have been. However, if between now and then we witness a transformation in the way we think about aging, and if we take advantage of the opportunities embedded in it, the link between the stock market and aging may become a virtuous one.

When it comes to banking services, the effects of aging will be quite extensive. For starters, the demand for mortgages and consumer credit is likely to decline, but there will be a greater desire for products that allow people to reduce the risks associated with investing their savings so that they last longer. In addition, there is growing demand among seniors to generate income from the house they live in. Airbnb, as we shall see in Chapter 7, is one such possibility. In many parts of the world banks now offer "reverse mortgages," or arrangements in which homeowners can agree today to give their home to the bank when they pass away, in exchange for a lump sum of money at the start of the reverse mortgage or a series of monthly payments. The homeowner gets to stay at home *and* receive some income from the property.

Traditional banks are under great pressure these days to rebuild trust, incorporate technology, and offer innovative products. Aging generates yet another challenge—a declining savings rate, since people beyond a certain age tend to be net spenders as opposed to net savers. It just so happens that taking deposits from customers is the cheapest source of funds banks traditionally have had. As a result, consumers may end up having to pay higher interest rates when they borrow.

On the brighter side, the aging of the population will stimulate the demand for advisory services, asset management, and annuities, among other products. The problem is that banks aren't alone in offering these types of high-margin products. All manner of financial intermediaries and "fintech" startups are now competing for the gray market. The fintech industry needs to "move beyond creating tech solutions for the 18–35 year olds, to focus on solutions to meet the needs of all as we age," says Theodora Lau, founder of Unconventional Ventures and former director of market innovation at AARP. Fintech represents a formidable opportunity to integrate services across many generations. "Central to that strategy is assisting the ecosystem that supports older adults, including their caregivers," she argues.

Another vexing issue that fintech can address is what to do when the spouse in charge of the family's finances becomes incapacitated or dies, as the newspaper *American Banker* emphasizes. What are the 40 million American widowed spouses who are in the dark about finances to do when their other half is no longer there to manage their money? Brad Kotansky faced this problem when his father passed away. "It took me three years to put the pieces of the puzzle together . . . there was just tremendous stuff accumulated over 80 years. . . . Step one for me was to speak to my mother," who had let her husband run the family's finances. He decided to found Onist in 2017, an app that helps family members and other stakeholders share financial data and documents like wills, powers of attorney, and titles to property so they can sort out the family's finances after the death of a relative. The company sells its software to banks and other financial institutions.

Or consider another all-too-frequent situation: an older adult loses his job and isn't financially prepared for early retirement. Navigating the options offered by Social Security and Medicare can be a daunting task, and figuring out a workable financial plan is difficult under duress; all of this can be made more difficult by the plummeting self-esteem that can accompany the loss of a job. Ramya Joseph started Pefin when her father lost his job. Each of the company's five thousand clients is modeled individually using artificial intelligence and big data to provide automated financial planning, advice, and investment options. "Ultimately, though money is the vehicle, this is about people achieving what matters most to them in life, then ongoing coaching and advice," notes CEO Catherine Flax. "When an incremental dollar comes in, should I be saving it, should I be paying down debt, should I be optimizing my 401(k)?" The company also sells its software to large pension funds.

Perhaps one of the most important areas to keep in mind for the future is financial abuse, a growing problem that tends to disproportionately affect the gray population. Alarmingly, it tends to be relatives, friends, neighbors, caregivers, attorneys, bank employees, and religious community leaders who most often perpetrate this type of crime. Predatory lending and identity theft are also rampant. According to the National Adult Protective Services Association, one in twenty seniors reports being financially abused, but only one in forty-four cases of such abuse is ever reported. The National Coalition on Aging estimates that financial abuse and fraud costs at least $3 billion and perhaps as much as $36 billion annually in the United States alone. The wide range of estimates shows how little is known about this growing epidemic. AARP reports that the loss per victim averages $120,000. As usual, technology may come to the rescue with apps that help people of all ages keep track of their income, spending, savings, and assets, but it may also exacerbate the problem. Financial cybercrime is difficult to curb, a sign that the rewards for finding a solution are huge. Perhaps robots can be programmed to provide care for those who need it without stealing from them.

And fintech can also come to the rescue of unsuspecting seniors duped by deceptive schemes. "My mother was an accountant, it wasn't that she wasn't financially astute," says Howard Tischler, co-founder and CEO of EverSafe. Because his mother was legally blind, "she brought somebody in to pay her bills who wrote herself a check every week. At the end of the day, she lost her entire life savings. Until I noticed she was having trouble with her memory [and was diagnosed with Alzheimer's], I had no idea she was being exploited." The co-founder of EverSafe is Liz Loewy, who ran the Elder Abuse Unit in the Manhattan District Attorney's Office. Among other prominent cases, she prosecuted Anthony D. Marshall, the only son of philanthropist and socialite Brooke Astor. He spent two months in prison for stealing millions from his mother. The reason? He had learned that his inheritance was going to be cut in half, to

$14.5 million, a small proportion of her $100 million fortune. His mother was helpless to defend herself, as Alzheimer's had ravished her mind.

EverSafe also uses machine learning to detect unusual changes in financial behavior that may be attributable to abuse by a third party. "The basic concept was to be able to deliver a personal suspicious activity report to the consumer and their loved ones or professionals so that they could be alerted that something is going on—before there's a crisis," explains Tischler. "We take into account the patterns Liz observed on elder financial abuse prosecutions, add observations from machine learning algorithms, and alert for things like missing deposits—things like Social Security or pensions—as well as changes in spending, unusual investment activity, and unauthorized account openings, to name a few."

THE GRAY LABOR MARKET

In the 2015 movie *The Intern*, seventy-year-old widower Ben Whittaker (played by Robert De Niro) asks, "How do I spend the rest of my days? You name it. Golf. Books. Movies. Pinochle. Tried yoga, learned to cook, bought some plants, [*switches to speaking Mandarin*] took classes in Mandarin. [*In English*] Believe me, I've tried everything." He ends up joining a Brooklyn online fashion startup under a new program to attract senior talent led by founder and CEO Jules Ostin (Anne Hathaway). Through a number of twists and turns, Ben becomes Jules's closest advisor and confidant.

Consider how much talent we waste by not fully utilizing the know-how and experience of the graying generations as their numbers grow bigger and bigger. Pause for a moment and dare to visualize a different world in which our grandparents are among the most active and productive members of society.

When the Prussian statesman Otto von Bismarck implemented the first national old-age social insurance plan, he was attempting to "domesticate" the working class by offering them something to look forward to. He came up with one of the great inventions of the late 1800s, which—along with the telephone, the internal combustion engine, and artificial fibers—would revolutionize modernity. In combination with universal schooling, another nineteenth-century innovation, retirement programs led to a radical compartmentalization of people's lives into three distinct stages: learning, working, and resting. It was no longer a matter of personal choice: the government told you what to do depending on your age, and social norms reinforced that regimented model of life.

It's astonishing to realize that for the longest time the government, the law, and even mainstream culture have told us that people above a certain age can no longer make genuine contributions to society and the economy. People above sixty-five (or some other arbitrary number) were deemed to be part of the "passive" population, neither takers nor givers.

But especially given the increase in life span—by 2030, the average sixty-year-old can expect to live for another twenty-two years; in the developed world, that number grows to twenty-five years—it's time to reconsider this so-called truism. "The desire to work, in part, comes from a financial place," says Catherine Collinson, CEO of the Transamerica Center for Retirement Studies, "but it also does transcend beyond that to a desire to be engaged in the world." Similarly, companies are becoming keenly aware of the loss they incur when an experienced worker retires. "As baby boomers retire, their institutional knowledge is walking out the door," says Susan Weinstock, a vice president at AARP. "Older workers are a great value to employers." Boeing, Michelin, and UPS have brought recent retirees back in during periods of peak demand for their products or services.

There are other potential benefits. Research shows that diversity in terms of gender or ethnicity tends to reduce group cohesion and performance but enhances creativity and non-routine problem-solving. While the impact of age tends to be blurred by its association with job tenure, there are some reports that groups formed by a cohort of varying ages may be more creative. For instance, BMW, the German car company, found that intergenerational work teams perform better when it comes to generating ideas and solving problems. "A multi-generational team offers a diversified way of looking at a project or problem," argues Helen Dennis, a specialist on the topic. "The more thoughts you have, the greater the advantage you have to accomplish your objective." *The Intern* brilliantly captured how the interplay of generations in the workplace can lead to win-win situations—and a few laughs. But what about the unintended consequences?

One largely unforeseen consequence of work beyond retirement age has been the increasing reluctance of governments in Europe and the United States to take full responsibility for the well-being of people beyond a certain age. The talk about discretionary spending and "gray is the new black" also has the effect of persuading politicians that seniors can do well without government handouts. For example, governments' fiscal difficulties, the ideology of self-reliance, and the discretionary spending power of a large segment of the senior population reinforce in some quarters the notion that state pensions not only cannot but also should not be the sole source of support. Many politicians now feel that seniors should take charge of their own destinies to a much greater extent than in decades past—say, by generating supplementary income by renting rooms in their homes or driving an Uber, as we shall see in Chapter 7. As the over-sixty demographic expands worldwide, this will surely become the subject of heated debates, especially as the smaller younger cohorts of taxpayers—millennials and Gen Z—weigh in politically.

AND MILLENNIALS WILL AGE TOO

By 2040, the first millennials will go into retirement. Initially dubbed Generation Y, they're frequently defined as the age cohort born between 1980 and 2000, although some identify them more narrowly as those born between the early 1980s and the late 1990s. They are far more than a mere age cohort in the sense that they were born at a time when information and communication technologies were undergoing a quantum leap that transformed the world. Not all millennials, however, are "digital natives," in the sense that only the second half of this generation was born into the networked digital age as we know it today. One can perhaps say that millennials were raised, if not born, digital.

Few millennials have ever purchased a CD, let alone a cassette tape, developed photographic film, used correcting tape to undo a typewriting mistake, asked for driving directions, watched broadcast TV, sent a fax, or used a rotary phone. They can barely imagine what life was like before 4G, let alone 1G. Under such conditions, childhood friendships are not limited by geography, and intimate relationships have been transformed by the mediating impact of social media and dating apps. The world of 2030 and beyond will be in part shaped by the attitude and behavior of millennials, and thus we need to understand this pivotal generation in order to be able to see what the world will look like a decade from now.

Some early analyses of millennials were controversial and caused quite a stir. For instance, Jean Twenge's 2006 book, *Generation Me: Why Today's Young Americans Are More Confident, Assertive, Entitled—and More Miserable than Ever Before*, advanced the argument that millennials are the most narcissistic generation ever, and that their parents were the reason for it. "We are doing kids a tremendous disservice when we lead them to believe that just because they are special to us (their parents), the rest of the world will treat them this way," she wrote. "The best preparation they can receive is not narcissism or even self-esteem, but your love and support—and your message to them that hard work and perseverance are more important to success than self-belief." Other critics highlighted different traits, like their desire to contribute to society, chase novel experiences, or prioritize jobs that satisfy their passions rather than offer financial security. While a 2016 study found that millennials score higher on the Narcissistic Personality Inventory than their parents, the comparison isn't particularly fair, especially when we consider that people's attitudes toward life change with age.

In fact, demographers and historians William Strauss and Neil Howe—who became successful consultants to companies, governments, and universities after penning the first analysis of millennials—argue that this generation appears to be as other-regarding as the Silent Generation. They characterize American millennials as sheltered, confident, team-oriented, conventional, pressured, and achievement-oriented. Others, like David Burstein, think that millennials are driven by a kind of "pragmatic idealism," which leads them to use practical tools to make the world a better place, without falling for radical or revolutionary approaches to social change. That perhaps explains why the Occupy Wall Street movement was relatively small and short-lived.

The problem with these characterizations of millennials—whether flattering or not—is that they seem to apply primarily to "white, affluent teenagers [and young adults] who accomplish great things as they grow up in the suburbs," as journalist Eric Hoover argues. These are young people "who confront anxiety when applying to super-selective colleges, and who multitask with ease as their helicopter parents hover reassuringly above them." Millennials from less privileged socioeconomic backgrounds are surely different in their attitudes and behavior. Overall, American "millennials are the first generation to have just a fifty-fifty chance of being financially better off than their parents," observes Jia Tolentino in *The New Yorker*. Their future well-being is not guaranteed in an increasingly competitive global economy. Flattering their ego, as many marketers seem intent on, might actually worsen their economic prospects.

According to statistics put together by the White House's Council of Economic Advisors during the Obama presidency, American millennials are on average less interested in home or automobile ownership, continue to live with their parents well into their twenties or even in some cases their thirties, and postpone or forgo marriage. One in four don't even care about getting a driver's license. We'll look further into these stunning behavioral patterns in Chapter 7.

One entirely inaccurate stereotype about American millennials is that they are compulsive job hoppers. In reality, millennials tend to spend more time in each job they hold than Generation X, though they prefer to do meaningful work rather than pursue the swiftest career path to the top. Some research indicates that their preference for team-based work is driven by their intensive use of social media, which also makes them long for more interaction with supervisors and demand a healthy balance between work and play.

Looming large behind millennials' work preferences is the fact that their early experience in the labor market was tainted by the 2008 financial crisis and subsequent recession (though the impact was different around the world; in most emerging markets, this was a time of sustained economic growth). Thus, there exist two realities within the global millennial population; that of millennials raised in rich countries, where middle-class incomes have been stagnant for two or three decades, and the reality of those raised in the emerging and developing world, for whom economic opportunities are so much better than what existed for their parents or grandparents. And within the European and American millennial generational unit, there's a subunit born into affluent households and another subunit born to low-income parents or to parents whose middle-class jobs may have disappeared as a consequence of globalization and technological change. Thus, companies and entrepreneurs should take any blanket generalization about the behavior of millennials as consumers, and its implications for the future, with a grain of salt.

Equally problematic are conclusions drawn from attitudinal surveys. The best source on international cultural values, the World Values Survey, found that millennials espouse higher self-expression values than most other generations in the world as a whole and in each region within it. This difference is driven by having more material means, higher intellectual skills, and wider social connectivity than their forbears. In turn, these lead to more independent behaviors, greater choice, and more room to actualize inner potential. (As with the other surveys I mention throughout this book, averages inevitably conceal major differences, in this case especially between affluent millennials and those of more modest family backgrounds.)

Values matter, of course, especially when it comes to making economic decisions. But much of the economic behavior of millennials has been driven by the rise in the costs of housing and higher education. Meanwhile, most wealth—and the income that can be derived from it—belongs to their parents and grandparents. Sociologist Kathleen Shaputis blames these economic issues for the tendency by millennials to delay rites of passage such as marriage and having children. In her book *The Crowded Nest Syndrome*, she writes about the "Peter Pan" or "boomerang" generation, which finds itself at a distinct stage in life between the teens and adulthood that she calls "emerging adulthood."

Under these circumstances, it should not come as a surprise that the aggregate savings rate among millennials is one of the lowest in recent memory. And there is no better window into the future than assessing how much people are saving today. Moody's Analytics rang the alarm in 2014 by showing that American adults under the age of thirty-five had a *negative* savings rate of –1.8 percent, meaning that they borrow to sustain their consumption rather than save for the future. Of course, as we move further away in time from the impact of the Great Recession, things will improve. According to a 2018 survey conducted by Bank of America, one in six American millennials ages twenty-three to thirty-seven have savings in excess of $100,000. That's very impressive. But other surveys have found that only 13 percent of those aged eighteen to twenty-four have more than $10,000 in savings, a percentage that marginally improves to 20 percent for those between the ages of twenty-five and thirty-four. Seventy-five percent of millennials believe that their generation overspends compared to other generations, and 20 percent say they cannot afford a home. With credit card and student debt at historic levels, it should be no surprise that most young millennials are finding it hard to save. Americans under the age of thirty-five in 2017 were shouldering educational debt at a level nearly twice that of what Americans in the same age group were carrying in 2001. Over the same period, the median net worth of young Americans plummeted from $15,000 to $10,400.

But beware of aggregate statistics. Remember that the millennial population in the world, and within specific countries like the United States, is not homogeneous. Companies keen on attracting millennials as customers need to recognize that essential fact and not assume that all millennials are cut from the same cloth. The world of 2030 will be shaped not by one monolithic generation but by the interplay among the various millennial generational subunits, defined by education, income, and ethnicity.

WHAT'S NEXT AFTER MILLENNIALS?

I always like to share one very interesting statistic. In some countries the number of people between the ages of fifteen and thirty-four will decline over time, especially in China, Japan, and Europe. In other regions, by contrast, it will increase at least for a generation or two, as in South Asia, the Middle East, and Africa. These trends are simply the result of the number of babies being born today. The United States, however, belongs in neither category. As of 2017 there were about 90.4 million people in that age group, and by 2030 the forecast is 89.5 million. That's roughly the same number, but it will be a very different cohort of young people. Let me explain why.

I like to argue that gauging the effects of immigration is tantamount to predicting the future. While in 1980 about 78 percent of those aged fifteen to thirty-four in the United States were non-Hispanic whites, by 2030 less than half will be. The young age group in the United States and Europe will become more ethnically and linguistically diverse. Since, on average, immigrant families tend to have more babies, the composition of our young will change very quickly, much faster than the population as a whole. What today we call "minorities" will be the majority in ten years.

This trend will bring about important behavioral changes. It just so happens that nowadays the desire of children of immigrants to marry and to own a home and car is greater than that of their native peers. It's the essence of the American dream. Because of this, the children of immigrants seem to constitute a separate generational unit. Unless millennial children of immigrants assimilate with the mainstream at a much faster rate than previous generations of immigrants, young Americans in 2030 will behave differently from young people today.

Let's think for a moment about the implications of a changing ethnolinguistic composition for the sharing economy, one of the most exciting new developments around the world. Surveys indicate that Hispanic Americans, African Americans, and Asian Americans are more likely to use ride-hailing apps and accommodation-sharing services than their mainstream counterparts. This makes sense when we consider the differences in purchasing power.

Another important trend involves entrepreneurship. Hispanic Americans are more likely than any other group, white or non-white, to be self-employed or own a business. In addition, Hispanic entrepreneurs are more likely than Hispanics in general to be English-dominant or English-preferred speakers. Although Hispanics' share of high-tech ventures is still low, that is also likely to change as more Hispanics attend college and graduate school.

While the numbers and diversity of Generation Z, the generation after millennials, are straightforward to calculate, what will their identity and behavior be like? In its extensive global survey and report on the subject, the London-based Varkey Foundation argues that their identity will be defined by inequality in all of its manifestations, from educational opportunity and gender and racial disparities to migration and the increasing wealth gap. It will also be the generation that will feel the brunt of the pension crisis: they are likely to be asked to pay more taxes so that their parents and grandparents will receive the benefits they were promised. Yikes!

And it will be the first generation of young adults entirely born into the networked digital age. Those in "Generation Z have grown up with the limitless opportunities provided by the power of computing and networking. They are more likely to have travelled across borders, have friends who are on the other side of the world, and know people from another religion or culture than that of their parents and grandparents," argues the Varkey report. "In their lifetime, attitudes and laws on social issues from same-sex marriage to transgender rights seem to have changed at lightning speed. Meanwhile, gender and race seem as divisive and contested as ever."

But are these perspectives shared by all members of Generation Z around the world? In 2016, the Varkey Foundation polled twenty thousand people between the ages of fifteen and twenty-one in twenty countries. (It's important to keep in mind that the respondents were all part of global online research panels, which biases the sample toward urban youth with relatively high educational standards.) The poll found that global values, as opposed to local or parochial ones, predominate among people in this group, with respondents in countries at different levels of economic development sharing similar views. They tend to have tolerant attitudes toward contentious issues such as immigration and same-sex marriage, and progressive views about inequality, climate change, and freedom of speech. The study concludes that this generation might be driven by the idea of "global citizenship," which stands in contrast with the spirit of nationalism and nativism trending across the world today.

CHINA'S BEWILDERING GENERATIONS

Nowhere in the world is the interplay between generations as complex as in China. The thing that makes this vast and diverse country such a fascinating social laboratory is that it has taken China a mere thirty years to accomplish what took Europe and the United States two or three centuries. In 1712, the

English inventor Thomas Newcomen designed the first steam engine (later perfected by the Scottish inventor James Watt, who also developed the concept of horsepower, which was later translated into terms of another unit of power that we know today as the watt). It unleashed the industrial revolution. It subsequently took Britain three hundred years to become the service economy it is today, something that occurred only after a considerable amount of turmoil and dislocation. It took the United States half as much time. China, by contrast, made the transition from agrarian economy to a technological and service-oriented one in less than two generations.

As a result of China's swift economic and demographic transition, by 2030 the country will have about 60 million *fewer* people between the ages of fifteen and thirty-five than in 2020, and nearly 114 million *more* people above the age of sixty. "If you say that the developed Western countries are strolling into the phenomenon of an ageing population," says Yuan Xin, a demographer at Nankai University in Tianjin, "China is sprinting into it."

Chinese seniors face a more challenging future than their American counterparts not only because their numbers are increasing rapidly, but also because so many young people have left the countryside. Zhang Fumin and Liu Xiuying are a married couple in their seventies. They live in Longwangtou, a small village some eight hundred miles south of Beijing. Their two sons moved to the nation's capital after graduating from college. Demographers call aging parents like Zhang and Liu "the left-behind elderly." In 2017 their first grandson was born, and they decided to temporarily move in with their younger son to help raise the baby, though they planned to return to the village after a few weeks. Of China's 215 million people above the age of sixty in 2015, authorities believe that about 50 million lived far away from their children. That number could nearly double by 2030. "A large-scale migration of younger workers from rural to urban China . . . has separated many adult children from their ageing parents and imposed significant challenges on traditional patterns of familial support," observes ethnographer Jieyu Liu in a recent study. "These challenges are augmented by the fact that in rural China the elderly have been deprived [of] a state pension and other welfare provisions available to urban residents."

Migration to the cities also taints the future prospects of millennials in

China's deep countryside. While in the United States the main divide among millennials has to do with socioeconomic background, in China it involves the rural-urban cleavage. Most urban youth are middle-class or outright rich, while most rural youth are poor. Another key difference is that urban Chinese millennials have outstripped American millennials in terms of their networked digital activity, even adjusting for purchasing power. They are way more digitally connected, shop online more assiduously, use electronic payments for everything, and seem not to care much about how their personal information might be used. We have little systematic data about the values and attitudes of Chinese urban millennials, but one can fairly say that they indulge in self-expression values (social toleration, life satisfaction, public expression, and an aspiration to liberty) and do not tend to see modernization, wealth, and progress as "Western." They save three times as much as their American peers, although that's true for other age groups in China as well—not a bad idea given how skewed the age pyramid will become, with 25 percent of the population over the age of sixty by 2030.

THE FUTURE OF "OLD" AND "YOUNG"

One imaginative way of creating new opportunities for intergenerational collaboration is the intriguing lateral idea of the "nursing home dorm," a long-term care facility for senior citizens where college students get a free room and a sense of purpose in exchange for a certain number of hours of work per month. In the Netherlands, where the first experiments took place, there is mounting pressure to find the resources to offer seniors the care and attention they deserve. "That's when I thought of a group of other people—in this case, students—that also don't have much money," said Gea Sijpkes, the director of a pioneering nursing home dorm. The students assist seniors with some of their daily tasks and also help them improve their digital skills. The potential for attracting more seniors to these types of facilities lies in their ability to reduce the feelings of loneliness that research associates with faster cognitive decline, worsening health, and higher mortality.

The analysis of generations—whether for fun or for financial gain—must proceed cautiously. Arthur E. Levine, former president of Teachers College at Columbia University and of the Woodrow Wilson Foundation, observed that "generational images are stereotypes." In his view, our constant search for contrasts blinds us to similarities. "There are some differences that stand out," he says, "but there are more similarities between students of the past and the present. But if you wrote a book saying that, how interesting would that book be?"

Each generation in history has contained a bewildering diversity of individuals. Thinking in terms of generations, generational units, and subunits provides some analytical rigor. But the main point of this chapter is broader than that. Understanding millennials today does not ensure that we will better understand them in the future, because their behavior will surely evolve. As members of a generation go through the many stages of life, they adjust their attitudes and behavior. The group of people above age sixty today is going to differ, sometimes considerably, from the same age group in the future. But one reason for this has less to do with which generation we're looking at and more to do with changing conceptions of what old age really means.

Wired magazine and Pfizer, one of the world's largest pharmaceutical companies, have joined forces to envision what getting old will mean in the future. "While there are still many uncertainties on the aging horizon," says Pfizer's head of medical strategy, Pol Vandenbroucke, "many of us can take steps now to make sure old age won't just mean living long, but living well." We can count on medicine and technology keeping us healthier as we age, but our own behavior will also be key to remaining physically and mentally alert. Here's an intriguing prediction: "The millennial generation is very different from their baby boomer and Gen X elders. Stereotypes aside, they represent an important cultural inflection point: the first generation exposed to the internet throughout childhood. Their penchant for constant connectivity and immediate access to information is defining characteristics that may already be setting them up for success in old age." Millennials may well be the generation to realize that longevity requires a lifelong commitment to staying healthy and active, and their strong inclination for hyperconnectivity may help them overcome isolation as they grow older. As Stephen Ewell, executive director of the Consumer Technology Association Foundation, argues, "Millennials . . . are really interested in preparing for longer health spans. We not only incorporate their ideas, we take those ideas, and they become part of our ecosystem of how we make a community stronger."

Millennials will live longer lives than previous generations, so the stakes regarding the definition of the gray way of life are getting higher. The good news, according to the Sightlines Project at Stanford University's Center on Longevity, is that "smoking rates are starkly down, and exercise is up. More than young people in the past, millennials have friends they count on in tough times. More millennials have college degrees than do prior generations, and there is no better predictor of functioning well at advanced ages than education." But there's also bad news, especially from the point of view of financial security. Many millennials will be well off by the time they reach retirement, but an equal, if not greater, number of them will find themselves in dire financial straits for most of their adult lives. Globally, we see a similar bifurcation of the fortunes of different groups, the subject of the next chapter.

Keeping Up with the Singhs and the Wangs

Being in the middle class is a feeling as well as an income level.

—MARGARET HALSEY, AMERICAN WRITER

In 2009, the Indian economy was booming. Ten million people would be lifted out of poverty that year, and an incipient middle class was emerging for everyone to see. Tata Motors, founded in 1945, was the leading car company in the country and was eager to remain on top. To do so, Ratan Tata, the great-grandson of the Tata Group's founder, unveiled their newest model, the Tata Nano. Priced at the equivalent of $2,000, it was a no-frills vehicle that had no air-conditioning and was powered by a tiny 634 cc engine. "Today's story started some years ago when I observed families riding on two-wheelers, the father driving a scooter, his young kid standing in front of him, his wife sitting behind him holding a baby," Tata told reporters. "I asked myself whether one could conceive of a safe, affordable, all-weather form of transport for such a family. This [has] been referred to as one man's dream and indeed it was." Driven by the chairman's vision, the company invested heavily and built a factory capable of producing 250,000 units a year. Ratan Tata personally delivered the first three Nanos. As the *Economic Times* reported at the time, Ashok Raghunath Vichare, a fifty-nine-year-old customs official from Mumbai, received the first and was "very happy" to drive the car "to a nearby Hindu temple to have the vehicle blessed." The second was purchased by Ashish Balakrishnan, a twenty-nine-year-old bank employee, who could not wait to go on a "joyride on the Bandra-Worli Sea-Link," a new 3.5-mile bridge in Mumbai. "This is my first car," he said. "The price was a major factor." The company hoped that this attitude was indicative of the emerging Indian middle-class's eagerness to replace their bicycles and motorcycles, as did the eighty-two-year-old former assistant commissioner of the Mumbai police, who replaced his scooter with the Nano.

But this didn't happen. Instead, consumers purchased Suzukis, Hyundais, Toyotas, and other foreign brands. When they saw billboards advertising the Nano as the "World's Cheapest Car," they associated the vehicle with the poor. Sales never came close to the company's expectations. "It became termed as a cheapest car by the public and, I am sorry to say, by ourselves, not by me, but the company when it was marketing it," Tata admitted. "I think that is unfortunate."

The Nano will go down in business history as one of the worst corporate blunders of all time. "I don't like the way the Nano looks to people and it's all about the look," twenty-two-year-old computer operator Shushank Sharma said. "I take the [motor] bike to work. But if I have to go hang out with my friends or go for a marriage, then I prefer a car. But I would prefer to sit at home if I have to go in a Nano." The new middle class in emerging markets like India is fundamentally aspirational. By looking backward rather than forward, Tata Motors created something that did not match that demographic's new class consciousness, and thus it failed to capture what should have been an exciting market opportunity. They didn't grasp that the Singhs, true to their middle-class status, were striving to keep up with the Joneses.

By contrast, consider the success of the American manufacturer of outdoor grills Weber-Stephen Products LLC as it entered the Indian market. Consider, too, the challenge: How do you sell barbecue grills in a country where people don't eat beef or pork, and the men don't traditionally cook?

Weber-Stephen was originally founded in 1893 as Weber Bros. Metal Works. In the early 1950s, George Stephen Sr., a part-owner of a sheet metal shop in Chicago, was looking for a way to improve the brazier he had been using for outdoor cooking. He imagined building a more practical barbecue composed of two metal hemispheres: the bottom serving as a receptacle for burning charcoal and the top as a lid. It was a hit. To further refine the product, Stephen joined forces with Weber Bros., and its round kettle grill is now a ubiquitous sight on many American patios and in backyards. The company has played a significant role in popularizing the outdoor BBQ, which at this point is very much a part of American culture. "The culinary tradition of cooking meat low and slow over indirect flame . . . has become so prevalent over the years," writes Natasha Geiling on Smithsonian.com, "that BBQ itself represents a sort of pop culture, spawning TV shows, historically focused road trips, and even fusion dishes like BBQ tacos."

In 2010, a couple of years after the fateful launch of the Tata Nano, Weber-Stephen decided to take a stab at the Indian middle-class market. They hired Sivakumar "Siva" Kandaswamy to manage the product launch. Kandaswamy understood the challenges ahead, and the team he assembled was attuned to the cultural differences between India and the United States. They learned everything there was to learn about how the new Indian middle-class consumer viewed food and cooking. But they also surmised that traditional attitudes and habits might shift as more people climbed up the socioeconomic ladder and started watching foreign movies and TV shows. Within a few years, "a backyard grilling culture has taken hold in India," noted Dave Sutton, a consultant with Top Right Partners in Atlanta. "License to Grill: India Takes to the Barbecue," was the headline of a 2011 article in the *Times of India*. "And you thought barbecuing was too American to appeal to Indians, who love their tandoor, thank you very much," the article went on. "The reality is that more and more urban Indians are taking to the grill, especially in centers with high homecoming NRI [non-resident Indian diaspora] populations such as Bangalore, Pune, Gurgaon and parts of Mumbai." Weber-Stephen knew it had to steer Indian consumers toward appreciating the fun of barbecuing. As its own literature attests, the company "helps deliver additional functional and emotional benefits by providing consumers with tips, tools, and localized recipes." Soon enough, Indian middle-class families were gathering around the grill to barbecue everything from tandoori chicken to plantain kebabs. That came about because Weber-Stephen did not shy away from the complexities of the Indian market; rather, the company embraced the opportunity.

▪

The Greek philosopher Aristotle once said that "the most perfect political community is one in which the middle class is in control, and outnumbers both of the other classes." The middle class is, indeed, the backbone of modern societies and economies. Louis D. Brandeis, the astute American Progressive reformer of the early twentieth century, once predicted that "we can have democracy in this country, or we can have great wealth concentrated in the hands of a few, but we can't have both." For the longest time, the United States and Western Europe managed to strike a delicate balance whereby the enormous wealth being generated by the global economy fell mostly to the American and European middle classes.

Not anymore.

While the American and European middle classes are still the world's richest, their economic fortunes are stagnant and their status is waning. By contrast, every year more than a hundred million people are joining the ranks of the middle class in emerging markets, and those already there are seeing their incomes increase very rapidly. They're on the upswing, while we're in the doldrums.

Shares of Middle-Class Purchasing Power (%)

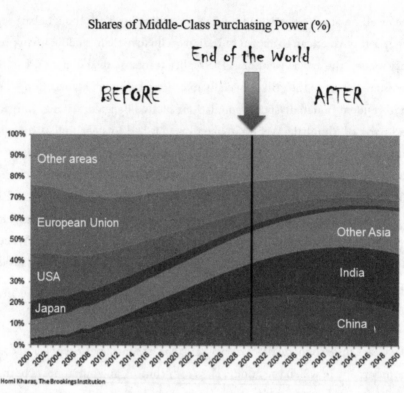

Homi Kharas, The Brookings Institution

Figure 5

Figure 5 shows the distribution of middle-class spending power in different parts of the world. On a global scale, the middle class includes individuals
who have an income of between $10 and $100 a day. For a family of four, that
would roughly translate into an annual income of between $15,000 and
$150,000.

The United States and Europe house the majority of the world's middle
class now, but by 2030, China, India, and the rest of Asia (excluding Japan)
will be home to more than half of global consumer purchasing power (adjusted
for inflation). That's a sea change between the 1920s, when companies such as
General Motors and Sears became the business titans of the day by catering to
the needs of an expanding American middle class, and the second decade of
the new millennium, when the likes of Alphabet and Amazon reign supreme.

We also don't need to wait until 2030 for certain fields of consumption
to shift toward Asia. Consider the Chinese dominance in online shopping.

Singles Day—celebrated mostly online—generated $25 billion in sales in 2017, dwarfing Cyber Monday's $7 billion in the United States. Or gambling: Macau, in southern China, annually generates gross gambling revenues of $33 billion, compared to $7 billion for Las Vegas.

But the trends indicate that the Chinese middle-class market will be the world's largest in terms of purchasing power just for a decade or two at most. India's young and increasingly well-educated population, due to its growth potential, will constitute the most attractive emerging market by 2030.

FROM *MADAME BOVARY* TO *THE SIMPSONS*

Business executives and politicians in Europe and the United States used to know what the middle class was all about. They actively contributed to creating that large segment of people who are neither affluent nor destitute. They catered to middle-class needs by delivering cheap goods, low inflation, and political stability. The middle class became the engine of the market economy. Because most economic activity is driven by the distribution and sale of consumer goods and services, no developed country could do without it. Hence the popularity of terms such as "consumer confidence," "consumer price index," and "consumer credit." If consumers don't spend, the entire economy tanks— and elections are lost.

Our modern understanding of the middle class goes back to a British government report from 1913, which defined it as people who are neither upper-class nor traditionally working-class. Recent Western history has been about broadening this middle ground. With rising inequality on both sides of the North Atlantic, however, this large segment is starting to shrink.

Another, somewhat earlier perspective on the middle class conceived it as a state of transition. Charles Dickens, who understood English nineteenth-century life better than most, argued that "though we are perpetually bragging of [the middle class] as our safety, it is nothing but a poor fringe on the mantle of the upper class." In 1937, another shrewd observer of British life, George Orwell, wrote in *Road to Wigan Pier* that "we of the sinking middle class—the private schoolmaster, the half-starved free-lance journalist, . . . the clerks, the civil servants, commercial travelers, and the thrice-bankrupt drapers in the country towns—may sink without further struggles into the working class where we belong, and probably when we get there it will not be so dreadful as we feared, for, after all, we have nothing to lose."

From an economic point of view, the middle class affords a cozy existence. "Comfort came in with the middle classes," wrote the British art critic Clive Bell. Economists define belonging to the middle class as enjoying a measure of discretionary income, above and beyond covering the basics of food, shelter, and education. Middle-class consumers take out mortgages to buy homes, purchase scores of convenient appliances, go on vacation, send their kids to good schools, and plan for retirement. In other words, being in the middle class meant being in a secure economic position, beyond living paycheck to paycheck—or at least it once meant that.

Defining the middle class by income may be convenient, but it can also blur the differences between, say, a nurse and a plumber, or a small business owner and an accountant, who can all be middle class yet have widely different educational backgrounds and careers. It's a commonly held belief that a college education is a passport to the middle class. But there are many members of the middle class who lack a college education.

In truth, "middle class" is much more than an economic or educational designation. "Being in the middle class is a feeling as well as an income level," says Margaret Halsey, the witty American writer. Middle-class status is as much a social-psychological state of mind as it is about money. The French novelist Gustave Flaubert captured the middle-class mindset as well as anyone could in *Madame Bovary* (1856), a novel in which a woman felt trapped by her middle-class status. "The middle class is so funny," argued author J. K. Rowling. "It's the class I know best, and it's the class where you find the most pretension, so that's what makes the middle classes so funny." The middle class is about not only aspiration but also ostentation, the theme of *Keeping Up with the Joneses*, the famous comic strip by Arthur R. "Pop" Momand that ran daily between 1913 and 1938, precisely when the American middle class went from its initial boom to its worst bust during the Great Depression. Status competition on the social ladder is as old as organized society itself, but it certainly acquired a new dimension as the middle class grew over the course of the twentieth century. "The Smiths like the new play; the Joneses go to see it, and they copy the Smith verdict," Mark Twain wrote in a 1901 essay called "Corn-Pone Opinions."

Fast-forward to *The Simpsons*. In this animated TV show, the Simpson family owns a home in a neighborhood filled with small business owners and professionals, the father tries out a series of white-collar jobs, the mother stays at home, they take vacations, they save for their children's college education, they have pets, and so on. It was not until season 6, episode 23 that Homer Simpson admits to being middle-class. He actually showed a pay stub indicating that he was making the equivalent of about $37,000 in 2016 dollars, which places the Simpsons squarely within the median income bracket.

Given that the middle class is such a large group, it's unsurprising that there's little agreement on the values shared by those in it. Historically, some notions that come to mind are propriety, balance, decency, and respectability. The American novelist and playwright Gertrude Stein put it best: "I simply contend that the middle-class ideal which demands that people be affectionate, respectable, honest and content, that they avoid excitements and cultivate serenity is the ideal that appeals to me, it is in short the ideal of affectionate family life, of honorable business methods."

There is also a tendency to associate the middle class with conformity, and research suggests middle-class individuals exhibit higher levels of status anxiety than those in either the upper class or the lower class. As Damon J. Phillips at Columbia and Ezra W. Zuckerman at MIT explain, "Conformity increases as actors value their membership in a group yet feel insecure in that membership." While high-status individuals tend to feel confident in their social position and therefore have little reason to conform, low-status people "feel free to defy accepted practice because they are excluded regardless of their actions." It is those in the middle who feel the pressure to conform, both so that they might move up the ladder and out of fear that they might slide downward.

Having said that, it is instructive to note that middle-class behavior does not tend to be as virtuous as some argue. One key distinction between middle-class and working-class values is the individualism of the former and the communitarianism of the latter. A middle-class upbringing emphasizes individual choice and independence, while the classic ethos of the working class is all about solidarity and interdependence. It turns out that unethical behavior is more prevalent among members of the middle class, while prosocial and altruistic behavior is more common among the working class. Research published in the *Proceedings of the National Academy of Sciences* found that "upper-class individuals were more likely to break the law while driving, relative to lower-class individuals ... exhibit unethical decision-making tendencies ... take valued goods from others ... lie in a negotiation ... cheat to increase their chances of winning a prize ... and endorse unethical behavior at work."

For now, the middle classes in the United States and Europe constitute a monumental enigma. While they're characterized by propriety, honesty, and respectability, they're also susceptible to unethical behavior because of the individualist ethos, pretentiousness, and pressure to conform. There's also the added layer of frustration and anger from the status lost in the wake of global and domestic economic stagnation.

WE'RE NOT ALONE IN THE UNIVERSE

Zhou Yuanyan was born in Inner Mongolia. She moved to a village on Beijing's sixth ring road and commuted an hour and a half for a job in the city, first as a waitress and then as a real estate agent. As things improved financially, her mother moved in with her, and together they enjoy the comfort that comes with her new job, life, and status. "I increased my commission income quite a bit ... so we were able to move twice," Zhou told the *Financial Times*. China will add another 400 million people like her to its middle class by 2030.

Thousands of miles away, in some countries and cities across Africa, another middle class is slowly taking shape. "I'm very, very, very excited," John Monday, a gas turbine operator, proclaimed as a friend photographed him in front of a supermarket located in a mall in Warri, a boomtown in Nigeria's oil region. According to the *New York Times*, Monday traveled nearly two hundred miles to visit a new shopping mall at Warri. "A middle-class person can come into this mall and feel a sense of belonging," Monday said. The country's fifth-largest financial group, Access Bank, whose branch managers have heard me speak about the outlook for 2030, estimates that more than 10 percent of Nigeria's population of some 200 million is now middle-class—and each year it grows by a whopping 1.5 million.

Though still small by Chinese or Indian standards, the African middle-class consumer market continues to grow. According to a recent report by Deloitte, this is mostly due to population growth, purchasing power, cities, and technology use. In surveys, a quarter to half of consumers living in the largest African economies—Nigeria, South Africa, Egypt, and Kenya—sense a material improvement in their lives from five years ago. They have discretionary income, aspire to buy well-known consumer brands, and would spend a bit extra to keep pace with the latest fashion or trend. Quality is more important than price, and international brands are preferred. While the market is currently ripe for American and European brands, it won't be long before local companies and entrepreneurs jockey for position.

In fact, according to Brand Africa, a nonprofit focused on leveraging a unified African image internationally, the one hundred most admired brands on the continent come from twenty-eight different countries, which include eight African ones. While twenty-four American brands are among the top hundred, as many as seventeen are African. And more African brands will succeed as the continent's consumer markets evolve.

The key to grasping the essence of the new middle class in emerging markets like China or Nigeria is to recognize how it differs from the old middle class of the United States, Europe, or Japan. For starters, the "old" middle class has remained so for generations. But the emerging middle class is all "new money," as the expression goes. While the *average* per capita income of middle-class people in the United States, Europe, and Japan is about three times higher than that of the middle class in China, India, or other emerging markets, it is stagnant. The generational and income differences between the old and new make middle-class consumers in emerging markets far more aspirational than middle-class consumers in developed ones.

MQAM2LL/A iPhone X, Space Gray, 256GB
Designed by Apple in California Assembled in China
Other items as marked thereon Model A1901

(1P) Part No. MQAM2LL/A

(S) Serial No. F17WN7XLJCL8

() ICCID 89014104270884584789

UPC
1 9 0 1 9 8 4 5 9 1 2 1

IMEI/MEID 354876090941985

FCC ID: 8CG-E3175A
IC: 579C-E3175A

Apple
Apple Inc., 1 Infinite Loop, Cupertino, CA 95014 USA
TM and © 2017 Apple Inc. All rights reserved. 602-01589-A

Figure 6

WHY THE IPHONE LOOKS LIKE AN IPHONE

The iPhone is the most iconic middle-class consumer product of the early twenty-first century. It's not just a phone—it's also a calendar, web browser, camera, calculator, flashlight, music and video playback system, e-book reader, and a myriad of other things jammed into one extremely versatile and easy-to-use device with more computing power than the Apollo mission computer or the fictional talking supercomputer HAL in *2001: A Space Odyssey*.

The touch screen on my iPhone is just marvelous. But look closely at the box my phone arrived in (Figure 6).

The "FCC" indicates that the product meets the technical and safety standards of the Federal Communications Commission, a U.S. government agency, and the "CE" indicates it meets the parallel standards for products sold within the European Union's borders. But why refer only to the United States and Europe, and not other countries or economic unions?

It's because at present those are the two biggest markets. Back in the 1980s, before Europe became the single (and second-largest) market that it is today, only the FCC logo would have appeared on electronic products. In other words, the largest markets write the rules of the game—simply because they are large and influential. Companies that vie for their share of the pie have no option but to comply with whatever product regulations these governments put in place.

By 2030, however, China and India will be the largest consumer markets. I'm ready to bet my entire pension fund that, alongside FCC and CE logos, our smartphones will also carry a Chinese, and possibly an Indian, regulatory stamp of approval.

There are other ways in which growing middle-class markets globally are changing how technological competition takes place. Let's consider patents.

In Article I, the U.S. Constitution gives Congress the power "to promote the progress of science and useful arts, by securing for limited times to authors and inventors the exclusive right to their respective writings and discoveries." For inventors, that exclusive right is protected through a patent, which can apply to a new pharmaceutical drug, mechanical device, or composite material. In the United States, a patent confers an exclusive right of use for twenty years. For decades, the U.S. Patent and Trademark Office has been the world's most important agency when it comes to protecting inventions, and it will likely continue to be for some time. But while in 2016 the number of patent applications filed in the United States was three times greater than in 1995, in India it was seven times greater, and in China a whopping seventy-two times greater. As China and India grow in prominence, so does their culture of patenting new products and inventions.

A CLASH OF THE MIDDLE CLASSES?

The Hooker Furniture Corporation offers everything from bed frames and dressers to sofas and armchairs. In 1925, four-year-old Clyde Hooker Jr. pulled the cord on the steam whistle to mark the first workday at the company. The company had been founded a year earlier in Martinsville, Virginia, less than ten miles from North Carolina, which became the heart of America's furniture industry. In the 1990s, after decades of growth, cheap imports from Mexico and elsewhere started to undermine the region's producers. "Increasingly, our customers weren't willing to buy domestically produced furniture," said Paul Toms, the chairman and CEO of Hooker. The company was forced to shut down five plants and its workforce was cut to two hundred employees, a 90 percent decrease. North Carolina's furniture industry as a whole lost about 60 percent of its jobs. "These were good, hardworking people that were doing everything that we asked of them and it was through no fault of theirs. There was no other alternative. We sold furniture below what it cost us to manufacture it." Meanwhile, the Chinese furniture industry is booming, not mainly because of exports but primarily thanks to burgeoning demand from the country's rapidly growing middle class.

The divergent fortunes of the middle classes in the developed world and the emerging markets will be a defining economic and political reality in 2030 and beyond. The Joneses will indeed have trouble keeping up with the Singhs and the Wangs in more ways than one. "Depending on who and where you ask, the middle class is either growing or shrinking, optimistic or anxious, getting richer or getting poorer, politically engaged or opting out," argues Clive Crook, a columnist and editor. Do the middle classes across the world compete for jobs and prosperity with one another? If they do, and there's unfair competition, then extraordinary measures—like protectionism—gain traction among the electorate.

In 2015, the Pew Research Center announced that the combined numbers of poor and rich households in the United States had, for the first time in two generations, exceeded the number of middle-class households. In 1971, there were 80 million middle-class households (compared to 52 million either above or below). By 2015 there were 120.8 million middle-class families, compared to 121.3 million in the two other groups. Aristotle would turn in his grave. Echoing the stagnation of the American middle class, Homer Simpson has tried nearly two hundred different jobs since the show first aired three decades ago—without showing any career progression whatsoever. Six hundred episodes—no improvement in his economic status.

The sluggish, if not declining, living standards of the American and European middle class have been recklessly blamed, by politicians and pundits, on immigration, unfair competition from emerging markets, and the elite indifference to the dark sides of globalization. The result has been Brexit and a Donald Trump presidency. The global economic and geopolitical order that emerged after World War II is under heavy fire from both sides of the political spectrum.

The clash is also taking place among companies. Those from emerging markets are growing bigger and bigger by the day, while those from Europe and the United States are downsizing—with some notable exceptions, such as tech. But even in the tech sector, Chinese and Indian companies are becoming larger not only because of the size of the population they serve but also because more people are online and using digital services. The truth is that there are more broadband, social media, and mobile payment users in China or in India than in the United States. This gap will only continue to widen.

How will European and American companies fare as the center of gravity of global middle-class consumption shifts to Asia? Can they compete for market share alongside their foreign counterparts? Alibaba is a bigger company than Amazon, Didi just purchased Uber's Chinese operations, and India boasts more technicians and engineers employed in the information technology sector than the United States. Strong companies are important to the middle class because they create well-paying jobs and offer careers and paths to professional advancement. This post-global economy is a tough competitive landscape for everyone, and especially so for the old middle class, precisely because companies like General Motors and Sears are on the decline.

Now consider new types of companies like Spotify and Airbnb. These two widely admired champions of the tech economy are "unicorns"—which, as mentioned earlier, are privately held companies valued at over $1 billion. For years they have been the darlings of angel investors and venture capitalists. And yet the vast majority of their customers and revenue are confined to Europe and the Americas. Airbnb has struggled to expand. Spotify doesn't report how many customers it has in China or India; remarkably, both nations are subsumed under the generic category "rest of the world." Something is awry when a company like Spotify fails to distinguish two national markets that are about to become the world's largest.

Even Netflix—a U.S. company that operates in more than 190 countries, has more subscribers and streaming revenue internationally than domestically, and accounts for 20 percent of total global online traffic—has so far postponed entering the Chinese market. It produces Mandarin-language content, but for the Chinese diaspora. In India, Netflix faces fewer hurdles, but it has been forced to cut subscription prices to accelerate its sluggish growth. "Already wrestling with global giants such as Walt Disney Co. and Amazon.com Inc.," the *Economic Times* of India reported in 2019, "Netflix now also contends with broadcasters and Bollywood powerhouses allied with billionaire-backed wireless carriers, who are luring users with free offers or as low as 40 cents a month. . . . The intense competition could derail Chief Executive Officer Reed Hasting's goal of 100 million customers in India." At the time the article was written Netflix had just 4 million customers there, in a video streaming market that's twice as big as America. Are U.S. companies dropping the ball?

More broadly, if a company has been successful with the old middle class, there's no guarantee it will be equally successful with the new middle class. There are numerous horror stories of American companies grossly misunderstanding the preferences and habits of consumers in emerging markets. It may seem obvious, but the new middle class does not necessarily love what Americans love. For example, eBay has consistently underperformed TaoBao in China because it failed to recognize that Chinese consumers prefer interacting directly with suppliers and care little about a rating system. Walmart carried skis in Brazil—a country without snow-capped mountains, let alone ski slopes!—and packaged items in wholesale sizes in South Korea, where consumers prefer to buy small quantities. It also ignored differences in consumer attitudes: large stores are perceived by Indian and Chinese consumers as expensive, whereas in the United States they're considered home to the cheapest goods.

And there's another, potentially disruptive effect involving the rise of middle-class consumption in emerging markets such as China: the younger generation of consumers isn't saving as much as its parents and grandparents used to. "For my parents' generation, for them to get a decent job, a stable job, is good enough—and what they do is they save money, they buy houses and they raise kids," observes Liu Biting, a millennial who has a marketing job in Shanghai. "We see money as a thing to be spent." An increasing number of Chinese millennials are taking short-term loans from multiple online lending platforms to service other loans they had previously taken to fuel their consumption. Yu Runting also works in marketing in Shanghai, but her monthly income of about $1,300 is just enough to cover her rent and basic necessities. Yet, as reported in the *Jing Daily*, she has purchased a "Celine's 'Medium Classic' Box shoulder bag (retail price, $4,400), Chanel's 'Gabrielle' Hobo Bag ($4,500), Bulgari's 'Serpenti Forever' shoulder bag ($2,100), and Tasaki 'balance eclipse' gold earrings

($1,800)—by maxing out four credit cards and topping it off with credit offered by Alipay's online lending system, Huabei." Yu asserts that "everyone working in my company, from receptionists to managers, owns at least two luxury handbags, and I know most of my colleagues at my level borrow." May Yee Chen, who heads the Innovation Group at J. Walter Thompson Intelligence for the Asia-Pacific region, observes that "many of these millennials and Gen-Z luxury consumers are single children . . . free from the practical or cultural constraints of their parents' generation, who were taught to save, save, save."

Clearly, Chinese young consumers are starting to behave as if they were Americans, a development that undermines the cozy arrangement whereby Chinese people saved while Americans spent. As of 2020 the proportion of Chinese household debt to GDP hovered at around 50 percent, compared to 76 percent in the United States. By 2030, both countries could be at the same level. Americans will need to tighten their belts if China's younger generation no longer does their saving for them.

CAN THE PLANET SUSTAIN SEVERAL MIDDLE CLASSES?

Satish and Arlene Palshikar live in Portland, Oregon, and are avid recyclers. In 2017 they drove their hybrid Prius to a waste sorting facility to deliver their recyclables. A worker told them that China would no longer recycle U.S. plastic. The Chinese government had recently notified the World Trade Organization that it would no longer accept certain types of solid waste, "to protect China's environmental interests and people's health." A key battle in the escalating trade war between the Trump administration and China is on the issue of recycling. In the past, China would ship manufactured goods to the United States while the United States would ship its waste and recyclable materials to China. It was a mutually beneficial arrangement. American middle-class consumers are the world's largest producers of waste. One-third of the country's recyclable waste is exported, and China receives nearly half of it. Each year, China used to accept roughly 47 million metric tons of discard plastics alone, which it then recycled.

But now China, India, and a host of other emerging countries have their own middle classes to look after—and their own trash to deal with. Without China's capacity to absorb the world's solid waste, it is unclear where that waste will go. "With plastic production and use continuing to rise, and companies and countries both committing to circular economies and increasing plastic recycling rates, the quantity of plastic waste needing a 'home' will continue to increase for the foreseeable future," concluded a University of Georgia study. "Where will the plastic waste go now? Absent bold new ideas and management strategies, current recycling rates will no longer be met, and ambitious goals and timelines for future recycling growth will be insurmountable." In fact, the renewed war against plastic waste in Europe and the United States has more to do with China's refusal to take our trash than with enhanced environmental awareness.

The growth of the middle class across the world means that the number of people below the poverty line globally continues to fall. That's a welcome development, but it also raises a staggering question for the future, as the *New York Times* pointedly asked in 2001: "Can the planet support more Americas?" Can you imagine a world in which 2 billion people in emerging markets consume like the average American? Total middle-class consumption in the world will grow by about 55 percent between 2020 and 2030. For example, as people see their incomes rise, they eat more protein, and they quickly develop a preference for beef over pork or chicken. Well, it takes an average of 1,800 gallons of freshwater to produce one pound of beef. Then think about the raw materials needed to manufacture a car or a washing machine, and the gas or electricity required to keep it running. We will need to come up with creative ways of avoiding conflict over scarce natural resources, including water, minerals, and energy. We will need workers, engineers, and entrepreneurs who design and deliver better systems for managing the limited resources available to us. And we might need to change our wasteful habits, as we shall see in Chapter 7.

MILLENNIALS STRUGGLE TO BECOME MIDDLE CLASS

"I'm currently a temp for an insurance/reinsurance company as a claims analyst," reads a post on Reddit. "The duration for my position was supposed to be 6 months . . . they told me they've submitted my information to become a permanent employee. It's been 10 months now and I still haven't heard back. I just want my salaried permanent position, not this hourly wage bullshit . . . I studied marketing and somehow landed a job in the financial risk management field. What am I doing wrong?" Another poster complained that, after spending four years studying for a degree in commerce, "I feel I could have worked straight out of high school and earned the same amount by now through yearly raises and not have had to spend 40K+." And a third asserted, "Things aren't going to happen just because you have a degree, despite what mom and dad told you. If you don't have relevant experience be ready for a salary cut if they hire you, that's if you are charming enough to get them to hire you."

Stories like these illustrate a general pattern: the middle class is shrinking in Europe and the United States not just because people are losing well-paying jobs to global competition or automation but also because the young cannot gain access to stable jobs in the first place; there are just fewer of those jobs to go around. "It has become more difficult for younger generations to make it to the middle class," concluded a 2018 study by OECD using data for several European countries as well as Mexico and the United States. "This is because older generations are often better protected from changes in the labor market and from low-income risks than the newer generations. Since the baby boomer generation, the middle-income group has grown smaller with each successive generation." For instance, while only 60 percent of thirtysomething millennials are part of the middle class, nearly 70 percent of baby boomers had been middle-class when they were at a similar stage in their lives.

And what's really alarming is that having children makes it harder for families to reach middle-class status, in a self-perpetuating dynamic that may push fertility rates further down. "Middle-class parents have been forced to invest more in their children while being guaranteed less by employers and the government," writes journalist Patrick A. Coleman in *Fatherly*. Again, the anecdotes aggregate to a trend with important implications for the future. "The share of households with children in the middle-income class has also fallen [in Europe and the United States]—from 72 to 68 percent for couples with children, and from 55 to 44 percent among single parents." By 2030, Europe and the United

States will be home not only to a smaller middle class but also to a more polarized society, with a larger share of children being born to either poor or rich families, and fewer of them enjoying the traditional comfort of the middle.

Another intriguing trend is that people over sixty now account for a greater share of the middle class in the United States and Europe than has historically been the case, because many have well-paying jobs, are finished raising children, and have managed to save some money. "The make-up of the middle-income class has undergone profound change," the OECD study concludes. "It has . . . aged faster than the population as a whole over the past three decades. . . . [C]hances to make it to middle incomes fell for each subsequent generation since the baby boom generation."

IS IT POSSIBLE TO BOUNCE BACK?

Buffalo, New York, used to be one of the country's richest metropolitan areas, populated by numerous thriving businesses, both large and small, and a vibrant middle class. It's home to architectural marvels designed by luminaries like Louis Sullivan and Frank Lloyd Wright. According to Frederick Law Olmsted, the designer of New York City's Central Park, Buffalo was "the best planned city in America, if not the world." He described it as "a democratic and egalitarian city." The city's 1804 plan featured a radial system of streets overlaid by a grid, like in Washington, DC. Its proximity to a lake inspired architecture critic Ada Louise Huxtable to name it "the greatest urban vista in America." The city boasts the nation's first museum of modern art, the Albright-Knox Art Gallery, which was founded in 1862. It was also the first city in the United States to use electric street lights. But since the 1950s, much of this history has been tarnished by the effects of manufacturing's decline and its heavy toll on the city's middle-class residents. Grain silos, factories, transportation facilities, and dilapidated office buildings have lain idle for decades.

In addition to the benefits of immigration discussed in Chapter 1, immigrants can become a resource for urban renewal. Originally built by European immigrants, parts of Buffalo have been revived by new waves of immigration—this time from Ethiopia, Somalia, Laos, Myanmar, and Serbia, among other countries. According to David Stebbins, who has written extensively about the revival of cities in the Great Lakes region, "These new residents bring with them a work ethic and entrepreneurial spirit that is helping repopulate teetering neighborhoods and creating new businesses to fill empty storefronts." This trend is part of a more general pattern. "Immigrant diversity appears to have widespread benefits across the labor force," notes a 2017 analysis by the bipartisan New American Economy think tank, which based its findings on a national sample of 33.5 million American workers. "When immigrants with diverse ideas and new skills arrive, employers can fill positions that would otherwise remain vacant, hit on better solutions to problems, and expand into new areas of business." As a result, the wages of both high and low earners grow on average by as much as 6 percent after an influx of immigrants arrives in a metropolitan area.

Buffalo has outperformed other cities in its region, including Rochester and Syracuse. The naysayers argue that any city of this size would have bounced back after an injection of $1 billion in state subsidies and grants. "Cuomo's 'Buffalo Billion': Is New York Getting Its Money's Worth?" read the headline in the *New York Times*, in reference to Governor Andrew Cuomo declaring in 2012 that "we believe in Buffalo. Let's put our money where our mouth is. That is a big 'B'—standing for Buffalo and standing for billion." As of 2018, nearly $1.5 billion has been invested, much of it in projects that have been criticized for creating very few permanent jobs, like the $750 million Tesla solar panel plant, which was highly automated. Throwing money at decaying cities can help if the funds are well spent, which doesn't always happen, but betting on renewal by attracting talent and hardworking people tends to be more successful over the long run.

There's no doubt that the economy of 2030 will be a tough competitive landscape for everyone, especially for people in places like Buffalo. But there are glimmers of hope. In a comprehensive study, Alan Berube and Cecile Murray of the Brookings Institution tracked the evolution of 185 urban counties with a significant history of manufacturing. These counties accounted in 2016 for about 12 percent of the United States population. Most of them are located in the Midwest and the Northeast. The researchers found that although more than half had managed to recover from the crisis, 70 percent had been unable to take advantage of opportunities emerging in new technology and service sectors between 1970 and 2016. Among the best-performing cities and counties were Brooklyn, Queens, and Buffalo, in New York; Philadelphia; St. Louis; and several around Boston. Others are still underperforming, including Albany, New York; Dayton, Ohio; and Detroit and Flint, in Michigan. Just a few factors account for the differences in success: the presence of major research universities, local political support for quality-of-life initiatives that attract a diverse pool of talent, and openness to immigration. Thus the fortunes of the American middle class differ by city and by geography, with some metropolitan areas experiencing growth while others remain stuck in neutral. Are there ways of restoring middle-class prosperity to a majority of the population?

FORD, AMAZON, AND THE IDEA OF A
UNIVERSAL BASIC INCOME

"On January 4, 1914, Henry Ford was a prosperous mechanic-turned-entrepreneur in the burgeoning Detroit automobile industry," wrote my Wharton colleague Daniel Raff. "His cars were very popular, but his name was unknown to the world at large save as that under which Model Ts were sold." The following day was characteristically cold in Detroit. Henry Ford and James Couzens, his vice president, were about to make an unprecedented announcement: the Ford Motor Company was going to double its workers' pay to $5 a day. Today, that's the equivalent of $126, or $14 an hour for a nine-hour workday, nearly twice as much as the 2019 federal minimum wage of $7.25 per hour. "'Gold Rush' Is Started by Ford's $5 Offer," read the headline in Detroit's *Times-Star*. "Thousands of men seek employment in Detroit factory. Will distribute $10,000,000 in semi-monthly bonuses. No employee to receive less than five dollars a day."

"One strand of popular reaction to the news," Raff recounted, "is well illustrated by a cartoon in the *New York Globe and Commercial Advertiser....* A number of fat men wearing top hats and overcoats with fur collars and smoking cigars are queued up at the pay window. Another such gentleman sits in the back of a chauffeured car.... 'Hawkins,' he says, 'will you step over to the pay window and get my wages? I quite overlooked the matter last week.'" The Five-Dollar Day catapulted Henry Ford to global celebrity. "The American Plan; automotive prosperity seeping down from above," wrote John Dos Passos in his 1933 novel *The Big Money*. "But that five dollars a day paid to good, clean American workmen who didn't drink or smoke cigarettes or read or think . . . made Henry Ford the automobileer, the admirer of Edison, the birdlover, the great American of his time."

Ford engineers had streamlined and standardized the assembly process. They had managed to trim the time it took to build a Model T from twelve hours to just ninety-three minutes. Such efficiency meant that the workday contracted significantly and workers got bored. As a result, employee turnover skyrocketed to 370 percent, meaning that the company employed nearly four different employees throughout the year to staff each assembly line position. "Ford reasoned that a bigger paycheck might make the factory's tedium more tolerable," wrote *The Henry Ford*, a publication that promotes the contributions made by Henry Ford to American innovation. In his research, Raff found "no evidence whatsoever that the company had any difficulty filling vacancies." Moreover, Ford's offer was not a straight wage increase; rather, it was a profit-sharing plan whereby a worker would get a bonus if certain requirements and performance milestones were met. According to *The Henry Ford*, the company created an infamous Sociological Department to "monitor its employees' habits beyond the workplace." To qualify for the Five-Dollar Day, "workers had to abstain from alcohol, not physically abuse their families, not take in boarders, keep their homes clean, and contribute regularly to a savings account." Such a paternalistic approach to labor management was actually quite common at the time. "Ford Motor Company inspectors came to workers' homes, asked probing questions, and observed general living conditions." The early cultural and economic development of the American middle class owes a large debt to Henry Ford's vision. He contributed to the formation of a large class of consumers, eager to purchase mass-produced goods like his own.

Fast-forward to October 2, 2018, the day Amazon announced it would pay all its U.S. employees—full-time, part-time, seasonal, and temporary—at least $15 an hour, more than twice the federal minimum wage. The company, which employs a quarter of a million people throughout the year (and an additional 100,000 during the holiday season), has been openly criticized for its labor practices. With the pay increase, the company "listened to its critics," according to CEO Jeff Bezos, and "decided we want to lead." Like Henry Ford, the richest man of his era chose a round number for its symbolic power. Even Senator Bernie Sanders, who had introduced the "Stop Bezos Act" to Congress, praised the decision: "Today, I want to give credit where credit is due. And I want to congratulate Mr. Bezos for doing exactly the right thing."

Consider the differences and similarities between the worlds Ford and Bezos occupied at the time each made his decision. Though the unemployment rate was about 14 percent in 1914 and only 4 percent in 2018, the context was similar in that workers and companies were coming to terms with dramatic technological change. Neither Ford nor Bezos ever lost sight of growth, but both were willing to make concessions to avoid the threat of an organized labor force. And both wanted to reduce turnover. Ford's move had a ripple effect throughout the automobile industry, and the rise of the American middle class is very much a product of the idea that workers double as consumers. Depressingly, assuming an eight-hour workday, Ford's Five-Dollar Day in 1914 was the equivalent of $15.69 per hour in 2018 after adjusting for inflation, 69 cents higher than Amazon's $15 per hour. In any event, very few companies are ever willing to increase wages unilaterally.

Today, as segments of the old middle class begin to suffer from impoverishment, support for a government-provided universal basic income is growing on both sides of the Atlantic. The idea has many fans in Europe and Canada. In the United States, by contrast, half the population regards it as heretical and a form of socialism. According to New Yorker magazine writer Nathan Heller, a government program to provide every family with a minimum income, "enough to live on—somewhere in America, at least—but not nearly enough to live well," has gained traction among not only academics but also labor leaders. Even libertarians support it, sensing a way to curb the government's bureaucracy and shrink welfare programs. In contrast to the current variety of government support programs, where government workers have to decide who is deserving of each particular form of government assistance and administer those benefits, the universality of such a program would reduce costs and eliminate bureaucracies. It is also a "hard budget line" in the sense that once a per-person or per-family income figure is set, you know how much the program costs. In fact, the libertarian economist Milton Friedman proposed a "negative income tax" (supplemental pay issued by the government for people under a certain income level) in his 1962 book *Capitalism and Freedom*. It just so happened that the Johnson administration found the idea so attractive that it decided to run a pilot program in New Jersey, the results of which raised more questions than answers. Other experts like the concept of a government-guaranteed minimum income because it would buffer the consumer-oriented economy from the ill effects of technology-induced unemployment—a trend that will only intensify between now and 2030. "There's a pretty good chance we end up with a universal basic income, or something like that, due to automation," said Elon Musk in 2016. "I am not sure what else one would do."

According to a February 2018 Gallup poll, Americans are evenly split as to whether a universal basic income is a good idea or not. The critics fear it would reduce the incentive to be productive, and undermine the pride and satisfaction that people derive from doing their jobs. "I think there's a certain dignity from work," argues Nobel Prize–winning economist Joseph Stiglitz, who often aligns himself with progressive policies. There are also doubts as to whether it would help the economy. The Roosevelt Institute, a left-leaning think tank, argues that, if funded through taxation, a universal basic income would bring no gains in terms of economic growth. But there are other potential benefits. A pilot program in Ontario, Canada, for single people earning less than $26,000 and couples earning less than $36,500 found that recipients felt empowered, less anxious, more socially connected, and able to invest in education and job-hunting.

Perhaps Alaska can provide the ultimate test as to the benefits and the costs of a universal basic income. Since 1982, Alaska residents have received an annual dividend from the Alaska Permanent Fund, financed by the state's oil revenue. In 2018 the payout was $1,600. A thorough study published by the National Bureau for Economic Research found no evidence that this dividend was a disincentive to work: "A universal and permanent cash transfer does not significantly decrease aggregate employment." Mouhcine Guettabi, an economist at the University of Alaska, Anchorage, corroborates this finding. In addition, he reviews other studies concluding that Alaskans spend more on goods and services for immediate consumption in the month when they receive the payment. In the four weeks after the distribution of the checks, incidents related to substance abuse increase by 10 percent but property crimes decrease by 8 percent. Other benefits included an average birthweight increase in the babies of low-income mothers and reduced obesity among three-year-olds. Intriguingly, the payouts reduce poverty but increase inequality, most likely because wealthier households reinvest the dividend while poorer ones spend it. Regardless of the balance of benefits and costs, the entire scheme rests on the assumption of steady oil revenues, which are threatened by price volatility and the depletion of existing oil fields. This uncertainty results in bitter political battles over how to allocate tax revenue across government programs.

UC Berkeley economists Hilary Hoynes and Jesse Rothstein present a bleak assessment of the future of universal basic income schemes. After reviewing pilot programs and policy proposals in Canada, Finland, Switzerland, and the United States, they conclude that "replacing existing anti-poverty programs with a universal basic income would be highly regressive, unless substantial additional funds were put in."

MIDDLE-CLASS INSECURITIES

In 2030, middle-class consumers in emerging markets will outnumber those in the United States, Europe, and Japan by five to one, which is a twofold increase from 2020. Instead of *The Simpsons*, we may well be watching the adventures of the Singhs, the Wangs, or the Mwangis. The action will take place not in a Springfield, Oregon, suburb like the Simpsons' but in Mumbai, Shanghai, or Nairobi. The leading brands of the world will no longer reflect the preferences of American consumers; rather, they will be tailored mainly to those of the aspirational middle class in emerging economies.

But the middle class is not the only transformational force nowadays. As we'll see next, the rise of women as earners and wealth holders is the other massive engine of change.

4.

Second Sex No More?

Women with money and women in power are

two uncomfortable ideas in our society.

—CANDACE BUSHNELL, CREATOR OF *SEX AND THE CITY*

A theocratic regime controls parts of the United States in the wake of twin environmental and fertility crises, and it has imposed ruthless measures in an effort to overcome them and to fight the holdouts who threaten the authority of the republic. Schools are empty for lack of children. Playing Scrabble or other unproductive games is forbidden. A "Compubank" has replaced all paper money in circulation. Women cannot have paid jobs or own property. Vanities such as cosmetics, jewelry, and magazines are considered banal and are shunned. Older women mysteriously disappear. The ruling patriarchs and their barren wives subjugate the lower castes of women. The lucky ones serve as walking wombs in a grand scheme to repopulate the land; the unlucky who cannot bear children anymore clean up chemical pollutants and radioactive waste. Both men and women know that even the slightest sexual peccadillos are punishable by amputation.

This is the dystopian plot of *The Handmaid's Tale*, a 1985 novel by Margaret Atwood (and since expanded into a Hulu series) that feels eerily contemporary. "Right now, it is both the best of times and the worst of times for women," Atwood observed in 2018. "Some women are fighting for the rights they've never had, but others are fighting the threat of removal of such rights."

Traces of the best of times are everywhere for people to see. Women receive the majority of undergraduate and graduate degrees in the United States, and more than 40 percent of married American mothers earn more than their husbands. Women are accumulating wealth faster than men—so much so that by 2030 more than half of the world's total wealth will be owned by women.

But the worst of times is also in plain sight. A study on gender equality funded by the Gates Foundation concluded that "with just 11 years to go until 2030, nearly 40 percent of the world's girls and women—1.5 billion—live in countries failing on gender equality." Women's advantage in life expectancy relative to men in the United States and other developed countries is on the decline. Moreover, women's fortunes tend to diverge based on several factors: whether they have kids, whether they are single or in a stable relationship, and whether they are married or divorced. This has created vast disparities among women themselves.

These momentous trends spell massive changes not just for society but also for capital markets, because women are different from men when it comes to investing; for companies, because women bring different perspectives to the workplace; and for innovation, because women are increasingly becoming entrepreneurs. Women are not yet on an equal footing with men, but large transformations are under way as a result of their new roles in the economy and in society.

Hollywood realized this early on. In the 1993 movie *Sleepless in Seattle*, a colleague at work tells Annie (played by Meg Ryan) that "it's easier to be killed by a terrorist than it is to find a husband over the age of 40." Horrified, Annie bursts out: "That statistic is not true!" Becky (Rosie O'Donnell) seeks to calm her down: "That's right—it's not true," she says. "But it *feels* true." This scene is based on real-world events that began with a study undertaken by three of the finest demographers in the world. In the mid-1980s, Neil Bennett, David Bloom, and Patricia Craig were investigating differences in marriage rates between American whites and blacks. Bloom was an economist at Harvard, where he still teaches; Bennett was a sociologist at Yale, and Craig was a graduate student of his. (I worked as Bennett's research assistant on this project during 1989.)

In 1986 a reporter with the *Advocate*, a small newspaper in Stamford, Connecticut, was looking for a good story to publish for Valentine's Day. He called Bennett, who mentioned, among many other things, that the estimated probability of marriage for a single female college graduate at age thirty was 20 percent, but by age forty was in the low single digits. The story ran on the first page of the *Advocate* and was picked up by an Associated Press reporter, who sent a dispatch over the agency's national wire with the headline "Women Who Tarry May Never Marry." The following June, *Newsweek* devoted a weekly issue to the topic: "The Marriage Crunch: If You're a Single Woman, Here Are Your Chances of Getting Married." The cover featured a chart showing a rather steep downward-sloping probability curve as women got older. Inside there was a story called "Too Late for Prince Charming?" It included a memorable line that generated a public uproar: "Forty-year-olds are more likely to be killed by a terrorist: they have a minuscule 2.6 percent probability of tying the knot." As Candace Bushnell, who later became famous for writing *Sex and the City*, wrote in the *New York Observer*, "That *Newsweek* cover struck terror in the hearts of single women everywhere."

The "Harvard-Yale Study," as the research became internationally known, had inspired one of the decade's most sensational stories. The media coverage—which often misstated the study's conclusions—resonated with educated women who were trying to balance their professional goals with their personal lives. The fact is, we've learned that less than 10 percent of American women in their fifties and sixties have never been married. And in the United States now, more unmarried than married couples live together and raise children. A growing number are same-sex couples.

The new socioeconomic position of women has far-reaching implications. As we saw in Chapter 1, on population trends, these transformational changes are mainly the result of several interlaced factors. Women increasingly pursue an education, work outside of the home, and have fewer babies.

In addition, it also matters that women tend to live longer than men—at least for the time being. I can't make promises to any women reading this sentence, but on average you will enjoy a lifetime between four and seven years longer than men, depending on where you live in the world. Longevity matters because it prolongs the years spent working and the time during which invested savings compound into greater wealth. It's also more likely that women will inherit wealth from their husbands or male partners rather than the other way around.

This is a roundabout way of saying that I have some very good news for the women of the world. Simply put, they will get rich before the world as we know it comes to an end in 2030. To be more accurate, the probability that a woman nowadays will accumulate enough wealth to enjoy a comfortable life is much greater than the probability that her mother or her grandmother ever did.

By the same token, I'm afraid I have very bad news for men, myself included. It's not merely that men will be poorer or see their wealth grow less quickly. On average—always on average—more men will be dead compared to women of the same age. And when they die, guess who will inherit the wealth?

"WOMEN TRY THEIR LUCK; MEN RISK THEIRS"

Does women's enhanced economic status actually matter for the future of markets around 2030? Yes indeed, if you believe that women come from Venus and men from Mars—that is, if they are behaviorally different in how they use their money. Let's examine the extent to which women differ from men when it comes to consumption, savings, and investment.

Who spends more money on luxuries, men or women? When I ask this question in class I almost always get a split response from the audience. Half say women, and the other half say men. But, as I frequently remind my undergraduate students, most of the time the correct answer to any question about the behavior of women and men is "It depends." In fact, this tends to be the best answer to most questions these days.

When it comes to luxuries, for instance, the statistics for most countries show that women prefer to spend their money on fashion, jewelry, and accessories, whereas men tend to go for big-ticket toys like sports cars. If you include sports cars as luxuries, men spend more than women. If you exclude them, women spend more than men, especially on fashion, jewelry, and accessories. Hence, the biggest behavioral difference between men and women is that the latter spread their luxury purchases over a larger number of items.

Women also differ when it comes to spending money on expensive yet vital services such as education, healthcare, and insurance. They are more willing than men to spend on education, not just for their own benefit but also for their children's and grandchildren's. They spend more on their own healthcare and are more inclined to ensure that their parents, children, and grandchildren get the healthcare they need. They prefer lower deductibles on property and casualty insurance and more comprehensive disability and death coverage, resulting in higher premiums. Overall, research indicates that women display a distinct preference for security.

So is the fast increase in women's wealth accumulation leading to a large transformation of the economy? Absolutely. Remember that spending on education, healthcare, and insurance account for about 30 percent of the American economy. As women accumulate more wealth over the next decade, those parts of the economy will benefit from increased spending.

When it comes to savings, it's also hard to generalize whether women save more than men or vice versa. Among single people with no plans to marry, women tend to save more than men. Research indicates that the reason lies, once again, in women's desire for security and independence. They also realize that they live longer (on average) than men, so they need to set more money aside for the future. However, the moment men decide to marry, they increase their savings, mostly because of cultural expectations and because they freak out: they haven't saved enough and they're about to take on major familial responsibilities. Before they have children, married women tend to save more money than married men of comparable backgrounds, but once they have their first baby the pendulum swings back yet again. Mothers, on average, save less than fathers because they spend more time with the children and thus face more unanticipated out-of-pocket expenses, including a snack, another pair of pants, a textbook, or a school trip. As these examples reveal, savings behavior depends on a person's stage of life and other circumstances.

Will faster female wealth accumulation change the rules of the game in terms of consumption and savings? This is an important lateral effect for the future. As the feminist writer Gloria Steinem once put it, "We can tell our values by looking at our checkbook stubs." (Translation for millennials: look at your Venmo transaction history.)

And when it comes to investing, women and men definitely come from different planets. Most people believe that women are more conservative or risk averse when it comes to investing. Research bears this out. As Lord Henry declared in Oscar Wilde's *The Picture of Dorian Gray*, "Women try their luck; men risk theirs." Attitudes toward risk shape most decisions in our lives, including consumption and savings. And they also affect what types of investments we deem conducive to achieving our financial goals. It's not much of a stretch to argue that if instead of Lehman Brothers we had had Lehman *Sisters*, the crisis of 2008 might have been averted.

There's actually an element of truth in that last statement. One unpublished study compared men and women doing trades for an investment bank in New York. They were similar in terms of education and experience. The researchers found that the men traded more frequently and took more risks than the women, and that the women obtained slightly better returns over the long run.

The era in which most of the wealth was generated by men, owned by men, and managed by men is nearly over. And financial markets are in for a huge transformation. Are you wondering why more people nowadays prefer stock funds linked to a market index as opposed to managed funds with more variability in their returns? You guessed it, I'm sure: more of those people investing are now women. The bottom line is that a better understanding of women as consumers, savers, and investors can provide companies with phenomenal new market opportunities. In fact, no company will be able to succeed if it fails to grasp women's preferences and decisions as they ascend and take control of the largest share of global wealth.

NOT ALL WOMEN (OR MEN) ARE THE SAME

Sadie Marie Groff of Missoula, Montana, gave birth to the first of her three children when she was twenty. She doesn't have a college degree and hasn't traveled the world. She attends to her children during the day; at night she works as a health aide. She dreams of getting a degree in radiologic technology. Ellen Scanlon, by contrast, lives in San Francisco. Her first, and only, baby was born when she had just turned forty, thanks to in vitro fertilization. After graduating from college, she attended business school, worked in finance, and founded a strategy consulting firm. She met her husband a decade before they had the baby. "We were just having a really good time," she says of their choice to postpone having a child.

Sadie and Ellen may both be American women living in the twenty-first century, but they inhabit two diametrically opposed universes, defined by place of residence and education. One common misconception when tracing trends leading to epochal transformations is to assume that everyone within a given social group is affected similarly by them. While it is certainly true that women's experiences are shifting, it is equally accurate to say that we are witnessing a huge bifurcation, with some women (and men) experiencing life in a dramatically different way than their parents, while for others the traditional pattern persists. This divergence helps explain why the economic fortunes and the political behavior of women and men in different parts of the world—notably Europe and the United States—have become so polarized. To put it simply, the opportunities available to different groups of people seem to be diverging over time, and so are their political views.

While women in general are increasing their fortunes and will be wealthier on average than men by 2030, there are two especially vulnerable categories: single moms and divorced women. In many cases, the two categories overlap. "When I was married, things were definitely better," said a forty-two-year-old divorced mother of three children in elementary school interviewed for Billfold, a personal finance website. "We were pretty solidly middle class. We had our financial struggles, but were doing fairly well. I used to have a savings and a small retirement fund, but I had to cash out and spend it during the divorce." She earns $40,000 a year working as an administrator at a small nonprofit organization in a suburb of Washington, DC. Her ex-husband, who shares custody of the children, contributes a small proportion of the expenses, $1,500 per month. To make matters worse, they had consolidated his student debt in her name because she had more favorable terms on a Department of Education loan. Now she spends $1,480 monthly on rent, $1,386 on childcare, and $400 on groceries. She can't make any payments on the student debt. "I have figured out how much I *have* to pay to keep the utility companies from shutting off my service."

The media are replete with stories about divorce settlements for women amounting to billions of dollars, as in the breakups of Jeff Bezos and Mac-Kenzie Bezos, Alec Wildenstein and Jocelyn Wildenstein, Rupert Murdoch and Anna Torv, Bernie Ecclestone and Slavica Radić, and Steve Wynn and Elaine Wynn. Contrary to myth, however, most women who divorce end up being much worse off financially. In fact, a comprehensive study found that staying married was almost always more financially advantageous than divorce for women. Even re-entering the workforce didn't return women to the economic situation they had enjoyed while married, and their economic situation worsened even if they remarried. The men, however, did not suffer a similar financial fallout once separated. In general, high rates of divorce among couples with kids is an important contributor to the stagnation of the middle class in Europe and the United States, as described earlier.

Teenage single motherhood also tends to limit women's lifetime opportunities. In the United States, each year nearly a quarter of a million babies are born to women aged fifteen to nineteen. Rates of teenage motherhood are more than twice as high among blacks, Hispanics, and Native Americans than among whites, and four times higher than rates among Asian Americans. While teenage pregnancy rates are dropping by 6 or 7 percent from year to year, it is most often women of lower income and education who become mothers during their teen years. Teenage motherhood imposes substantial costs on both the teen and her parents, often leading to the young mother dropping out of school and falling into poverty.

As we look toward 2030, perhaps no other factor will help improve women's economic well-being as much as avoiding dropping out of high school, especially if the reason for dropping out involves a pregnancy. "Everything changed for me in tenth grade," writes Jamie Rush of her pregnancy at age fifteen. "My relationship with the father pretty much ended when I told him I was going to have the baby." Her parents help support her and the baby, but unfortunately, Jamie's case is not typical, as more than 60 percent of young unmarried American mothers live in poverty. Conversely, poverty is a risk factor for teen pregnancy.

Lauren's mother died of cancer when she was twelve; her father was mostly absent. Lauren became pregnant shortly before graduating from high school in southeastern Massachusetts. Now she is homeless.

Creionna's mother died when she was two years old. Her father raised her until she was seven, when he went to prison on drug offenses. Various relatives raised her at homes where drug customers routinely visited. She became pregnant when she was sixteen. Both her boyfriend and her father wanted her to get an abortion, but she chose not to. After the baby was born, she and her child checked into a shelter. "Despite all this, she did have an edge over many of her peers," the *Atlantic* reported. "She had finished 11th grade. She had not resorted to prostitution, and she did not have a criminal record. She was not mentally ill and had not abused drugs." She persevered: she finished high school, started college, and landed a job at a health clinic. She moved with her toddler to a modest apartment.

While the opportunities available to women are expanding, workplace discrimination, divorce, and teen pregnancy continue to affect millions of women in the developed world every year. While a few of them, like Creionna, manage to overcome the odds, others are thrown into permanent poverty and homelessness. According to the federal government, about 45 million Americans live below the poverty line. Sixteen percent of women are poor, compared to 14 percent of men. Among women raising children by themselves, the poverty rate jumps to 27 percent.

And then we have the rising phenomenon of childless women (and men). In the mid-1970s about 10 percent of American women between the ages of thirty-five and thirty-nine had not yet had a baby; by 2016 that figure had nearly doubled. Among people in their forties, 16 percent of women are childless, compared to 24 percent for men; the difference is largely due to some mothers remaining single. Women and men without children will become more common in all parts of the world as the decline in fertility continues. By 2030 a third of American men and nearly as many women will retire childless.

Most American women who resolved not to have children are at peace with the decision. "I'm a retired woman, 66, and never had children. I went to college on the G.I. Bill and always worked a white-collar job. Women like me were considered oddities when I was in my 20s through 40s," one observes. Others go through ups and downs: "Over my life of 62 years I have gone from being heartbroken, to relieved, to proud that I never had children!" "Implying that women who don't have children are doomed to loneliness is ignorant. There are plenty of seniors whose adult kids want nothing to do with them or who get in contact only when they want to mooch off them," defiantly notes another. "It's possible to create a happy, richly fulfilled life without having kids. Or a husband, either," concludes another.

Paul Dolan, a professor at the London School of Economics who uses American data on happiness, goes one step further: "We do have some good longitudinal data following the same people over time, but I am going to do a massive disservice to that science and just say: if you're a man, you should probably get married; if you're a woman, don't bother." The difference lies in how marriage and having kids changes the life experiences of women and men. "You [i.e., men] take less risks, you earn more money at work, and you live a little longer. She, on the other hand, has to put up with that, and dies sooner than if she never married," observes Dolan, based on the data. "The healthiest and happiest population subgroup are women who never married or had children."

Intriguingly, the "happiness gap" between childless adults and parents is greater in the United States than in any other developed country. Research led by sociologist Jennifer Glass highlights that "children increase adults' exposure to a variety of stressors," but that "more generous family policies, particularly paid time off and childcare subsidies, are associated with smaller disparities in happiness between parents and non-parents." In some countries parents actually feel happier than nonparents, perhaps because of more generous parental leave and childcare programs: France, Finland, Sweden, Norway, Spain, Portugal, Hungary, and Russia. Government support for families with kids makes all the difference in the world. And while family support programs raise the happiness of fathers but not childless men, they increase the happiness of all women, whether they have children or not. Politicians who propose new family programs can expect to ingratiate themselves with women more so than with men.

By 2030 the trends toward better education and lower fertility will have solidified the differences among four categories of women: childless women, single moms, married women, and divorced women. And within each group, some will be in a comfortable financial situation while others will struggle.

"MY HUSBAND BROUGHT ME UP"

A similar divergence in women's experiences is taking place in developing countries, although the trend there is for more women to become much better off over time thanks to the growth of the middle class. Poverty continues to afflict more than half of women in both urban and rural areas throughout sub-Saharan Africa and in parts of Latin America, South Asia, Southeast Asia, and the Middle East. Adding to poor economic conditions are practices such as female genital mutilation, a human rights violation that has been inflicted on at least 200 million living women. Arranged marriages of girls are also a major problem. The advocacy organization Girls Not Brides estimates that one in five girls is married before age eighteen, and about 650 million women were married as minors, a practice that is most prevalent in Africa, South Asia, and Latin America. A South Sudanese woman by the name of Helen was forced to marry a fifty-year-old man when she was fifteen, a decision that meant she had to leave school against her will. Girls aged fifteen are five times more likely to die in childbirth than women in their twenties. "I was given to my husband when I was little and I don't even remember when I was given because I was so little," says Kanas from Ethiopia. "It's my husband who brought me up." Even in a country such as Switzerland, the government estimates that around fourteen hundred minor women are forced into marriage every year.

Despite lingering problems, many women in developing areas now enjoy opportunities unthinkable a generation ago. In Tanzania women who need equipment to pursue their entrepreneurial dreams—coolers and freezers, sewing machines, baking ovens, gravel-making machines, tractors, trucks—but lack the funds to purchase them outright can lease them through a company started by Victoria Kisyombe. Kisyombe, a UK-educated veterinarian by training, decided to go into entrepreneurship after her husband died, and she organized what eventually became SELFINA, Tanzania's largest leasing company, with over 22,000 lease contracts.

Even highly educated women like Kisyombe face obstacles and rampant discrimination. A World Bank report covering 128 developed and developing countries found a considerable degree of legal discrimination against women in areas that thwart entrepreneurship. For instance, as of 2009, women in forty-five countries did not have the same legal capacity to act or engage in economic transactions as men; in forty-nine countries, women were prevented from working in certain industries; and in thirty-two they did not have equal inheritance rights. Equal legal rights were found to result in a greater percentage of businesses owned or managed by women.

More broadly, women entrepreneurs have been long neglected by policymakers. That is, until 1970, when a Danish economist working for the United Nations, Ester Boserup, published an influential book, *Woman's Role in Economic Development*, which provided a detailed analysis of both how women contribute to economic development and how they are affected by it. She forcefully argued that women play a key role in development with their activities both inside and outside the household. Her work inspired the United Nations Decade for Women (1975–1985) and laid the foundations for a new wave of programs focused on promoting women's role in the economy as a way to accelerate economic development. The new approach aimed not only to advance gender equality as a goal in its own right but also to explore ways in which women's economic activities could contribute to economic growth and development.

At long last, policymakers realized that without women entrepreneurs countries would be wasting or underutilizing half of the talent pool. As Helen Clark, the administrator of the United Nations Development Programme, put it in 2009, "By unlocking the tremendous potential of women entrepreneurs and addressing the obstacles they face, such as access to credit and finance, and their inability to inherit or hold land titles or benefit from government budgetary allocations, we can reduce inequality and stimulate economic growth." These observations are echoed by Sibongile Sambo, founder of the airline company SRS Aviation. "Historically, women in South Africa, particularly black women, have not been afforded the opportunities of starting and running their own enterprises and making a full contribution to our economy," she says. "At SRS Aviation we are taking advantage of the new political freedom to create economic freedom. It is an opportunity that my mother and aunt did not have. But I do, and intend to grab it."

For women, entrepreneurship can be liberating and conducive to economic well-being, but it can also become a frustrating experience due to the barriers they face along the way, many of which are unique to being a woman in this space. As Azza Fahmy, the Egyptian founder of a famous jewelry company with 165 employees, observed, "My new experience was out of the ordinary for any conventional, young Egyptian woman in a traditional environment, but I was determined to go on." Or consider the example of Wu Huanshu, whose company manufactures clothing accessories and who is widely considered to be the first female entrepreneur in China to have incorporated her own company: "I still remember an official from the Dongcheng district office . . . said I should get a permit for my business to make it legal." Fahmy and Wu faced innumerable obstacles to realize their dreams.

Men and women differ in terms of their path to entrepreneurship. Women tend to go into fields of activity related to their most frequent previous experiences, such as personal services, retail, the creative crafts, and traditional industries. In addition, ventures founded, owned, and/or managed by women tend to grow less quickly over time, mostly as a result of structural constraints of various sorts. One of them is lack of knowledge of, and experience in, business. As Aissa Dionne, a Senegalese interior designer, notes, "At the beginning I didn't even know how to do an invoice. I was asking friends for advice."

Researchers have not been able to find consistent evidence of gender differences in terms of the motivations to become an entrepreneur, attitudes toward entrepreneurship, the social or psychological characteristics of entrepreneurs, the process of starting the business, management or leadership style, or even ongoing access to finance—though women do face discrimination when applying for startup funding. "I started working in Santiago, in a textile company," says Isabel Roa, a Chilean entrepreneur. "I then began to knit myself and to sell from door to door. The biggest problem I had was that when I started I did not have capital. I solved this by saving and getting loans."

Perhaps one important reason why women experience hurdles on their way to launching and growing their venture is that they are more likely than men to become entrepreneurs out of necessity. Says Nasreen Kasuri, who founded a school in Pakistan, "I realized the limited choice [of schools] available and also the fact that since the time when I myself went to school, the number of schools and seats had not increased." She adds, "I also realized that my children would not be fortunate enough to benefit from the quality of instruction that I had benefited from. The only way I could meet such a challenge was to set up a school which could provide quality education to my children and others." In fact, the Global Entrepreneurship Monitor, an annual survey of entrepreneurial activity around the world, documents that most women who become entrepreneurs do so for lack of other alternatives to make a living.

As we approach the year 2030, an important debate has emerged over whether women entrepreneurs have distinct preferences for how to imagine, organize, and manage ventures, and whether success should be defined in terms of goal achievement, a better work/family balance, or community benefits as opposed to growth, profits, and fame. In this vein, Rwandan handicrafts entrepreneur Janet Kkubana takes pride in the benefits that her venture brings to women facing difficult circumstances. "I have survivors, I have widows, I have women whose husbands are in prison. To see them sitting under one roof weaving and doing business together is a huge achievement," she says. "These women are now together, earning an income. It's amazing." Similarly, Annette Zamora, a Rapa Nui social entrepreneur focused on preserving and popularizing the ancient culture of the secluded volcanic isle known to Europeans as Easter Island, reflected: "I don't know if I have been successful. I have received recognition but I don't know that I have a clear concept of what 'successful' means."

SQUARING THE CIRCLE AROUND WORK AND FAMILY

In 2030 nearly half of all new business ventures in the world will be launched by women. Consider the case of Anu Ancharya. After graduate study in the United States, she decided to return to India—following the pattern of brain circulation we encountered in Chapter 1—to launch a genomics outsourcing company, Ocimum Biosolutions. After fifteen years of operation and three acquisitions in Europe and the United States, her firm is one of the leading players in the global biomedical outsourcing industry. A mother of two preteen girls, Anu has had to make very hard choices about balancing work and family: "My kids now are pretty much used to the fact that I am not available half of the time." The family lives with Anu's in-laws, who help raise the girls. Her company offers employees three months of paid maternity leave. "It's a very good place to work, especially for ladies. We have flexible office timings," says Jaishree Ravi, assistant vice president of quality systems and one of Ocimum's first employees. "If we have a PTA meeting to attend, I can go out and come back; all I have to do is log in nine hours of work."

Anu and Jaishree are not alone in feeling the pressures of combining motherhood and work outside of the home. "In 2007, I went through a difficult (and unexpected) divorce," says Melissa, whose is approaching fifty. She has a son in college and twin teenage daughters. A schoolteacher, she took time off until the kids started school, and subsequently worked part-time to spend as much time as possible with them. "One of the things I've learned in this process of reentering the workforce and balancing family life," she says, "is that I will not sacrifice being present to get my kids off to school in the morning." Like so many other educated women of her generation, Melissa has had to confront difficult trade-offs, many of which men simply don't have to face.

About 70 percent of American moms work full-time outside the home. For more than half of them, it's not a choice: they can't afford to stay at home or work only part-time. Helen Bechtol is a twenty-three-year-old mother of two children, ages five and four. She hopes to attend community college in North Carolina. "Right now I bartend Monday through Friday from noon to 6 p.m. at a little country bar," she explains. "And I'm a photographer part-time on the weekends." She lives with her parents, who help out as much as they can. "I'm paying about $650 or $700 on day care a month. I'm on food stamps. . . . I get about $300 a month from their father in child support."

"I don't want my son to think that working as a sales associate and making $8.50 an hour is OK," says Wileidy Ortiz, a high school dropout who works at a retail outlet in Boston's Prudential Center shopping mall. She got pregnant when she was nineteen. When she was three, her father was shot and killed in her native Puerto Rico, and her mother died from cancer after they relocated to Boston to be closer to relatives. The father of her child does not provide child support. She is on food stamps and fuel assistance. As with Bechtol, for Ortiz staying at home with her child is simply impossible.

For the women who can afford to stay at home, the decision isn't easy either. There's a social stigma attached to staying at home, and a fear that returning to the labor force might be difficult or impossible. "I couldn't imagine the emotional pain of having to leave your baby with someone else," explains Terry Spraitz Ciszek, a nurse by profession. Her children are now in their thirties. Staying at home "caused some self-esteem and ego difficulties because I watched people move ahead and have exciting careers. . . . It was ego-deflating, and it was all in the news. In the 70's it was all about, 'women can do it all,' and I remember the Virginia Slim[s] commercials." Terry's husband is a physician, and they can afford the upper-middle-class luxury of one income providing for them all.

When women interrupt their careers, their earnings suffer. A study of University of Chicago MBAs found that women who leave the workforce for three or more years suffer a compensation disadvantage on the order of 40 percent relative to comparable men. Some career advisors and authors like

Joanne Cleaver argue that "stepping off the career track completely is career suicide. Don't do it." Surprisingly, the decline in the number of babies offers mothers who would like to relaunch their careers a unique opportunity. The reason lies in population aging, which continues to shrink the pool of qualified workers. For decades, millions of highly educated Japanese women left their jobs after getting married. Now they're returning to the labor force in droves as companies desperately seek to fill vacancies. As of 2018 a greater percentage of Japanese women within each age group work outside of the household than American women, except for those below the age of twenty-four. About 71 percent of working-age Japanese women are now gainfully employed, the highest proportion in decades, and one of the highest in the world. Given the trend over the last decade, by 2030 Japanese women may come close to men's labor force participation rate, which hovers around 86 percent. However, pay discrimination is still rampant, and mothers continue to do most housework and childcare. "The awareness of men is still so low," complains a graphic designer with two children. "My husband does not have a gender equality concept."

The issue of work-family balance has made it onto the national agenda in many countries around the world, especially those concerned with population aging and the future viability of the welfare state. In 1996 the United Nations reported that only 35 percent of governments in countries with low fertility—about seventy in total—had policies in place to address such issues. By 2015, however, the proportion had grown to 59 percent. The most common policies are paid maternity leave (all countries but one), public childcare (88 percent), child or family allowance (85 percent), and paid paternity leave (64 percent). It is worth mentioning that the UN estimates that women spend an average of four hours a day doing unpaid domestic work, including taking care of children. Men, meanwhile, spend only 1.7 hours.

Work-family balance as a concept and as a policy is the subject of many controversies. Perhaps the most important one is whether people prefer to address the problem by integrating their work life with their family life or by keeping the two separate. My Wharton colleague Nancy Rothbard, along with Katherine Phillips and Tracy Dumas, asked nearly five hundred employees in the United States about their preferences. They found that people who prefer keeping work and family separate are less satisfied and less committed to the company when they are offered integrating programs such as workplace childcare. But they are more satisfied and committed when the company offers segmenting programs such as flextime, which allows employees to shift the start and end times of their workday.

Another useful way of thinking about the issue is to note the benefits to the economy from greater labor force participation by women. As Danish sociologist Gøsta Esping-Andersen has argued, the incorporation of women into the labor force triggered the growth of all manner of market-oriented service activities that women used to perform in the household without pay. If by 2030 more women in the developing world are gainfully employed, the economies of Africa, the Middle East, and South Asia will go through a phase of more rapid growth, accelerating the expansion of the middle class that we discussed in Chapter 3.

DOES WORKING INCREASE WOMEN'S MORTALITY RATE?

As more and more women take advantage of the opportunities in the labor market and navigate the trade-offs between work and family life, the difference in life expectancy between women and men is shrinking. In 1995 women enjoyed an average advantage over men in life expectancy of about 7.8 years. By 2018, the gap had narrowed to 6.8 years, and the United Nations estimates that it will decrease to 6.3 by 2030. As Figure 7 shows, this phenomenon is seen only in the most developed countries since the late 1990s, precisely when ever larger numbers of women began pursuing jobs and careers.

In the United States, a country where women have made greater inroads into the labor market, the decline has been precipitous: women's advantage in life expectancy over men peaked in the early 1970s at 7.7 years, but in 2019 it hovered around 5 years, and by 2030 it will be 4.3 years.

What exactly is responsible for this decrease? In order to answer that question, we need to understand why females live longer than men in the first place. Men experience higher mortality rates than women at every age. "Female

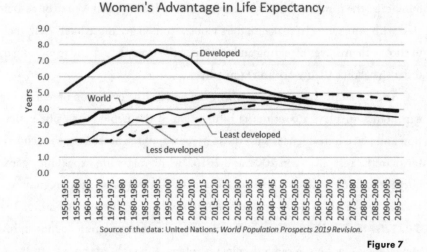

Women's Advantage in Life Expectancy

Source of the data: United Nations, *World Population Prospects 2019 Revision.*

Figure 7

hormones and the role of women in reproduction have been linked to greater longevity," observes *Scientific American*. "Estrogen, for example, facilitates the elimination of bad cholesterol and thus may offer some protection against heart disease; testosterone, on the other hand, has been linked to violence and risk taking." As if that were not enough, "the female body has to make reserves to accommodate the needs of pregnancy and breast feeding; this ability has been associated with a greater ability to cope with overeating and eliminating excess food."

Historically, another reason women have lived longer than men has to do with their lesser exposure to what's called "man-made diseases," including "exposure to the hazards of the workplace in an industrial context, alcoholism, smoking and road accidents, which have indeed increased considerably throughout the 20th century." But women are now increasingly exposed to those same conditions, especially in the most developed countries.

As Lisa Berkman, director of the Center for Population and Development Studies at Harvard, notes, women's new role in the U.S. economy has created a "perfect storm": they are more exposed to the stresses of the workplace, marriage, and in some cases single motherhood. "Chronic stress may promote earlier onset of chronic diseases," said UC San Francisco psychiatry professor Elissa Epel. She is famous for helping to discover that stress tends to wear down telomeres, the protective tips of chromosomes, which are believed to be associated with longevity. To make matters worse, women are more likely than men to soothe themselves by eating and to reduce the time they spend exercising in order to balance their work and family lives.

And for some women, it's getting even worse. The evolution of female life expectancy displays a continuing bifurcation in the United States by education and place of residence, with those in metropolitan areas faring much better than the rest. Between 2009 and 2016, "white men's life expectancy gains outpaced white women's life expectancy gains" in forty American regions analyzed by a team of demographers led by my Penn colleague Irma Elo. The data refer to non-Hispanic white women. Worse, women saw a decline in life expectancy—not just a reduction in advantage—in eight of those forty areas: women in non-metropolitan areas in Alabama, Arkansas, Kentucky, Louisiana, Missouri, Oklahoma, Tennessee, and Texas "lost nearly a year in life expectancy" between 1990 and 2016. The culprits? Smoking, mental and nervous system disorders, and drug overdoses.

The changes in women's roles also affect those who drop out of high school. Duke University's Arun Hendi found that "life expectancy increased or stagnated since 1990 among all education-race-sex groups except for non-Hispanic white women with less than a high school education," for whom there was a sharp decline of 2.5 years over two decades. Crystal Wilson of Cave City, Arkansas, where most residents are white, passed away at thirty-eight. A stay-at-home mom, she suffered from obesity and diabetes. She "dropped out in the tenth grade because she had married," writes Monica Potts in the *American Prospect*. "That was the way things were." According to Julie Johnson, the technology coordinator at the local school district, "If you are a woman, and you are a poorly educated woman, opportunities for you are next to nothing. You get married and you have kids. . . . You're better off if you're not working. . . . It's a horrible cycle." Her answer to what's killing white female high school dropouts? "The desperation of the times. I don't know anything about anything, but that's what kills them."

Overall, mortality continues to increase rapidly among Americans ages twenty-five to forty-four. "Young adults today have experienced difficulties coming of age during the Great Recession, that is, delayed transition to adulthood, declines in marriage, and increased rates of co-residence with parents," note Elo and her coauthors. "Adults in this age group have increased rates of drug and alcohol abuse and may experience increased morbidity and mortality related to these behaviors in future decades." That's the future awaiting a sizable number of millennial women and men who aren't benefiting from the tailwinds we've been discussing.

A GLASS CEILING—OR A THICK LAYER OF MEN?

"There's no such thing as a glass ceiling for women," argues author Laura Liswood. "It's just a thick layer of men." Even when women devote their entire lives to their careers, they find their progression hindered by innumerable obstacles. In 2015, the *New York Times* published an article titled "Fewer Women Run Big Companies than Men Named John." Among Standard & Poor's largest 1,500 companies, "for each woman, there are four men named John, Robert, William or James." In spite of the gains that women have experienced in educational and job opportunities, their numbers at the helm of major corporations around the world are meager. At the Fortune 500 ranking of America's largest corporations in terms of revenue, less than 5 percent of CEOs are women.

The situation is no better elsewhere. Among the largest publicly listed companies in the rich countries that make up the membership of the OECD, women are only a very small fraction of CEOs: 4 percent in the United Kingdom, India, and South Africa; 3 percent in Australia and Mexico; less than 3 percent, on average, in the European Union; less than 2 percent on average throughout Latin America; and exactly *zero* percent in France and Germany, the two most important economies in the EU. Only in China are women CEOs above the 5 percent mark—5.6 percent. When it comes to gender balance on boards of directors, there's only one country (Norway) that comes close to parity (with 42 percent women), and just fifteen countries have a proportion greater than 10 percent (the United States is at 17 percent). In several Asian countries half of publicly listed companies have all-male boards.

The International Labour Office has found that there are only three countries where women fill more than half of all senior and middle management positions: Jamaica, Colombia, and St. Lucia—all three in the Caribbean. In the United States, the number was 43 percent in the late 2010s. In 20 percent of the countries surveyed the proportion was less than 20 percent. In many Muslim countries it drops below 10 percent. Thus we see that while women are working in greater numbers and even accumulating wealth faster than men, the upper echelons of companies are still dominated by men.

When it comes to women in politics, the data are equally discouraging. As of the end of 2017, the only two countries with more women than men in the legislative branch were Rwanda (64 percent) and Bolivia (53 percent). At the other end of the spectrum, several countries had no women in their parliament: Tonga, Micronesia, and Vanuatu in the South Pacific, and Qatar and Yemen in the Middle East. Twenty-six countries had less than 10 percent women, and sixty-four countries had less than 20 percent. The average in the world has grown from 10 percent in 1990 to 21 percent in 2017. The United States, at 19 percent, is slightly below the global average; shockingly, Saudi Arabia, at 20 percent, has a higher proportion. In the executive branch, women represent more than half of cabinet ministers only for departments of health, culture, employment, trade, education, women's affairs, environment and energy, family and children, and social affairs, most of them fields in which women have a stronger presence throughout the economy and society.

It is only when it comes to senior civil service positions within the state bureaucracy that women seem to be represented well. Women represent 50 percent or more of such employees in Hungary, Russia, Lithuania, and Estonia, and more than 40 percent in Canada, Sweden, Slovenia, and Kazakhstan—all countries with a legacy of state socialism or a strong welfare state. Clearly, when recruitment is based on competitive examinations, women do well. By 2030 most senior career positions in government bureaucracies will be held by women with college degrees.

Once on the job, women continue to confront a wage gap, which is estimated to be greater than 30 percent relative to men even in developed countries with long-standing laws against discrimination, including Austria, the United

Kingdom, South Korea, and New Zealand. In Japan and other European countries the gap is at least 20 percent. In the United States the gender wage gap is about 22 percent across all occupations, 19 percent for managers, and as high as 33 percent among top executives.

As 2030 approaches, more women will be in managerial positions, though they will still be in the minority. In the private sector they will be grossly underrepresented, while in the public sector they may be nearing parity with men. It is unlikely, however, that the gender wage gap will disappear, given how persistently high it has remained over the last two or three decades. But will it make a difference if more women are in command?

ARE WOMEN "BOSSY" AS LEADERS?

The late British prime minister Margaret Thatcher and the current German chancellor Angela Merkel have a few things in common. Both led a conservative party to electoral success and reached the highest levels of power in their respective countries. Both were chemists by training. After graduating from Oxford, Thatcher worked briefly for the food conglomerate J. Lyons & Company, where she was part of a team that developed a process to turn ice cream into soft-serve, to the delight of children everywhere. She was dubbed the "Iron Lady of Soft Serve" by the *Atlantic*, a twist on her more famous nickname, the "Iron Lady." Thatcher had other nicknames as well throughout her time in politics: the "Grocer's Daughter," the "Milk Snatcher," and "Attila the Hen." The late French president François Mitterrand went as far as calling her the woman with "the eyes of Caligula and the lips of Marilyn Monroe," in a stunning display of misogyny.

Merkel's career, while very different from Thatcher's, also elicited sexist commentary. She earned a doctorate in quantum chemistry and worked as a research scientist for a few years. She decided to enter politics when the Berlin Wall crumbled, and within a year she had been elected to the German Federal Parliament. She has been variously described as the "World's Most Powerful Woman," "Mutti" ("mommy" in German) for her bland and unobjectionable approach to politics, and "Frau Nein" (Mrs. No) for her insistence on austerity policies during the eurozone crisis.

The key similarity that binds Thatcher and Merkel together is that they are both women with power. The unfortunate tendency is for women with power, whatever their personalities, to be seen first and foremost as women, and oftentimes as "bossy." The website Ban Bossy argues that "when a little boy asserts himself, he's called a 'leader.' Yet when a little girl does the same, she risks being branded 'bossy.'" The problem with the differential treatment is that "words like bossy send a message: don't raise your hand or speak up. By middle school, girls are less interested in leading than boys—a trend that continues into adulthood." As Facebook chief operating officer and best-selling author Sheryl Sandberg has put it, "That little girl is not bossy. That little girl has executive leadership skills."

But there is an even more profound aspect to the careers of the (few) women like Thatcher and Merkel who reached the pinnacle of power. While teaching at Yale University in the 1970s, Harvard Business School professor Rosabeth Moss Kanter, a sociologist by training, found that women behaved differently, and were perceived differently, when working in an environment in which they were "tokens," or in the minority. In those numerically skewed situations, token women are more visible, tend to be caricatured by the majority, endure more pressure to perform, and are expected to behave within strict, predefined gender roles. Given the structural forces at play in situations of tokenism, it's no wonder that many women give up before they reach the top; if they do make it to the prime minister's office or the CEO's suite, their behavior and performance are always seen in a different light than men's.

Writing before Thatcher and Merkel came to power, Kanter identified four "role traps" for women in organizations: the pet, the seductress, the battle-axe, and the mother. The pet is viewed as "cute, sweet or girly" and is rarely taken seriously. The seductress is "a bitch, witch, cow, vamp or man-eater" and is disliked by both men and women. "The most opprobrium is reserved for a woman who falls into the battle-axe role-trap," explains Judith Baxter, a professor at Aston University in the UK. "She has historical form in the tradition of Lady Macbeth or more recently, Margaret Thatcher. She is caricatured as scary, tough, mean, bossy, or just like a man." And Merkel fits the last of the four stereotypes, that of the mother or schoolmistress, "routinely described as schoolmarmy, bossy, frumpy or mumsy."

As we approach 2030, it seems that some attitudes toward women as leaders are changing rapidly. "For the first time since Gallup began measuring Americans' preferences about the gender of their boss," the famed polling organization reported in 2017, "a majority [55 percent] say their boss's gender makes no difference to them." Twenty-three percent of respondents said they would prefer a male boss if they had a choice, while 21 percent preferred a female, a difference well within the margin of error of plus or minus 4 percent. Gallup has been asking this question since 1953, when 66 percent preferred a man and only 5 percent a woman, with 25 percent of respondents being indifferent. Intriguingly, in 2017 only 44 percent of women were indifferent compared to 68 percent for men, suggesting that, as we have discussed, women differ massively in their attitudes and behavior depending on their age, education, and place of residence.

Although the poll was conducted a month after the Harvey Weinstein scandal came to light, and thus during the intense cultural reckoning of the Me Too movement, there are reasons to believe that women may be starting to overcome the curse of tokenism—that is, the tyranny of small numbers. As women become more numerous in a wide variety of workplaces and continue to advance to the highest levels, their roles and positions will shift quickly. By 2030, significant proportions of women will be in positions of political, social, and business leadership, thus potentially undermining once and for all the basis for one of the most blatant forms of discrimination.

Kanter's theory also helps explain dynamics in the marriage market. Back in the 1940s American women were told not to be ambitious when it came to their career aspirations. "Warning! Be careful not to seem smarter than your man," recommended one self-help book. "It's one thing to be almost as smart, but to be or seem smarter—that is taboo." That kind of advice was dispensed at a time when the United States faced a shortage of men due to wartime fatalities. The underlying assumption was that women who stood out for their smarts would be shunned in favor of those who were more "feminine," according to the conventions of the time.

Imagine now if the shortage actually went in the other direction, as in China. There women with a doctoral degree are often referred to as *di san xing*, or the "third sex," referring to the idea that few men want to marry them.

Chinese magazine articles routinely argue that "for the competent career woman, *sajiao* [the art of being shy, cute, and affectionate] is an indispensable tool for appearing neither too independent nor too self-sufficient for her boyfriend." The advice goes as far as suggesting that "*sajiao* allows her to appear soft and feminine rather than hard and powerful, traits that challenge traditional notions of womanhood." And if that weren't enough, here's the icing on the cake: "By playing up to the male ego, she accomplishes the near-impossible: making her man feel like a man."

Let's examine what happens to gendered stereotypes when there are sudden changes to women's opportunities and freedoms. Saudi women were first allowed to drive in 2018, and their car-buying behavior has taken everyone by surprise. "Showrooms in the kingdom stocked cars they thought Saudi women would be drawn to, such as brightly colored mini-SUVs," reported the *Wall Street Journal*. "Instead, they're opting for models that are loud and fast." The conventional wisdom says that men are interested in power and acceleration, while women are keen on comfort and safety. "We expected women to begin with small cars with small engines," said an Audi saleswoman. But Sahar Nasief, sixty-four, a grandmother of sixteen and an activist committed to a woman's right to drive, wanted a Mustang convertible, saying, "It's always been my dream car." When the Ford Motor Company heard about her preference, they offered to give her one, and she chose one that was yellow and black, the colors of her favorite soccer team. "I love this car because of its roar," Nasief said.

Kanter's theory can help explain this behavior too. There are still few women driving on Saudi Arabia's roads. As early adopters, Saudi women behave in ways that attempt to break with the stereotypes and that make them appear to be on an equal footing with men.

WILL WOMEN RULE THE WORLD IN 2030?

Women's hard-won new status in society can potentially lead to a transformation of the power structure, and perhaps fewer scandals, less corruption, and diminished violence, as a growing number of researchers have found. Or it can produce a sharp bifurcation whereby only a segment of women enjoy the benefits while the rest are pushed to the fringes, resulting in more social conflict rather than less. Regardless of their influence in managerial or governmental positions, however, women will control more of the wealth, and perhaps steer it toward areas that concern them, including education and healthcare, in a world with fewer babies and aging populations.

As the number of women of influence grows, will it become the new normal for women to be accepted as leaders? It's likely that 2030 is too soon for the utopian ideal of complete gender equality, especially given how slowly current trends are moving and how many women are still discriminated against or deprived of opportunities.

The most imponderable factor, however, has little to do with the balance of power and status between the sexes. As cities grow, women gain access to new opportunities. But global warming also accelerates with urban sprawl, as we shall see in Chapter 5. And climate change tends to hurt women and children the most.

Cities Drown First

Any city, however small, is in fact divided into two,
one the city of the poor, the other of the rich.

—PLATO

As 2030 approaches, cities will become a microcosm of what's to come. Each of the trends discussed in the previous chapters progresses faster in a city: fertility plunges earlier and more quickly; millennial behavioral patterns are quintessentially urban in nature; the new middle class lives in large agglomerations; and women's life chances and behavior evolve more quickly in more densely populated areas. Cities have become a gigantic engine of change, a catalyst for the end of the world as we know it.

Cities occupy 1 percent of the world's land yet are home to about 55 percent of the human population. Told another way, the total landmass on Earth is 196.9 million square miles and cities account for roughly 2 million of those. With 4 billion urban residents, that's an average of 2,000 people per square mile in cities, which is quite a crowd. Cities account for 75 percent of total energy consumption and 80 percent of total carbon emissions. They also disproportionately contribute to global warming with their closely packed buildings and surfaces paved with asphalt and concrete, which trap more heat—a process known as the "heat island effect."

And these are based on current figures.

Looking ahead, trends indicate that urbanization is on the rise. Each week, the population of cities around the world grows by 1.5 million people, which means a new round of construction, pollution, and greenhouse gas emissions. In 2017, there were twenty-nine cities with more than 10 million people. By 2030, there will be forty-three of them, and fourteen will be home to more than 20 million. Cities tend to exacerbate inequality. As they become the norm worldwide, we will be inching closer to potentially catastrophic social and climate crises. What might be done about urban poverty and global warming? Do we need large-scale changes or small behavioral adaptations? Should cities attempt to grow their own food? Can declining cities in the rustbelts of Europe and the United States turn their fortunes around?

CITIES ARE HOT IN MORE WAYS THAN ONE

In October 2018 the Inter-Governmental Panel on Climate Change, convened by the United Nations, warned in a new report that in order to avert catastrophic climate change, "global net human-caused emissions of carbon dioxide would need to fall by about 45 percent from 2010 levels by 2030, reaching 'net zero' around 2050." In other words, decisive action to avert the flooding of coastal areas, reduce the frequency of extreme weather events, and prevent widespread disruption to agriculture must be under way before 2030, or else . . .

"The next few years are probably the most important in our history," said Debra Roberts, co-chair of one of the working groups that produced the report. And in May 2019, the United Nations published another gloomy report predicting the demise of 1 million (out of 8 million) existing animal and plant species within a few decades if climate change is not reversed. As global temperatures rise, urban residents may experience something like hell. "The trends are very harmful to an increasing share of people living in the cities," notes Belgian scientist Hendrik Wouters. "Hot temperatures lead to excessive mortalities, hospital admissions, energy usage and economic loss, which are exacerbated by the urban heat island [effect]."

At this pace, we may not only compromise our future but also obliterate our past. According to Egyptologist Sarah Parcak, there are some 50 million unmapped archaeological sites in the world, and as cities expand, at least half of them may be destroyed by looting, climate change, and unregulated construction. This will all happen before 2030. In response, Parcak launched the crowdsourcing platform GlobalXplorer. In *The New Yorker,* Nick Paumgarten wrote about the platform's democratic ethos and how "citizen Indiana Joneses can scrutinize satellite maps and identify potential new sites. . . . The idea is to deploy more eyeballs (and, ultimately, more benevolent shovel bums) in the race against carbon and greed."

Cities will be more affected by climate change and rising sea levels than rural or uninhabited areas. About 90 percent of urban areas in the world lie along a coast, and by 2025 as much as 75 percent of the world's population will live on or near a coast. Asia, which has the fastest-growing middle class in the world and is home to 60 percent of the global population, will be very vulnerable to seawater flooding in megacities including Jakarta, Manila, Ho Chi Minh City, Bangkok, Osaka, Dhaka, and Shanghai. Outside of Asia, New Orleans, Miami, Venice, and Alexandria (in Egypt) are the most exposed.

Urban growth also aggravates another key feature of the world of 2030: inequality. This is a problem long in the making. "Any city, however small, is in fact divided into two," Plato wrote two and a half millennia ago. "One the city of the poor, the other of the rich." *Metropolis,* the 1927 futuristic silent movie by German filmmaker Fritz Lang, brought Plato's reflection to the silver screen. It portrays a society split in two; workers toil underground as the wealthy enjoy a seamlessly glittering city above, with futuristic vehicles, trains, airplanes, skyscrapers, overpasses, and underpasses. The two main characters—Freder, a wealthy son of the city's master, and Maria, beloved by the workers—attempt to bridge the gap between the haves and the have-nots. The film's overall aesthetic, as well as its visual themes and motifs, were inspired by Cubism, Expressionism, and Art Deco, just like many of our cities nowadays. It ends with an intriguing title card: "The Mediator between the Head and the Hands Must Be the Heart." While its reception was mixed when it first appeared, *Metropolis* today is considered a pioneering classic, one that anticipated what large cities would eventually look like, with their layers of splendor and squalor.

The massive growth of cities we see today is a relatively modern phenomenon. For some perspective, consider that in the 1920s no city in the world was home to more than 10 million people; in fact, only a handful had more than 1 million inhabitants. In the years following the first moon landing, in 1969, there were only three cities with more than 10 million residents: New York, Tokyo, and Osaka. At the turn of the twenty-first century, urban growth accelerated, and city life became the new normal. Are these changes all for good? As the Greek philosopher Aristotle, Plato's most influential disciple, pointed out, "A great city is not to be confounded with a populous one."

In fact, many big cities in the world have become dehumanized, soulless, and alienating. The twentieth-century Italian metaphysical painter Giorgio de Chirico captured it best with his paintings depicting futuristic, desolate cityscapes. The modernist architects and urban planners declared that "less is more," to quote the famous twentieth-century architect Ludwig Mies van der Rohe, streamlining designs to the point of turning cities into exercises in geometry and repetition, with an endless succession of avenues, street blocks, cube-like buildings, columns, windows, and so on. The simplicity of modernist architecture quickly degenerated into the Brutalist trend of unwieldy masses of concrete and glass. "There is nothing more poetic and terrible than the skyscrapers' battle with the heavens that cover them," said the poet Federico García Lorca after living in New York City in 1929. It would take decades before Robert Venturi turned the tide against modernist architecture with his whimsical "Less is a bore!" approach.

The reality is that as large cities grow larger, our problems will continue to multiply: everything from traffic congestion to air pollution, waste disposal to poverty and inequality. Cities are ground zero in the fight against global warming and the widening wealth gap. But we can't afford to feel overwhelmed by those mounting problems. Charles Dickens once said that "the most important thing to be successful is to stop saying 'I wish' and start saying 'I will.'" Consider nothing impossible, think laterally to confront the problems facing cities, then treat possibilities as probabilities.

CITY LIGHTS—AND SHADOWS

Satellite imagery helps create "luminosity maps," as cities turn on their lights during the night, such as Figure 8, provided by NASA.

The intensity of the skyglow is highly correlated with global standards of living, and researchers use it to triangulate and verify information from official statistics collected through conventional means. But satellites can't tell us that beneath the exhilarating glitter of city lights lie enormous pockets of poverty, the result of rising income and wealth disparities. The UK House of Commons Library has made the depressing forecast that by 2030 two-thirds of the world's wealth will be owned by the richest 1 percent, most of them living in cities. In 2018 Hong Kong had 10,000 ultra-rich residents with a net worth of at least $30 million each, topping New York's 9,000 for the first time. Tokyo, Los An-

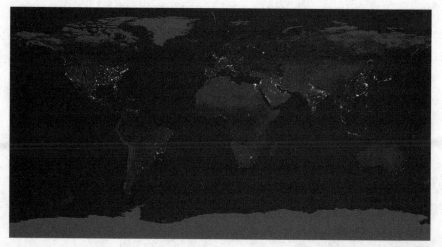

Figure 8

geles, Paris, London, Chicago, San Francisco, Washington, DC, and Osaka rounded out the top ten ranking of cities with ultra-wealthy people. But Hong Kong also has a sizable share (20 percent) of people living in poverty, and so does New York City (19 percent), according to municipal government data.

In 2019 the U.S. federal poverty line stood at $28,100 in annual income for a family of four. By that measure, 30 percent of the residents of the McAllen-Edinburg-Mission metropolitan area in Texas are poor. In Valdosta, Georgia, the percentage is 26 percent; in Visalia-Porterville, California, nearly 25 percent; and in Bloomington, Indiana, almost 23 percent. In 2017 the average nationally was 12.3 percent. And that's five decades after President Lyndon Johnson launched his war on poverty. At that time, the national poverty rate was 19 percent. Poverty—like wealth—is disproportionately concentrated in cities. The point is that cities amplify the highs and lows of life as we know it, and they polarize us into extremes of opportunity and disadvantage.

·

Within a few blocks of Capitol Hill lies one of the poorest urban neighborhoods in America. In 1932, Rosa Lee Cunningham's grandparents, who were share-croppers, migrated to that part of Washington, DC, from rural Rich Square, North Carolina. "Her life story spans a half-century of hardship in blighted neighborhoods," wrote *Washington Post* investigative journalist Leon Dash. "Not far away from the majestic buildings where policymakers have largely failed in periodic efforts to break the cycle of poverty," Rosa Lee became pregnant with the first of her eight children when she was thirteen, married at sixteen, and moved back to her parents' home a few months later when her husband started beating her. It took years for her to move into her own house. "Rosa Lee lived in a world defined by her poverty, illiteracy and criminal activities," Dash wrote. Two of her children eventually found stable jobs. They lived in a cramped apartment, along with her oldest son, who slept in the living room. Another son worked long hours at a KFC cleaning ovens. He smoked crack after work. Rosa shared a bedroom with one of her daughters, whose teenage son had spent time in a group home for young offenders. Another of her daughters— who had served an eleven-month term for cocaine possession—occupied the only other bedroom, along with her three children. That's a total of nine people from three different generations.

"Rosa Lee is a safety net for most of her children," Dash observed, who "live a kind of nomadic existence, bouncing from friends' apartments, to jail, to the street, to Rosa Lee's." She moved eighteen times during her forty-five years in the nation's capital. Hers was "the only steady income, not all of which is legal. She receives $437 a month from the Supplemental Security Income program for the disabled poor. . . . The rest of her money comes from selling shoplifted goods." She was diagnosed with AIDS in 1988 and died in 1995. "Poverty is a phenomenon that has devastated Americans of all races, in rural and urban communities, but it has disproportionately affected black Americans living in the nation's inner cities."

Eric was one of Rosa Lee's two sons to make it into the middle class. He drove a Jeep and lived in a DC suburb. Eric and his brother Alvin are the only ones of Rosa Lee's eight children who never used drugs or served prison time. They both joined the Army. At the time of their mother's death, Alvin was a bus driver, while Eric, a heavy-equipment operator, worked several temporary jobs. "In their family, drug abuse has become the dividing wall that no one can scale," Dash wrote. "Alvin and Eric don't spend holidays with their brothers, and neither one can remember the last time that [their siblings] came to their homes for a visit. If they see each other at all, it is usually when Alvin or Eric comes to straighten out a problem at Rosa Lee's apartment."

While the urban poor and the impoverished middle class toil and struggle, the rich live the good life. "I spent my Saturday nights in New York because those gleaming, dazzling parties of his [Jay Gatsby's] were with me so vividly that I could still hear the music and the laughter, faint and incessant, from his garden, and the cars going up and down his drive," wrote F. Scott Fitzgerald. "One night I did hear a material car there, and saw its lights stop at his front steps. But I didn't investigate. Probably it was some final guest who had been away at the ends of the earth and didn't know that the party was over." In their rarefied world, the rich compete with the rich for social esteem. "As wealth accumulates," wrote Thorstein Veblen in 1899, "the leisure class develops further in function and structure, and there arises a differentiation within the class. . . .

Those who stand near the higher and the highest grades of the wealthy leisure class, in point of birth, or in point of wealth, or both, outrank the remoter-born and the pecuniarily weaker."

COUCH POTATOES AND SOCIAL MEDIA

But it's mostly the middle class that will shape the future of cities. The expanding urban middle class constitutes the backbone of the modern consumer economy we discussed in Chapter 3, and its members lead very different lives than rural folk. The middle class tend to be interested in spending money on leisure and entertainment. They leave behind much bigger carbon and digital footprints. Urban residents and their lifestyles will shape the future of technology and consumption precisely because they have become the majority of the population—companies will develop new products and marketing gimmicks based on their behavior. More urban consumers beget more urban-style consumption in an endless, self-reinforcing cycle.

And as cities grow, the phenomenon of the "urban couch potato" proliferates. In 2017 there were more people in the world suffering from hunger (821 million) than from obesity (650 million). By 2030, the estimated obese population of 1.1 billion will far exceed the number of people going hungry, conservatively projected to be under 200 million as the middle class expands in Asia and Africa. The escalation of obesity has been driven by the population explosion in cities, with their characteristically sedentary lifestyles. Changes in our diet and the consumption of processed foods are also to blame. As obesity rises, so will the number of people suffering from heart problems, diabetes, and joint and muscle afflictions, among many other health issues. There will be higher demand for plus-size clothing and extra-room seating, for gyms and dietary advice.

The World Health Organization defines overweight people as those with a body mass index between 25 and 30. Obesity is defined as a body mass index in excess of 30. The prevalence of obesity in the world has more than doubled since 1980. In 2016, more than 1.9 billion adults were overweight, and 650 million of them were obese. Taken together, that's a fourth of the world's total population.

What's worse, 41 million preschool children were overweight or obese. That year, at least 2.8 million people of all ages died due to health problems related to excessive weight. A much larger number were unable to lead normal, productive lives: they lost their jobs, became socially ostracized, or suffered from other ailments. According to the OECD, "Adult obesity rates are highest in the United States, Mexico, New Zealand and Hungary, while they are lowest in Japan and Korea.... Adult obesity rates are projected to increase further by 2030." Obesity afflicts women more than men, and the poor more than the middle class.

The obesity epidemic is particularly acute in the United States, a country that represents just about 4 percent of the world's population but nearly 18 percent of total human body mass. According to the National Center for Health Statistics, a whopping 70 percent of Americans are either overweight (32 percent) or obese (38 percent), compared to global averages of 39 and 13 percent, respectively. Put another way, the excess weight of Americans is equivalent to about one billion average human beings on the planet. By 2030 nearly half of the American population is projected to be obese. Extreme obesity, as measured by a body mass index greater than 40, affects 5.5 percent of American men and an astounding 9.9 percent of American women. Among American children and adolescents, 17 percent are obese and 6 percent extremely obese. One in five American teenagers is obese, and nearly one in ten is extremely obese. These trends will only increase over time.

Economic growth in China, India, and other emerging economies in Asia and Africa (where malnutrition was historically a larger threat than obesity) has translated into higher protein and processed food consumption, more sedentary lifestyles, and other unhealthy facts of urban living. Still, the highest rates of obesity, sometimes approaching 80 percent of the population, are to be found in the island nations of the Southern Pacific, including American Samoa, Nauru, the Cook Islands, Tokelau, and Tonga. "Previously, it was thought that Pacific Islanders were genetically predisposed to obesity," the website Healthcare Global reported. Recent studies, however, indicate that Western diets are the culprit. "Traditional foods of the islands such as fresh fish, meat and local fruits and vegetables have been replaced by rice, sugar, flour, canned meats, canned fruits and vegetables, soft drinks and beer."

Lifestyles in the city are also shaped by the hectic nature of the urban experience, especially when it comes to traffic. About a third of the time that people spend driving their cars through the downtown areas of major U.S. cities is dedicated to finding a parking space. Research indicates that in those urban parts of the globe where the middle class has grown to prominence, people spend 20 to 30 percent of their awake time in traffic. It is no surprise that many cities have become synonymous with smog or acute air pollution.

And urban lifestyles have become synonymous with the use of all sorts of smartphone apps, which further contribute to a bifurcation in behavior between urban and rural residents. Social media apps are the most frequently used. As of January 2019, more than 80 percent of the population age thirteen and above in the United States, Latin America, and East Asia regularly engaged with digital social media like Facebook, Twitter, Instagram, or WeChat. In Europe and the Middle East the proportion was above 70 percent. By contrast, in sub-Saharan Africa it was below 20 percent, and in India about 30 percent (two parts of the world in which not all smartphone owners use social media). The large rural populations in these countries are why the social media numbers are relatively low. Even when they have access to digital networks and apps, people in small villages prefer to interact with other people face-to-face. The proportion of the population that live in the countryside is about 59 percent in sub-Saharan Africa and 65 percent in India, compared to just 17 percent in the United States, although these numbers are declining fast as people migrate to the cities.

CAN "LIBERTARIAN PATERNALISM" SAVE OUR CITIES—AND THE PLANET?

People often wonder what can be done about global warming short of putting the entire economy on a draconian carbon-free diet. The answer is that small, ordinary adjustments to our daily behavior can actually go a long way in averting catastrophe. There are two basic principles involved in making each city's life friendlier toward the environment, more tolerable, and more enjoyable for a larger share of its population. Without implementing them, it will be very difficult to cope with pollution, environmental decay, and climate change. They both involve lateral thinking.

The first lateral principle is the "mundanity of excellence," or the idea that high performance is not normally a result of quantum leaps or innate talent but rather comes about because of a series of tiny improvements. Sociologist Daniel Chambliss coined the term after conducting an extensive ethnographic and quantitative analysis of competitive swimmers, concluding that "superlative performance is really a confluence of dozens of small skills or activities, each one learned or stumbled upon." According to three-time Olympic gold medalist Mary Meagher, "People don't know how ordinary success is." It's a long list of little things that produces superior results when done simultaneously. "There is nothing extraordinary or superhuman in any one of those actions; only the fact that they are done consistently and correctly," says Chambliss. In other words, excellence is essentially mundane. Here's how it works.

Swimmers improve by learning how to perform "a proper flip turn," to execute "a streamlined push off from the wall, with the arms squeezed together over the head," to position "the hands in the water so no air is cupped in them," to use weights in the gym "to properly build strength," "to eat the right foods," "to wear the best suits for racing," and so on. Peter Drucker, one of the most influential management consultants ever, once wrote that becoming a successful executive "does not require special gifts, special aptitude, or special training. Effectiveness as an executive demands doing certain—and fairly simple— things." As we shall see, small behavioral adjustments on our part can go a long way in terms of slowing down climate change and preserving the environment for future generations.

The second principle involves what behavioral scientists call "nudging"— behavioral modification through either positive reinforcement or indirect suggestion to influence the motives, incentives, and decisions of groups or individuals. The "art of the nudge" was first developed in an article titled "Einstein Meets Magritte" written by the British scientist D. J. Stewart in 1999. In 2008 Richard Thaler and Cass Sunstein's book *Nudge: Improving Decisions About Health, Wealth, and Happiness* catapulted the "science of nudging" to worldwide attention. The basic problem, in their view, is that people tend to act in ways that are not only inimical to the common good but also against their own self-interest. Thaler—who subsequently won the Nobel Prize in Economic Sciences—and his coauthor argued that the true beauty of nudging is its potential for creating behavioral change that promotes the common good as well as individual interests. Nudging has nothing to do with regulation, enforcement, or coercion. Thaler and Sunstein refer to it as "libertarian paternalism." As they write, "To count as a mere nudge, the intervention must be easy and cheap to avoid. Nudges are not mandates. Putting fruit at eye level [next to the cash register] counts as a nudge. Banning junk food does not."

Nudging works by making small, subtle, and inexpensive changes. To take one example: by etching the image of a housefly in men's urinals at Amsterdam's Schiphol Airport, the designers "improve[d] the aim" of users, which reduced janitorial costs. Nudging has found widespread application in the fields of marketing, talent management, healthcare, all kinds of therapy, and politics, with candidates using its techniques to improve fundraising, engagement, and election day turnouts.

Let me share with you a practical example. Depending on the number of red lights I encounter on my daily commute in Philadelphia, the time I spend commuting can double or even triple, and with it my carbon footprint. I face a big incentive to accelerate through an intersection when the light is about to turn red—a very dangerous type of behavior that increases the risk of an accident. But the city could install panels above traffic lights to inform drivers about the status of the lights farther ahead. If I am approaching a light that is turning yellow but see that lights down the road will also be turning yellow and then red, racing to get through the intersection before the light turns red becomes a less desirable option given that I will need to stop at the next light anyway. As another example, painting lines and arrows on the pavement sometimes helps people drive more fluidly, especially when making turns. Similarly, retailers have known for years that accelerating the tempo of the background music when the aisles in the store get crowded helps reduce lines and maximize sales.

Research indicates that mundane adaptations and libertarian paternalism can be more effective at helping cities deal with pollution, congestion, and climate change than can punitive fines, carbon taxes, or monetary incentives. Pro-environmental behaviors such as choosing a less polluting transportation mode, participating in recycling programs, or using environmentally friendly detergents proliferate when people feel a moral obligation to do something about climate change. It's true that people need to be made aware of the problem and of its consequences, to be encouraged to assume personal responsibility, and to be motivated to take action. But research also shows that pro-environmental behaviors are largely driven by habit. The gap between intention and action can be bridged by nudging that encourages people to develop positive habits. For example, thermostats should display how much it is costing to warm the room as opposed to what the temperature is. Energy bills that compare your monthly bill to that of the average in your neighborhood have also been proven to reduce energy consumption—it's as if they spur people to keep up with the Joneses in righteousness instead of conspicuous consumption. Making it easier to pay for the bus by accepting credit cards and mobile payments might also increase the use of public transportation.

"WHEN THE WELL IS DRY, WE LEARN THE WORTH OF WATER"

The quote in the heading of this section is from Benjamin Franklin, and although it's intended to be a general observation about not taking things for granted, a literal interpretation of that aphorism is especially apt today. Water is almost always a renewable resource, but its quality and distribution around the world are the subject of considerable friction and conflict. Cities in particular tend to face recurrent water shortages. What's more, one out of four urban residents, or 1 billion people, don't have access to piped water in their home. The changing geographical distribution of population growth, the process of urbanization, the growth of the middle class, and climate change will fundamentally reshape the economics and politics of water. As my Penn colleague Irina Marinov, an oceanographer and climate modeler, points out, "We have changed the system more in the last 200 years than nature usually does in 100,000-year cycles."

Our water problems will multiply by 2030. "In the western United States, there is an old saying that whiskey is for drinking, and water is for fighting," says Ian Lyle, director of federal affairs for the National Water Resources Association. According to McKinsey & Co., water is the third most important and costly area for future infrastructure development, after transportation and energy. Water is difficult (and costly) to store and transport over large distances. The future of cities hinges on building new water infrastructure and on encouraging everyone—consumers, farmers, manufacturers, and energy producers—to be more mindful about water use.

Water and water management are essential to large-scale human society. Every major ancient civilization—Egypt, Mesopotamia, the Indus Valley, China, Rome—developed water management infrastructure and technologies to feed and sustain large concentrations of population in urbanized settings. Throughout history, major calamities have occurred in the wake of water shortages. According to the United Nations, most natural disasters, perhaps as many as 90 percent, are related to water. Major refugee crises have erupted as a result of droughts or conflicts over water, as in Somalia in 2011 or Sudan and Mali in 2012. The OECD has estimated that by 2030 almost 4 billion people—half of the world's projected population—will live in areas with serious water shortages, mostly in East Asia, South Asia, and the Middle East, precisely where cities are growing the fastest.

Consider the challenge: More than two-thirds of the earth's surface is covered with water, but 97.5 percent of it is undrinkable. That leaves just 2.5 percent for human consumption. Most of that, perhaps as much as 70 percent, is beyond easy reach—frozen in ice sheets, glaciers, permafrost, and permanent snow cover. About 30 percent is groundwater, and less than 1 percent is in rivers, lakes, wetlands, and other reservoirs. Around 1.2 billion people presently lack access to clean drinking water, and about 2.8 billion face water scarcity during at least one month a year. The scarcity problem can be driven by physical or economic reasons. Some parts of the world just lack enough water to support present and future population levels, while in other areas, especially sub-Saharan Africa and parts of South Asia, water scarcity is due to lack of infrastructure, mismanagement of resources, or other economic factors. In some of these regions, people—mostly women and children—can spend up to five hours per day procuring water for their families during droughts.

The situation is especially dire in South Asia. "Even in Chennai, Bangalore, Shimla and Delhi, water is being rationed and India's food security is under threat. With the lives and livelihood of millions at risk, urban India is scream-ing for water," notes a report from India's National Commission for Women. "For instance, water is rationed twice a week in Bangalore, and for 30 minutes a day in Bhopal. . . . Mumbai routinely lives through water cuts from January to June, while some areas get water once in three days in Hyderabad." The cities mentioned in that quote are among the world's fastest-growing places.

REINVENTING THE WHEEL

In the poorest parts of the world, women and girls walk long distances to pro-cure water for their families, a task made all the more difficult by how heavy water is. The World Health Organization recommends 5.3 to 13.2 gallons per person per day for drinking, cooking, and washing. In parts of Asia and Africa, women walk an average of 3.7 miles per day carrying about 3 gallons of water at a time.

Cynthia Koenig decided to solve this problem. After graduating from the University of Michigan with an MBA and a master's degree in global sustain-ability, she launched Wello WaterWheel, a social venture that manufactures and distributes plastic water barrels that can be easily rolled on a variety of surfaces and terrains. Her invention aimed at replacing the traditional Indian head-carried 2.2-gallon water pot with a 24-gallon plastic drum resembling a fat wheel with a very long U-shaped handle that can be pushed as if the contrap-tion were a shopping cart. That's ten times more water and much less effort at transporting it over several miles.

While Koenig didn't invent the concept, her price point distinguished her product in the marketplace. "The vision for Wello was born out of years of per-sonal experience living and working in water scarce environments," she recalls. "While based in a remote village in Mexico, I struggled to haul enough water to meet my daily needs." She started to brainstorm solutions while on an exploratory trip to Rajasthan, India. "Our early ideas were all over the place—from water-carrying balloons to ergonomic panniers for donkeys." By the end of 2016 more than 10,000 WaterWheels were in daily use across Bangladesh, India, Kenya, Malawi, Pakistan, and Zambia, servicing both rural and urban areas.

On a much larger scale, the biggest threat to the future of water comes from poor farming practices, since agriculture accounts for roughly 70 percent of worldwide human-related water consumption. Industrial usage accounts for about 20 percent, leaving the remaining 10 percent for households. In Chapter 1 we assessed the potential for an industrial-agricultural revolution in Africa, a transformation that cannot take place without better water management.

THE WATER-ENERGY NEXUS

Cities also stand a better chance of getting the water they need if we become more mindful about the role of water in energy production. We need water to extract, wash, and sort raw materials and fossil fuels, cool thermal power plants, cultivate biofuels, and power hydroelectric turbines. According to the United Nations, about 90 percent of all electric power generation is water-intensive. But what happens when energy needs and the need to preserve water supplies collide? Pollution of aquifers because of mining or hydraulic fracturing (known as "fracking") is on the rise. Climate change will be a disruptive force as well. Policymaking and planning need to take into consideration the constraints and the risks inherent in the increasing demand for both water and energy from a growing urban population. Thus there is a "water-energy nexus," as well as a "water-energy-food nexus," according to Ralph Exton, chief marketing officer for GE Power, Water & Process Technologies. "Water is the most overused, abused, and underpriced resource in the world, and a large fraction of it is not renewable or is returned [to the watershed] undrinkable," notes my Penn engineering colleague Noam Lior. "Governments are reluctant to intervene. Nobody wants to undertake a thorough cost analysis and to formulate policies based on it."

Climate change will inevitably affect the water cycle in unforeseen ways, magnifying episodic droughts and floods. In addition to these recurring challenges of water management, global warming poses new threats and will have several immediate effects. Higher temperatures mean increased evaporation, which will divert water that would otherwise fill streams, rivers, and lakes to the benefit of both urban and rural residents. Changes in vegetation will alter rainwater patterns. Warming will make glaciers recede and eventually disappear, thus depriving streams and rivers of their steady flow of water. Water available for irrigation will become scarcer. Sporadic heavy rainfall in warmer areas will lead to temporary accumulations that will provide mosquitoes with new breeding areas, posing significant new public health challenges.

FARMING INSIDE A SHIPPING CONTAINER

If cities are the main source of carbon emissions and the most heavily affected by climate change and water shortages, perhaps we should think laterally and bring to the city some of the things that make the countryside so much more environmentally friendly. One tantalizing prospect for 2030 and beyond is that cities may turn to producing the food needed to feed their growing population, thus becoming "green islands" rather than heat islands. Such a development would also reduce carbon emissions by reducing food imports, and an increase in urban vegetation would help absorb some of the emissions from cars and energy production facilities.

The concept of "vertical farming" is taking hold in the most developed countries. Originally proposed by Dickson Despommier at Columbia University, vertical farming involves growing food inside a building two stories high or taller. "Food is now been grown in such unlikely places as old factories, abandoned warehouses, and industrial buildings," notes Ravindra Krishnamurthy, an expert on the subject. Jack Ng built Sky Greens, one of the world's first large and commercially viable vertical farms in Singapore. He grows vegetables like lettuce and spinach in A-shaped towers soaring thirty feet high. Thirty-eight tiers of growing troughs rotate at a rate of one millimeter per second, "which ensures uniform distribution of sunlight, proper air circulation and irrigation for all plants." The breakthrough is the efficient use of resources. Each tower costs as little as $3 per month to operate, with an extremely low carbon footprint given that it needs "the energy equivalent to illuminating a 40-watt light bulb"; the water is recycled and "all the organic wastes are also composted and reused."

Vertical agriculture has the potential to help revitalize cities in decline. "Entrepreneurs are taking advantage of inexpensive former warehouses and factories in Detroit and transforming them for agricultural use to produce local foods," reports the *Detroit News*. For instance, "Green Collar Foods mists the bare roots of kale, cilantro and peppers using an aeroponics system under fluorescent lights in its 400-square-foot plastic-encased greenhouse. The system is built vertically, stacking plants on shelves to grow above each other." Jeff Adams launched Artesian Farms in 2015 in a 7,500-square-foot vacant warehouse. He uses twenty times less water to grow a head of lettuce than his California competitors. Most importantly, vertical agriculture in cities promises to reduce the carbon emissions involved in transportation and to shorten delivery times. "The food you're eating right now, it's seven to 10 days before it reaches Michigan," Adams notes. But his produce gets "from here to the market in a day, at most, 48 hours. . . . It's going to be much more flavorful and much more nutritional."

Urban agriculture—whether vertical or not—will be crucial for meeting the needs of the rapidly growing cities of Africa, where transportation from the countryside represents a key bottleneck in the supply chain. For instance, city officials in Kampala and Nairobi, the capitals of Uganda and Kenya, respectively, have encouraged agricultural activities for years, with varying degrees of success. Some studies indicate that already "800 million people are engaged in urban agriculture worldwide, producing 15–20 percent of the world's food." Most of these are in the developing world. In Africa, as many as 35–40 million people receive their food mostly from urban farms.

Farmers are coming up with unusual ideas for meeting Africa's food needs. "We're farming in a shipping container," says Oluwayimika Angel Adelaja, a Nigerian entrepreneur who founded Fresh Direct Produce. She moved her farm to the Nigerian capital, Abuja, thus cutting transportation costs and ensuring that most of the produce would reach market in perfect condition. Too, container farming is much more efficient in its use of water, and solar panels provide the power. One step at a time, Africa is edging closer to addressing the food-related challenges of its population growth to 2030 and beyond by developing urban agriculture techniques.

HIP CITIES, FROM BILBAO TO PITTSBURGH

Lateral thinking will also be required to reverse one of the most important urban challenges in the developed world: the decay resulting from deindustrialization, a process that has increased poverty and wreaked havoc on the middle class.

In 1997 the Guggenheim Bilbao Museum opened to the public in a decrepit industrial city in the Basque country of northern Spain, a region where ironworks and shipbuilding flourished in the second half of the nineteenth century— a standard story of boom and bust similar to what happened in hundreds of cities in the derelict rustbelts of Europe and the United States. The building was designed by superstar architect Frank Gehry. Its curved, voluptuous, platinum-colored forms became an instant sensation around the world. "Bilbao has lately become a pilgrimage town," wrote the renowned architectural critic Herbert Muschamp in the *New York Times Magazine*. "The word is out that miracles still occur, and that a major one has happened here.... People have been flocking to Bilbao for nearly two years, just to watch the building's skeleton take shape. 'Have you been to Bilbao?' In architectural circles, that question has acquired the status of a shibboleth. Have you seen the light? Have you seen the future? Does it work? Does it play?" Much of the building's appeal to the average observer is its irregular, complex form. My friend Rafael del Pino, executive chairman of Ferrovial, the construction company that erected it, once joked to one of Gehry's partners, "If we had built it slightly different, would you have noticed?"

The Guggenheim Bilbao became a global symbol of urban revival. "There was a decay of the industrial system, high unemployment (between 25 and 30 percent, reaching 35 percent in certain areas of the greater metropolitan area), degradation of the environment and the general city framework, emigration and stagnation of the population, and problems of social exclusion," recalls

Ibon Areso, an architect by training. He served as deputy mayor, as head of urban planning, and (briefly) as mayor, and spearheaded his city's transformation. "In contemporary societies, cultural activities, the arts, sport, and leisure constitute a genuine thermometer of collective vitality, determining the attractiveness of a city, contributing to its image abroad," he notes. "I am convinced that, in the future, there will not be cities that are not simultaneously financially strong and culturally important. This double function is already true of large capital cities such as London, Paris, and New York."

The Guggenheim Bilbao cost 132 million euros to build (about $150 million). The plan was widely criticized by locals who couldn't understand why the government would spend so much money on a museum when there were so many other needs and priorities. "The feasibility survey carried out estimated that 400,000 visitors per year would be required to justify the investment," recalls Ibon. "During the first year after its opening, the museum received 1,360,000 visitors." Nowadays, the average is about a million visitors per year. The economic activity induced directly or indirectly by the museum has created about four thousand jobs, about the same as the most important shipbuilding yard in the city during its heyday. The infrastructure built to transform the city—using Basque, Spanish, and European Union funding—revolved around the new, sparkling downtown area. However, "these figures don't take into account other factors such as the positive publicity that this action brought to the city, or its effect to gain other investments." The museum's success also contributed to the "recovery of Bilbao's self-esteem."

These revitalization projects have been equally controversial in the United States. "The post-industrial U.S. 'legacy' cities are experiencing a renaissance," editorialized *Fast Company* in 2018, a magazine intended for entrepreneurs. "But lower-income, majority-black enclaves are struggling more than ever."

Consider the case of Pittsburgh, Pennsylvania, the hometown of Andrew Carnegie and Andrew Mellon, the "robber barons" of the industrial era. For five generations, Pittsburgh supplied the nation's steel for building skyscrapers, highways, and intercontinental ships; the city was far more successful than Bilbao ever was during the first industrial revolution. But Pittsburgh, too, suffered from the decline of industry. Now, though, in a vacant lot along the

Monongahela River, Uber is testing self-driving cars. A nearby decrepit building, once part of a steel mill, is being turned into the Advanced Robotics for Manufacturing Institute. Caterpillar has set up a facility to develop autonomous heavy construction and mining equipment. Billions of dollars of venture capital money are pouring in. Longtime residents have noted that property prices are rising after decades of decline. "The transformation of the city by new, young people working in AI and robotics has been spectacular," according to Carnegie-Mellon University's Andrew Moore, "but it has been more of an approach of gentrification rather than an inclusion of the community."

Reversing decades of urban squalor isn't easy. That's what makes the path to 2030 and beyond so challenging for many cities. "Pittsburgh is hip right now," observed *Fast Company* in 2018. However, "look more closely at the enthusiasm around Pittsburgh, for instance, and you find that it's clustered in a handful of neighborhoods." Alan Mallach, author of *The Divided City: Poverty and Prosperity in Urban America*, notes that in cities like Baltimore, Cleveland, Detroit, and Pittsburgh, "the revival is ignoring the poor." His conclusion is that "from one legacy city to the next, as some areas gentrify, many other neighborhoods, including many that were pretty solid, relatively stable working-class or middle-class neighborhoods until fairly recently, are falling off a social and economic cliff." In *The New Urban Crisis*, Richard Florida notes the dualistic nature of cities: "Are cities the great engines of innovation, the models of economic and social progress, that the optimists celebrate, or are they the zones of gaping inequality and class division that the pessimists decry? The reality is that they are both." By 2030, more and more cities will experience a similar bifurcation between the areas inhabited by the upwardly mobile, highly educated professionals and those home to the functionally illiterate, who make up about 15 percent of the adult population. How will cities deal with this widening chasm?

•

"Pardon me boy, is that the Chattanooga Choo Choo?" Thus begins one of the most famous American songs, originally recorded in 1941 by Glenn Miller and his orchestra, and featured in the movie *Sun Valley Serenade*. It became a number-one hit and was the first record to go gold, selling 1.2 million copies within its first nine weeks. Chattanooga, Tennessee, was then a prosperous textile and furniture manufacturing and metalworking town. Located on the banks of the Tennessee River, bordering Georgia, it was dubbed the "Dynamo of Dixie." All trains heading south stopped there.

The population peaked at about 130,000 in the late 1950s, but even then middle-class white people were beginning to move in droves to the suburbs. Shortly thereafter, manufacturing jobs began to dwindle in number. In 1969 the federal government determined that the city had the "dirtiest air of any city in the United States," as the scenic surrounding mountains trapped the industrial pollutants within the valley. In 1971 passenger rail service to Chattanooga came to an end.

The city's recovery during the 1990s was equally dramatic. Thanks to local philanthropic funding, efforts to rebuild the meandering Tennessee riverfront received a boost: in 1992, the world's largest freshwater aquarium opened, followed by a park, a school, and a housing complex. Chattanooga became one of just eighteen American cities to witness population growth during the 1990s. Jobs in tourism, finance, and insurance grew at double-digit rates. The city was already on the upswing when Volkswagen announced in 2008 that it would invest $1 billion to build a major assembly facility in the area.

But perhaps the most visionary action taken by Chattanooga officials and their private backers was to invest in a citywide high-speed fiber-optic Internet network, the first in any American city (fewer than two hundred have built one). Known as "the Gig," for its gigabit-per-second speed, it boasts the fastest connection in the country. "Chattanooga has turned itself from what could have been another failing mid-sized city into a startup hub that's filling up with exiles from Manhattan, San Francisco, and Austin," writes Jason Koebler of Vice. "Over the period 2011–2015, the fiber infrastructure has generated incremental economic and social benefits ranging from $865.3 million to $1.3 billion while additionally creating between 2,800 and 5,200 new jobs," concluded a study by Bento Lobo, an economist at the University of Tennessee at Chattanooga. Among many other companies, Knoxville-based Claris Networks decided to set up shop in Chattanooga because "in Knoxville a 100 Mbps service from AT&T would cost $1,400 per month whereas a comparable service through [Chattanooga's fiber network] costs $300, a $1,100 savings." The savings are even greater for gigabit service: "Whereas such service might cost between $5,000 and $7,000 per month through AT&T, the same costs $1,400 per month through [Chattanooga's EPB], a savings of between $3,600 and $5,600 per month." As we shall see in Chapter 6, the Gig has helped Chattanooga attract numerous startups that depend on high-speed Internet.

GAYS AND BOHEMIANS

When people think of an urban creative hub, what comes to mind is usually Silicon Valley or Manhattan's Silicon Alley. Chattanooga is very different in many respects. "You look at the startup havens and typically you see those in blue states, very liberal, very young. That's typically what you see," notes Jack Studer, head of a Chattanooga startup accelerator. "This is a southern city. The people at [the tech-enabled Chattanooga-based moving company] Bellhops, they all hunt, they all fish, they all watch SEC football. You don't see that at Facebook. It's just different."

Global cities like San Francisco and New York City play a different role in the economy, "doing the work of globalization," to borrow from sociologist Saskia Sassen's pathbreaking research on the subject. They are magnets for the so-called creative class, a term proposed by University of Toronto professor and best-selling author Richard Florida to capture the phenomenon of the knowledge professionals—from scientists and engineers to architects, artists, and designers. Cities compete with one another to attract and retain them. The creative class, in turn, attracts all manner of businesses, in a virtuous cycle. Most crucially, many cities have become hubs of innovation.

Nowadays, the creative class accounts for about one-third of the American workforce, a proportion expected to reach 50 percent by 2030. Creative workers "draw on complex bodies of knowledge to solve specific problems." Florida summarizes what it takes for a city to develop a dynamic creative class with his concept of "the three T's": talent, tolerance, and technology.

Of the three, "tolerance" has attracted quite a bit of attention. Florida argues that cities that score high on what he calls the "Gay Index" and the "Bohemian Index" eventually do better. He defines tolerance in terms of a melting pot of diverse people, including members of the LGBTQ community, artists, and musicians, among others. More broadly, the entire creative class is associated with a distinct lifestyle that fosters open-mindedness. "Tolerance and openness to diversity is part and parcel of the broad cultural shift toward post-materialist values," he writes. They provide "an additional source of economic advantage that works alongside technology and talent." The three T's work together to attract the people who power the knowledge economy. One of Florida's specific arguments concerns urban renewal. His "street-level culture" refers to the "teeming blend of cafés, sidewalk musicians, and small galleries and bistros, where it is hard to draw the line between participant and observer, or between creativity and its creators."

The growing importance of creativity manifests itself across a large number of occupations. David J. Deming, an economist at the Harvard Graduate School of Education, found that an increasing amount of jobs require nonroutine analytical skills. More importantly, social skills involving coordination, negotiation, persuasion, and social perceptiveness are in high demand. Deming's research suggests that by 2030 a majority of jobs will require the use of social skills and creativity.

Florida and his colleagues have ranked the thirty most creative cities in the United States. Cupertino and Palo Alto in California, McLean, Virginia, and Bethesda, Maryland, topped the list in 2015. (Chattanooga was not on it.) It is worth noting that one of the two states with the largest number of cities that score low on their creativity metric is California (the other is New Jersey). Thus, "cities with ultra-high and ultra-low shares of the creative class exist side-by-side," concludes Florida's CityLab in one of its reports. "It appears that the growing economic gap between regions is less profound than the divide between have and have-not places in some of America's most robust economic centers."

CityLab has also classified cities and metropolitan areas around the world into three categories. The "global giants" include New York, Los Angeles, London, Paris, Tokyo, and Osaka-Kobe. San Jose, Boston, Seattle, San Diego, Washington, DC, Chicago, Austin, Dallas, Atlanta, Portland (in Oregon), Denver,

Amsterdam, Stockholm, and Zurich are "knowledge capitals." A few others are categorized as "Asian anchors": Hong Kong, Singapore, Seoul-Incheon, Shanghai, Beijing, and Moscow. Amy Liu, who heads the Brookings Institution Metropolitan Policy Program, observes one key aspect about the continued growth of global cities. "The irony now is that all this energy and progress comes amidst a new environment: growing skepticism about global trade, concerns about immigrants and refugees, and pessimism about a slow-growing world economy," she writes. "How can cities deepen their efforts to be globally engaged and competitive while addressing head on the disparities and negative consequences that come with greater global integration?" Remember that most of Rosa Lee's drug-addicted children and grandchildren live in Washington, DC, a metropolitan area categorized as one of the knowledge capitals of the world, where 45 percent of the workforce belongs to the creative class.

Florida's theory of the creative class dovetails with the evolution of societies from traditional to secular-rational values, and from survival to self-expression values, as identified by Ronald Inglehart, a political scientist at the University of Michigan and a mastermind of the World Values Survey. Although societies do not tend to fully converge over time in terms of cultural values and norms, people report an increasing adherence to the values associated with secularization, rationality, self-expression, and post-materialism, and an increasing acceptance of divorce, abortion, euthanasia, suicide, different sexual orientations, and gender equality. The caveat is, however, that the data on the evolution of cultural values shows that people in at least half of the countries in the world are still either mostly traditional or mostly survival-oriented. A significant minority score high on both traditional and survival values, especially in South Asia, the Middle East, and North Africa.

WILL CITIES BE LIVABLE IN 2030?

The movie *Metropolis*, the Bilbao revival, and the gentrification of Pittsburgh and so many other American cities remind us about the highs and the lows of urban living. So do the stories of Rosa Lee Cunningham and those of the highly educated engineers, artists, doctors, and financiers who inhabit the world's global cities. By 2030 there will be four hundred cities that have populations of more than 1 million people. Those urban agglomerations will be dualistic in nature and populated mainly by overweight or obese people hooked to their favorite streaming services and social media apps, a trend that leads to social isolation as opposed to engagement. Many will be home to a vibrant creative class of knowledge-intensive workers. A majority will face formidable challenges related to pollution, congestion, and security. The cities most exposed to climate change will suffer from a shortage of freshwater and an excess of saltwater in the form of flooding. Will our behavioral adaptations make a dent? Will vertical agriculture develop fast enough? Will a technological breakthrough come to the rescue? Chapters 6, 7, and 8 explore the coming revolution in invention and innovation, and its potential for improving the quality of life in cities and elsewhere moving forward.

More Cellphones than Toilets

REINVENTING THE WHEEL, THE NEW CAMBRIAN

EXPLOSION, AND THE FUTURE OF TECHNOLOGY

Creative destruction is . . . the process of industrial mutation that
incessantly revolutionizes the economic structure *from within*,
incessantly destroying the old one, incessantly creating a new one.

—JOSEPH SCHUMPETER, ECONOMIST

Inventors and entrepreneurs churn out new ideas, products, and technologies by the minute—but just a handful catch on and even fewer prove truly transformational. Consider the toilet.

After she graduated from Stanford University with a degree in comparative literature, Virginia Gardiner's first job was for a design magazine. She was assigned to write about the kitchen and bath industry. "The first article I wrote for the magazine was about toilets—about the fact that they don't change."

According to the British Association of Urological Surgeons, the oldest toilet we know of dates back to a Neolithic settlement in Scotland around 3000 BCE. Earthenware pans, possibly flushed with buckets of water after each use, can be admired at the Greek Palace of Knossos (1700 BCE). In her article, Gardiner noted that the modern flush toilet with a raised cistern was invented in 1596 (or perhaps a few years earlier) by Sir John Harington, an English courtier and godson of Elizabeth I, the queen who laid the foundations for England to become a European—and eventually global—power. The S-shaped pipe to keep out odors, called a trap, was invented in 1775 by the watchmaker Alexander Cummings. The toilet's design didn't change much over the ensuing centuries, and in the developed world we have no reason to complain. That's because the true innovation is below: our sewer system.

Which leads us to the predicament of Eleonore Rartjarasoaniony, a forty-seven-year-old mother living in Antananarivo, Madagascar's capital city, where she owns a small shop. Her home has no connection to the sewer, making a flush toilet useless. A few months ago she replaced her pit latrine with a brand-new waterless toilet, which uses a white biodegradable film to seal the waste and store it underneath the toilet (added bonus: it's odorless). The manufacturer of the toilet collects the waste once a week. "My family of four uses it, and so do my three tenants who rent the next house over—it's included in the rent," she notes. "Even my son can use it." Like many other mothers throughout Africa and the rest of the developing world, she lives in fear that her child might one day drown in a pit full of human excrement.

The maker of Eleonore's toilet is Loowatt, a company based in London. The founder? Virginia Gardiner. After her stint as a magazine writer, she went on to pursue a master's degree at the Royal College of Art in London, where she wrote her thesis on a waterless toilet system. She founded the company in 2010. A year later she obtained a grant from the Bill and Melinda Gates Foundation's new Reinvent the Toilet Challenge, aimed at encouraging innovation in sustainable sanitation. A Canadian living in Madagascar got wind of her venture and became the first investor. Within a year Gardiner had launched a pilot program and built a small processing facility, which turned the waste into biogas to generate electricity to charge—you probably guessed it—cellphones. Malagasy women such as Gloria Razafindeamiza see another benefit to waterless toilets. Before, she had to share an outhouse with several neighbors, but now, "with this toilet I feel safe and secure."

"In a lot of communities all over Africa, people can talk on their cell phones, but they can't turn on a light or a water faucet. Never mind flush a toilet. And they may be going hungry," says Winnie V. Mitullah, director of the Institute for Development Studies at the University of Nairobi. "As far as the most basic services that many of us take for granted—water, sewage, electricity, roads—an awful lot of people might as well be living in the nineteenth century." Mitullah argues that a lack of reliable access to electricity and running water is more than a mere inconvenience. "Kids get sick and die when there's not enough clean water to wash with and there's no safe disposal of sewage. And without lights to study in the evening, or no way to connect to the outside world—except your cell phone—your opportunities for education and success are limited."

Zafar Adeel, director of the United Nations University's Institute for Water, Environment and Health, warns that "anyone who shirks the topic [of sanitation] as repugnant, minimizes it as undignified, or considers unworthy those in need should let others take over for the sake of 1.5 million children and countless others killed each year by contaminated water and unhealthy sanitation." All in all, there are 1.5 billion people who own or share a cellphone *and* must relieve themselves in the open or go to a shared outhouse. And the gap continues to widen: investments in mobile telecommunications have soared while those in basic sanitation dwindle throughout sub-Saharan Africa and South Asia. Among the bottom 20 percent of Indian households by income, for instance, three times as many have a cellphone as a toilet.

In the developed world we take both sanitation and cellphones for granted. The use of mobile telecommunications has expanded swiftly in sub-Saharan Africa because it happens to be a relatively cheap technology to deploy. Given that upward of 60 percent of the population is rural, cell towers are far cheaper and faster to install than fixed lines—let alone sewers and flush toilets. And because less than 10 percent of the population in most sub-Saharan African countries have a bank account or a credit card, the cellphone has become the de facto instrument for making and receiving payments. There are in fact more people in that part of the world who use mobile payment platforms than in East Asia, South Asia, Europe, or the Americas. More to the point, many of them don't use physical money at all.

It's no surprise that technological change has come to pervade the economies and the cultures of the world, or that it alters the rules of the game. As both the cellphone and the waterless toilet illustrate, technology also has the potential to improve the quality of life of billions of people, especially in cities. When it comes to consumer applications of new technology, however, the most consequential aspect is not what technology can accomplish but how it interacts with demographic and societal trends, creating highly unexpected patterns and outcomes, some good and some bad.

Before I delve into all that, however, I'd like to tell you the story of the watch.

IT ALL BEGAN WITH DICK TRACY AND SUPERMAN

If the cellphone feels ubiquitous, the watch is more so: more people around the world own a watch than a cellphone. The history of the modern wristwatch— encompassing both Rolex and the Apple Watch—shows that successive technological waves transformed everything from how the device is made to how it is sold and used. Martin Cooper, who pioneered wireless communications and invented the first cellphone while working for Motorola in the 1970s, got his inspiration from the two-way radio wristwatch worn by the detective Dick Tracy in 1946 in the eponymous comic strip. (Coincidentally, an episode of the radio program *Superman*, "The Talking Cat," featured a similar device that year as well.)

Before the phrase "Swiss made" became synonymous with the watch, England was home to the most innovative timepiece industry. Portable clocks first appeared in the 1400s. History tells us that pocket watches did not become common until the 1600s. Perhaps the first major technological breakthrough in watches occurred in 1657, when either Robert Hooke or Christiaan Huygens came up with the idea of adding a balance spring to the balance wheel, which significantly increased accuracy (an innovation we forget nowadays, when we expect our timepieces to be right). Who is responsible for this idea is hotly disputed. Hooke was an English natural philosopher, architect, and polymath. Huygens was a Dutch physicist, mathematician, and astronomer who discovered Titan, Saturn's largest moon. He was one of the giants of the Scientific Revolution: he invented the pendulum clock and is widely regarded as the founder of mathematical physics. (Incidentally, Titan Watches Limited, an Indian company in operation since 1984, whose name honors Huygens, is nowadays one of the world's largest watch companies.)

To make matters more complicated, the Brazilians claim that aviation pioneer Alberto Santos-Dumont invented the concept of wearing a pendant watch or a pocket watch around the wrist. However, most histories of this ingenious wearable tech give credit to the Swiss, whose army needed a means of coordinating tactics in the rugged, mountainous terrain known as the Alps.

Regardless of the murkiness surrounding the watch's origins, it wasn't the English, the Dutch, or the Brazilians who came to dominate the industry, but the Swiss. They happened to have excellent jewelers and craftsmen thanks, in part, to the arrival of persecuted French Huguenots, many of whom were very adept at making sophisticated mechanical gadgets. They manufactured luxury wristwatches in small batches and sold them all over Europe. The Swiss were so successful that even Rolex, originally founded in London in 1905, moved its base of operations to Switzerland in 1919 to take advantage of this highly skilled labor force in the beautiful valley of Jura, just north of Geneva.

Then came a revolution. Based on the techniques developed during World War II, American companies hit upon the idea of mass-producing the watch. All one needed to do was use alloys instead of precious metals and a battery instead of a spring as a power source. The company that came to dominate this technology—and make a ton of money—was Timex. How they read the times! Mass consumption in the United States was defining the era. People demanded vast quantities of everything, from refrigerators and washing machines to cars and watches. Price took priority over quality and durability. Rolex languished while Timex surged ahead.

A second wave of technological change hit the industry in the 1960s. A Swiss engineer invented an ingenious mechanism to simplify the design and thus make it cheaper to manufacture. It was based on a tuning fork, a two-pronged metallic part that vibrates when struck. The frequency of the vibration could then be converted into a much more accurate measure of time than the traditional escapement, which consisted of an intricate mechanism of gears. And it was another American firm, Bulova, that took advantage and profited from the innovation. The Swiss, by contrast, did not, as they were too proud to stop making the watch by hand, one piece at a time—it was, after all, a work of art.

The third gale of innovation took place when the Japanese decided to join in the fun. They further simplified the design by incorporating a new technology based on quartz. It was, once again, a Swiss engineer who discovered that if an electrical current runs through a piece of quartz, this natural crystal produces vibrations, which can be used as an extraordinarily accurate measure of time. By the 1970s, the likes of Seiko, Citizen, and Casio had taken the piss out of Timex and Bulova. From the 1970s to the late 1980s, most quartz watches were made in Japan, not in Switzerland or the United States.

It wasn't until the late 1980s that the Swiss managed to finally react to the successive ripples of technological transformation by coming up with the Swatch, a product that not only told time accurately but doubled as a fashionable accessory and collector's item. Celebrities were recruited to sell them via advertising. The Swiss watch industry, which had lost nearly all its jobs, recovered on the back of Swatch's rise. All of sudden, the Japanese watches looked boring.

Then came the cellphone. If there is a radical disruption that undermines the necessity of a watch, it's a portable device that tells the time *and* makes calls. All of a sudden, the watch becomes a luxury, useful for social occasions or simply for fun. And now we come full circle, as technology companies like Apple, Samsung, and Xiaomi, all of which brought us smartphones, are now trying to sell us smart watches.

A key lesson from this history is that each time a new technology replaced an old one, jobs were created and destroyed, different national watch industries rose and fell, and new modes of consumption emerged. And the watch is but one of many examples. Refrigeration displaced ice as a coolant, the telephone proved superior to the telegraph, incandescent lamps replaced gas lamps, the

transistor did away with the vacuum tube, the jet engine outdid the propel-
ler, the CD turned vinyl into a collector's item, the word processor rendered the
typewriter obsolete, digital imaging supplanted chemical photography, and
video games proved more entertaining than traditional toys. We use the term
"disruption" to refer to such dramatic transformations, with the wristwatch being just one illustration of this pervasive pattern.

A NEW CAMBRIAN EXPLOSION OF CREATIVE DESTRUCTION

Technology disrupts the status quo by changing one or more of the following:
the concept of the product, the way it is made, how it is sold, who uses it, how
people use it, or how people interact with one another. The average lifetime of
a company on the Standard & Poor's 500 stock index has declined from sixty
years to a mere ten years over the last half century. By 2030, technological change
will usher in a new reality in which there will be billions of computers, sensors,
and robotic arms in factories, offices, hospitals, schools, homes, vehicles, and all
types of infrastructure. For the first time, there will be more computers than
human brains, more sensors than eyes, and more robotic arms than human
labor in manufacturing. We're going through the technological equivalent of
the Cambrian explosion, which took place 541 million years ago and lasted between 13 million and 25 million years. It was during the Cambrian that complex animal species appeared on land and marine ecosystems developed. Until
that moment, most organisms were single-celled. During the Cambrian, small
organisms every bit as intricate as today's animals emerged, including a five-
eyed carnivore and a lace crab with a head, spine, thorax, legs, and two pairs of
antennae.

From virtual reality to 3-D printing, and from artificial intelligence to
nanotechnologies, it is only a mild exaggeration to compare today's transformation to the Cambrian explosion. These new technologies promise to address all manner of otherwise intractable problems, from poverty and disease
to environmental degradation, climate change, and social isolation. They are
giving rise to a new class of mostly young, visionary entrepreneurs, many of

them in their twenties, self-described as "masters of the universe," to borrow a line from Tom Wolfe.

Each technological wave of disruption is accompanied by the illusion that technology can liberate us from our problems, small and large. In fact, it is a force that tends to both create problems and generate solutions. Automation, for instance, frees humans from the boredom and often dire physical and psychological consequences of repetitive work, perhaps best illustrated by Charlie Chaplin in the classic movie *Modern Times*. However, it also has the effect of displacing workers from jobs that provided a reliable path into the middle class decades ago. If workers lack the flexibility or the resources to rotate into other occupations, they may find themselves displaced without a plan B, something that can be further complicated by one's age or ability to travel in search of new opportunities. Entire job categories and communities can be sunk because someone invented or innovated in a space traditionally reliant on human labor, oversight, and expertise.

The Austrian economist and political scientist Joseph Schumpeter came up with one of the most felicitous metaphors of all time—"creative destruction"—to describe the essence of what we've been exploring. He argued that the market economy's tendency to incorporate new technologies and their cascading impacts, which then displace older, inefficient ones, is both its corrosive aspect and its strength. "The fundamental impulse that sets and keeps the capitalist engine in motion," he wrote in 1942, "comes from the new consumers' goods, the new methods of production or transportation, the new markets, the new forms of industrial organization that capitalist enterprise creates." He described this dynamic as "the process of industrial mutation that incessantly revolutionizes the economic structure *from within*, incessantly destroying the old one, incessantly creating a new one." He concluded that "this process of Creative Destruction is the essential fact about capitalism."

Schumpeter thus reminds us that disruption is as normal as it is ubiquitous; it has reshaped human life since the beginning of the agricultural revolution about twelve thousand years ago. While it is not a new phenomenon, it seems to happen more frequently and more quickly as time goes on. It's a force that transforms not just the economy but every aspect of life, from politics to interpersonal relationships.

"COMPUTERS ARE USELESS—THEY CAN ONLY GIVE YOU ANSWERS"

When technological disruption arrives—as happens time and again; witness the watch—the diabolical dynamic of creative destruction ensues: lives are dislocated, careers are derailed, and communities are shattered.

In terms of its potential consequences, the field of artificial intelligence (AI) is fertile ground for analysis. As with the watch, there are competing interests and beliefs regarding where we are right now and where we're headed. Back in 1992, the *Economist* editorialized about "Artificial Stupidity," saying that "there is no practical reason to create machine intelligences indistinguishable from human ones" because "people are in plentiful supply." They also observed that "should a shortage arise, there are proven and popular methods for making more of them." (That's assuming people want to procreate, which we now know was wishful thinking back in the 1990s.) In a similar vein, Elon Musk recently tweeted that "excessive automation at Tesla was a mistake," adding that "humans are underrated." And Pablo Picasso once observed that "computers are useless—they can only give you answers."

In reality, AI opens up a whole array of new opportunities, and that's one big reason why the world as we know it is coming to an end. AI includes a wide array of applications to perform tasks that have traditionally been the province of the human brain, such as speech recognition, visual perception, and decision-making. It is being deployed in self-driving cars and trucks, efficient and responsive infrastructure, and smart medical and living systems. In our lifetime, AI has accelerated considerably. In 1997 IBM's Deep Blue computer defeated chess champion Gary Kasparov. A year later, Tiger Electronics developed a robotic toy with voice-recognition technology. In 2000 Honda launched ASIMO, a humanoid robot serving as a multifunctional personal assistant. In 2011 Apple incorporated a virtual assistant, Siri, into its smartphones. From targeted social media advertising to photo tagging, AI is already all around us. In China the state security apparatus is using AI-enabled face-recognition technology to monitor people in small villages in their everyday endeavors. The goal of this program, known as Sharp Eyes, is to calculate a score for each citizen based on actual behavior. It's eerily reminiscent of George Orwell's Big Brother in *1984*.

Some visionaries predict that the world will come to an end, literally, when the "singularity" arrives—that is, the point when AI is sophisticated and smart enough to take over and render us humans, as a whole, useless. It's a future in which machines program and control other machines. It would be, as the computer scientist Irving Good argued in 1965, "the *last* invention that man need ever make." His colleague Alan Turing, who led the effort to break Germany's Enigma secret code during World War II and helped pioneer the computer itself, declared in 1951 that AI would "outstrip our feeble powers" and "take control." Theoretical physicist Stephen Hawking added his two cents by saying that it "could spell the end of the human race."

Apocalypse aside, there is little doubt that AI will bring about epochal change. There are, as we speak, hundreds of thousands of programmers advancing the reach and power of intelligent machine learning and its applications.

·

Meanwhile, back on the ground at a truck stop somewhere in the American heartland, tractor-trailer drivers are taking a quick rest. They do an essential job for the economy: hauling merchandise around the country. They labor long hours for little pay, especially if they are independent contractors. For those engaged in long-haul trucking, belonging to any one community is difficult. Truck drivers constitute the largest occupational group in twenty-nine of the fifty states of the Union. The only exceptions are most of New England, the Mid-Atlantic, California, and Texas, where either software developers, primary school teachers, farmers, secretaries, nursing aides, retail clerks, customer service representatives, or lawyers take the top spot. According to one study commissioned by the Obama White House, between 1.5 million and 2.2 million light- and heavy-truck drivers are at risk of losing their jobs as a result of autonomous vehicle technology. That's between 60 and 90 percent of the total number of drivers employed in 2015. If one adds bus drivers, taxi drivers, chauffeurs, and self-employed drivers, the total potential job loss from this technology could top 3 million.

Current experiments with autonomous vehicles indicate a bright future because human beings are sloppy and unreliable. We can get distracted, bored, or tired. A computer can optimize a complex trip and adapt to traffic and road conditions, all while being fuel-efficient. Most importantly, computers can communicate with other computers. We communicate with each other on the road by relying on primitive means like lights, horns, and hand signals. By contrast, a self-driving car, in tandem with other cars in its vicinity, can collectively manage traffic flow (and reduce accidents) in a coordinated manner.

And it doesn't end there. In manufacturing, a single robot can displace an average of five to six workers. The number of people employed in repetitive manual labor jobs in the United States stood at 28 million in 1983. By 2015 that number had only increased to 30 million. During that time period, 300,000 robots were installed, doing the work of nearly 2 million workers. Technology is partly responsible for the stagnation of the American middle class of routine manual and non-manual or cognitive workers we discussed in Chapter 3. And now that 35,000 robots are being installed each year, the impact will accelerate over the next decade. By 2030 the manufacturing sector will employ more programmers and controllers than day laborers.

Similarly, the number of routine cognitive jobs grew from 28 to 33 million, including primarily office workers and shop attendants. By contrast, non-routine manual jobs such as skilled mechanics increased from 14 million to 27 million, and non-routine cognitive occupations like teachers, designers, programmers, and healthcare workers rose from 28 million to a whopping 57 million. At least for now, it seems as if there are certain jobs beyond the reach of technology's powers of creative destruction.

But it won't be long before routine cognitive occupations such as office and administration work are affected by AI, and in numbers as seismic as big data itself. Surgeons performing routine procedures, young lawyers helping put together a legal case, and professors teaching introductory subjects are at risk of seeing their jobs performed by intelligent machines. The next, and perhaps final, step would be the elimination of some non-routine jobs, especially if the singularity does in fact arrive.

Consider the tasks performed by a surgeon, among the most complex and sophisticated in the world, for which nearly ten years of advanced education and on-the-job training are required. "In a robotic surgery breakthrough," the Institute of Electrical and Electronics Engineers reported in 2016, "a bot stitched up a pig's small intestines using its own vision, tools, and intelligence to carry out the procedure." More importantly, "the Smart Tissue Autonomous Robot (STAR) did a better job on the operation than human surgeons who were given the same task." The sutures made by human surgeons were less consistent and less resistant to leaks than the robot's stitches. In the words of Peter Kim, a pediatric surgeon who participated in the research, "Even though we surgeons take pride in our craft at doing procedures, to have a machine that works with us to improve outcomes and safety would be a tremendous benefit." He thinks robots will first offer human surgeons a helping hand, just like self-driving cars "started with parking, then a technology that tells you not to go into the wrong lane." In that sense, robotics would not necessarily displace workers, but it could help them be better at what they do.

Another attractive feature of robots is that they aren't judgmental—at least not yet. "We spend a lot of time talking to Alexa and Siri," argues journalist Laura Sydell. "Imagine if such artificial personalities were put inside a cute, adorable robot." Alexander Reben, a researcher at MIT, built a robot out of cardboard called Boxie. One day he found a man sharing his troubles with Boxie. He "just started talking to this thing like it was another person." Reben decided to team up with artist and filmmaker Brent Hoff to design a cute robot that would encourage people to open up. "It's the perfect smile," Hoff says. "It's open and engaging to make sure [it is] as nonjudgmental and nonthreatening as possible." And early results show that it's working. Sherry Turkle, an MIT expert on human-machine interactions, says that it isn't difficult to get humans to open up to a robot: "We are kind of cheap dates."

THE TROLLEY PROBLEM IN THE
AGE OF THE INTELLIGENT MACHINE

Technology brings benefits—and ethical dilemmas. Imagine a driverless car approaching an intersection and planning to make a right turn. The sensors on the vehicle carefully monitor the biker on the right. Suddenly a toddler frees himself from his mother's hand and darts across the street. The computer must decide in a split second whether to spare the biker or the child. There's no time to collect more data or to make elaborate calculations about how to inflict the least damage, or to consider how to prioritize one life over another, the young child's or the biker's. What will the computer do?

This is a modified version of the classic thought experiment known as the "trolley problem." In this problem, a runaway tram speeding down the tracks is about to hit and kill five people. If you could switch the trolley to a different track where it would hit and kill one person, would you do it? The trolley problem reveals a conundrum that cannot be resolved on simple moral or ethical grounds. In the movie *Sophie's Choice*, Meryl Streep plays a Polish mother of two who was part of the resistance during the German occupation. She is captured and sent to Auschwitz, where a Nazi officer puts her in the impossible position of having to choose which of her children will go to the gas chamber and which to the labor camp. In the spur of the moment, Sophie has to make a terrifying choice, and so would the driver in our illustration above. This type of moral dilemma helps explain why drone pilots experience higher rates of post-traumatic stress disorder than conventional pilots. The drone pilots make decisions about life and death from the comfort of a control center thousands of miles away, while real pilots are actually putting their own lives at risk. In a *New York Times* article about a drone operator named Aaron, Eyal Press writes, "What unspooled before Aaron's eyes was jarringly intimate: coffins being carried through the streets after drone strikes." Although he was an experienced military drone operator, Aaron began to feel sick and emotionally distressed. He developed debilitating symptoms including nausea, skin welts, and chronic digestive problems. "I was very, very unwell," he told Press. He was reeling from the decisions about whom to kill and whom to spare that he had made on a routine basis.

In 2016 and 2017, a team of international researchers convened by MIT conducted a project they called the Moral Machine experiment to assess how people in different cultures deal with these kinds of dilemmas. Using an online platform, they gathered nearly 40 million decisions about driving from more than 2 million people in over two hundred countries and territories. Respondents were presented with thirteen scenarios in which someone's death was inevitable. Some of the decisions were arguably easier to make than others. For instance, should the driver spare a pet or a human? Should a greater or a smaller number of lives take priority? But others were very tough ethically and morally. Should the fit or the physically challenged be spared? What about a criminal or a law-abiding citizen? In the experiment, people displayed a marked tendency to spare humans over animals, more lives over fewer lives, and young lives over older lives. "Accordingly," the researchers reasoned, "these three preferences may be considered essential building blocks for machine ethics."

As would be expected, there were some differences. Both men and women were more inclined to spare females, with women displaying a stronger preference. People who were more religious had a stronger leaning toward sparing humans over animals. And the research unveiled some stark differences across countries. "The preference to spare younger characters rather than older characters is much less pronounced for countries in the Eastern cluster [Confucian countries in Asia and a few Muslim ones], and much higher for countries in the Southern cluster [Latin America and Francophone Africa]. The same is true for the preference for sparing higher status characters." In the Southern cluster people displayed "a much weaker preference for sparing humans over pets." Interestingly, "only the (weak) preference for sparing pedestrians over passengers and the (moderate) preference for sparing the lawful over the unlawful appear to be shared to the same extent in all clusters." In countries with more individualistic cultures people were more likely to spare the young, and in poorer countries people were more tolerant of jaywalkers than pedestrians who observe the rules.

Disturbingly, respondents in countries with more economic inequality were more willing to spare higher-status people.

One troubling implication of the research is that "people who think about machine ethics make it sound like you can come up with a perfect set of rules for robots," said Iyad Rahwan, one of the authors of the study. "What we show here with data is that there are no universal rules." Another co-author, Edmond Awad, noted that "more people have started becoming aware that AI could have different ethical consequences on different groups of people. The fact that we see people engaged with this—I think that that's something promising." As Barbara Wege, a manager at Audi's autonomous vehicle unit in Germany, puts it, "We need to come up with a social consensus about which risks we are willing to take."

The moral dilemmas involved in the trolley problem are not the only ones brought about by the rise of AI. As Srikar Reddy, the chief executive officer of Sonata Software, and I recently argued in a World Economic Forum blog, one must distinguish between deontological and teleological ethical standards, with the former focusing on the intention and the means, and the latter on the ends and outcomes. Which approach is best depends on the technology and the context. "In the case of autonomous vehicles, the end of an error-free transportation system that is also efficient and friendly towards the environment might be enough to justify large-scale data collection about driving under different conditions and also experimentation based on AI applications." By comparison, medical trials based on big data are hard to justify on teleological grounds, given the horrific history of medical experimentation on unsuspecting human subjects. A deontological approach based on intention and means makes more sense.

The ethical and moral dilemmas posed by automation, AI, and big data are becoming hard to ignore. "Never in the history of humanity have we allowed a machine to autonomously decide who should live and who should die, in a fraction of a second, without real-time supervision," the Moral Machine researchers concluded. "We are going to cross that bridge any time now," which, if you're betting on my opinion, is by 2030. "Before we allow our cars to make ethical decisions, we need to have a global conversation to express our preferences to the companies that will design moral algorithms, and to the policymakers that will regulate them." The issue is that the ethics and morals of automation cannot be automated or laid out in algorithmic form.

"WHO NEEDS THE PARIS CLIMATE ACCORDS WHEN YOU HAVE 3-D PRINTING?"

That's the provocative question posed by Richard A. D'Aveni, a professor at Dartmouth College's Tuck School of Business. New 3-D printers create a three-dimensional object by printing ultra-thin sheets in sequence and stacking them on top of each other to form a three-dimensional shape; the technical term is "additive manufacturing." This technique reduces waste by using only the precise amount of material needed to make everything from plastic parts to dental pieces or human replacement tissue. Like traditional manufacturing, it needs energy, but "it gives off less smoke and other toxic fumes." And the biggest benefits of all will come from the possibility that with "printer farms and mini-factories closer to customers, companies will need much less shipping." We've too readily accepted the idea that in manufacturing, economies of scale are essential to delivering low-cost goods. Mini-mills and flexible production methods began a trend in the 1980s that 3-D printing will accelerate and enlarge, much to the benefit of the environment. "We're going to move away from the throwaway ethic of the 20th century," he predicts. "People will buy less, and be happier with what they get—just what environmentalists have been telling us to do. As we make fewer goods with less material, we'll put much less carbon in the atmosphere."

In other words, 3-D printing will catch on if managers and customers abandon old assumptions and change their habits; if they step out of well-trodden territory to imagine new possibilities; if they think laterally. Instead of manufacturing to stock (storing what they produce in a warehouse so that it's ready to use), companies should learn to produce to real-time demand. Industrial customers should also learn how to wait until they actually need something. "Freight transportation . . . accounts for about a quarter of all carbon emissions in the affluent countries," D'Aveni notes. And the shipping behemoth UPS relies on an extensive network of warehouses to cater to the needs of its industrial customers. "It recently installed a hundred large 3-D printers at its central hub in Louisville, with the goal of reducing warehouse space and shipping distances. More and more parts will be made only as needed." In 2017 UPS launched a partnership with SAP, the German technology consulting firm, to print spare parts for clients on demand. UPS is effectively reinventing itself "as a logistics company, not a shipper."

The technology of 3-D printing is ideal for customized parts, but don't limit your thinking to dentures. Cities increasingly under the threat of flooding (see Chapter 5) can benefit from 3-D-printed seawalls, Volvo, the Swedish car company, notes, with "complex curved cement surfaces that disperse wave energy in many directions." It has partnered with local organizations in Sydney, Australia, to build an artificial reef resembling mangrove trees, providing a locus for marine life the way a real reef would. The ensuing biodiversity helps remove heavy metals and particulate matter such as plastic from the water. The tiles are made of concrete using 3-D-printed molds.

And there are many other applications that may help us avert the worst of a future climate crisis. As an architect, Platt Boyd grew increasingly frustrated by the limitations of traditional building materials and how wasteful the construction industry is. He decided to become an entrepreneur in the incipient field of 3-D printing. In 2015 he moved his company, Branch Technologies, to a startup accelerator in Chattanooga, Tennessee, because it was the only such facility wired to a citywide gigabit network, as we saw in Chapter 5. Branch uses "a revolutionary technology that combines industrial robots, sophisticated algorithms, and a novel 'freeform' extrusion technology that allows material to solidify in free space," he proudly explains. "This technology, called Cellular Fabrication (C-FABTM), draws inspiration from the way that nature creates form and structure and stands to revolutionize the construction industry through unprecedented design freedom and resource stewardship." The advantages of 3-D printing are manifold. "Branch is democratizing design freedom and developing a new construction product than can be lighter, stronger, faster on-site, and with ten times greater design freedom through a process that is inherently waste-free (additive manufacturing vs. 'subtractive' manufacturing, which is what nearly every construction method to date has been)." At its head-quarters, the company boasts the biggest freeform 3-D printer in the world and holds the record for the world's largest 3-D-printed structure: a bandshell at a Nashville park commemorating the United Nations' Sustainable Development Goals.

Annie Wang and Zach Simkin decided to seize opportunities in 3-D printing as well. They met as MBA students at Wharton. Like most of her classmates, Annie was intent on pursuing a traditional career path upon graduation, working for a large company or bank, whereas Zach was focused exclusively on entrepreneurship. They knew little about 3-D printing. Their first encounter with it occurred while they were taking an innovation class shortly before graduating in 2013. They saw an opportunity to combine artificial intelligence and machine learning to help industrial clients design parts and components that could be made using a 3-D printer. Annie gave up a coveted full-time position with the cosmetics firm Estée Lauder to pursue this visionary but risky project. Seven years later, their company, Senvol, counts multiple U.S. defense agencies, the U.S. Navy, and industrial corporations among its clients. It is one of hundreds of companies, ventures, and initiatives that are contributing to a revival of American manufacturing.

Another revolutionary application for 3-D printing involves some areas of healthcare, including dentistry and "printed tissue" for transplants. And Chinese companies are printing entire homes, a move that may speed up disaster relief and recovery after events such as hurricanes—which are becoming more frequent and devastating because of climate change. Perhaps the most tantalizing prospect for 3-D printing will be space exploration and colonization. Imagine a human settlement on Mars that, instead of asking for equipment, parts, and components to be shipped from Earth, has a 3-D printer available to create everything it needs using local raw materials. That would save not only money but also time, given that it takes seven months to travel from Earth to Mars.

There may be a panoply of benefits from 3-D printing, but it will also endanger some of the most skilled and best-paying blue-collar occupations, especially those involved in certain parts of the supply chain. The political implications could be significant as well (consider the fact that simple firearms can now be made using 3-D printers). What's essential to grasp about automation, AI, and 3-D printing is that they truly change the rules of the game. Automation redefines the relationship between people and work. AI replaces human mental activity with machine learning and human speech with natural language processing. The 3-D printing technology reconfigures the very way in which buyers and suppliers interact in the economy, and it reshapes our existing transportation ecosystem.

MAKING INSURANCE MORE EXCITING—AND FAIR

Insurance companies are expected to err on the safe side. They calculate risks meticulously, carefully picking and choosing the customers they insure. They are boring because their role in the economy is to shield everyone and everything from catastrophic loss. Unlike manufacturing, nothing truly revolutionary ever happens in the insurance industry. For centuries, insurers have charged higher premiums to people in "high-risk categories" such as smokers, male drivers under the age of thirty, and extreme-sports enthusiasts. This type of classification frequently results in biases and outright discrimination against disadvantaged groups. But in the future, real-time data collection will enable insurance companies to charge pay-as-you-drive rates depending on people's actual behavior on the road, as opposed to generalized stereotypes of certain "at-risk" groups. Bad or high-risk individual drivers will end up paying more for insurance, regardless of whether they are men or women, young or old. The Big Brother connotations are ominous, but many people might agree to the real-time monitoring of their driving behavior if it means lower rates.

The constellation of technologies behind these potential advancements is called the "Internet of Things"—all of the interconnected sensors and other devices designed to run factories, mines, energy systems, transportation systems, retail facilities, vehicles, homes, offices, and even people. It has the potential to revolutionize not just insurance but the entire economy and society. By 2030 there will be about 200 billion devices and sensors connected to it. The fastest areas of growth include factories, cities, healthcare, retail, and transportation. The ecosystem required to implement a comprehensive Internet of Things is expansive, including not just the devices themselves but data transmission and storage facilities, analysis hubs, and feedback loops. Arguably, a large number of jobs will be created to support this mammoth infrastructure. This wave of creative destruction promises to both eliminate and generate jobs.

TRAINING YOUR BRAIN TO
MAKE YOU HAPPIER AND HEALTHIER

Until a few years ago, I thought that virtual reality (VR) appealed only to addicted video game players. Turns out it's far more useful and revolutionary. In healthcare, surgeons and their assistants are now starting to wear VR goggles to visualize the best way to perform complex types of surgery. Psychologists are using VR as a therapy for patients with fear of heights, vertigo, anxiety disorders, and post-traumatic stress disorder. Two researchers at the University of Oxford are using VR to help patients with persecutory delusions, a form of paranoia. "The most effective way to do that is to help the individual learn from experience that the situations they dread are actually safe," they explain. "As the feeling of safety increases, so the delusion diminishes." Their patients experience rapid improvement, even after just one session. "Virtual reality isn't merely here to stay in the gaming world," they note. "We believe it's likely to play a central role in assessment and treatment in the mental health centers of the future." This technology is also being used to reduce anxiety at the dentist's office or while undergoing an MRI.

VR is proving to be effective at stimulating motor functions for people with lesions in certain regions of the brain. Researchers in South Korea have found that "VR equipment can be used to carry significant and appropriate stimulations to an individual's nervous system and thus take advantage of neuroplasticity to stimulate both motor and cognitive systems." In a similar vein, VR is helping some children manage autism. "Both kids and adults use smartphones, computers, smart watches, TVs, and gaming technology on a daily basis and think nothing of it except that it's a good time," notes VR Fitness Insider, a website dedicated to VR applications in the area of well-being. "Some kids and adults with autism who are minimally verbal or are non-verbal use iPads and voice apps to speak for them and as an educational tool every day." By monitoring brain activity during a VR session, doctors can study the cognitive and social aspects of behavior in kids with and without autism. A therapist can then help patients practice facial and body cues to overcome barriers in social interaction. VR can also help children with autism build social skills in school so that they can learn more easily and effectively. By 2030, this type of technology—coupled with the experience accumulated by doctors and therapists over the decades—might reduce the prevalence of psychological disorders by several orders of magnitude.

ARRESTING CLIMATE CHANGE WITH NANOTECHNOLOGIES

One of the biggest contributors to climate change is the clothing industry. Estimates indicate that it is responsible for about 8 percent of total carbon emissions. That's more than international flights and maritime shipping combined. The new field of nanotechnology could vastly reduce our dependence on synthetic fibers made from fossil fuels. The process of making a T-shirt from polyester emits more than twice as much carbon as making it from cotton. The phenomenon of "fast fashion," with new designs appearing every few weeks, has exacerbated the problem. "There are 20 new garments manufactured per person each year and we are buying 60 percent more than we were in 2000," noted an editorial in *Nature* in 2018. "Each garment is worn less before being disposed of and this shorter lifespan means higher relative manufacturing emissions. . . . There will be continued growth as the middle class expands and purchases increase to match this demographic shift." In addition, there has sometimes been a stigma attached to buying used clothes. By contrast, savvy automobile buyers shop for "pre-owned" vehicles as opposed to new ones.

Nanotechnologies offer other paths to addressing the issue of clothing's contribution to climate change. These technologies involve the manipulation of matter on an atomic, molecular, or supramolecular scale. We're talking here about designing particles as tiny as one-billionth of an inch in size with the goal of arriving at stronger, cheaper, or more environmentally friendly materials. Perhaps the most pervasive application of nanotechnologies will be programmable matter—materials endowed with the ability to change their physical properties, such as shape, density, conductivity, or optical properties, in response to signals or sensors. By 2030, we may not have to rearrange our closets seasonally; the same garment might provide us with warmth in the winter and relief from heat in the summer. It could even change color in response to the temperature outdoors. The MIT Self-Assembly Lab holds that "clothing that you can wear whatever the weather is no longer a sci-fi dream." Researchers have created "a smart material that works just like the pores on human skin, expanding and contracting depending on the surrounding temperature." The material tightens in cold weather to provide insulation and loosens as the temperature rises, thus allowing for air to circulate.

Nanotechnologies may also help avert the climate tipping point of 2030 by improving energy efficiency. Higher-strength composites are already being used in all manner of goods, from aircraft and automobiles to skis and tennis racquets. They help reduce the amount of energy needed to do the job. The building industry will change as a result of the use of materials that are more durable and energy-saving. "Nanotechnology promises to make thermal insulation more efficient, less reliant on non-renewable resources," and will be "an important strategy on the pathway to green buildings," recent research indicates. "The application of nano insulation materials to limit the wall thickness is one of the greatest potential energy-saving characteristics for the existing buildings, as well as for the architectural heritage."

Programmable matter can also be used as a "universal spare part." The Defense Advanced Research Projects Agency (DARPA) is focused on military applications. Mitchell Zakin, a program manager there, explains that "in the future a soldier will have something that looks like a paint can in the back of his vehicle . . . filled with particles of varying sizes, shapes and capabilities [such as] small computers, ceramics, biological systems—potentially anything the user wants them to be." If in the midst of battle "the soldier needs a wrench of a specific size, [he] broadcasts a message to the container, which causes the particles to automatically form the wrench. After the wrench has been used, the soldier realizes that he needs a hammer. He puts the wrench back into the can where it disassembles itself back into its components and re-forms into a hammer." Similarly, programmable matter would enable an aircraft to change the shape, density, or flexibility of its wings, making them more energy-efficient under changing flight conditions. Such uses of nanotechnologies will certainly help slow down the rate of climate change.

A new field of "nanomedicine" has emerged to diagnose and treat a wide variety of diseases. In 2018 the National Foundation for Cancer Research announced a potential breakthrough in terms of delivering drugs to cancerous cells with extreme precision. "These nanorobots can be programmed to transport molecular payloads and cause on-site tumor blood supply blockages, which can lead to tissue death and shrink the tumor," said one of the members of the Sino-American research team. In the case of ovarian cancer, nanotechnologies can help with early detection when the disease is affecting just one hundred cells. And nanotechnologies promise to offer cheap, biodegradable substitutes for plastic to avoid polluting fisheries with tiny, harmful particles, which harm wildlife and may enter the food chain.

E-BOOKS, WINES, AND FROGS

The recent evolution of technology seems like a triumphant litany of progress. Digital alternatives have displaced the traditional consumption of news (the physical newspaper), music (the record), or movies (rest in peace, Blockbuster). The Buggles memorialized this process with their 1979 song "Video Killed the Radio Star." E-books, by contrast, haven't yet supplanted the physical book in the United States and other developed countries. So what's behind the extraordinary resilience of this format made possible by Johannes Gutenberg's five-hundred-year-old innovation?

One might suspect that the use of e-books hasn't supplanted physical books because millennials don't read books anymore. But according to the Pew Research Center, this group reports reading more books across all formats than any other age group. Another possibility is that book publishers are prisoners of "structural inertia," which discourages individuals, organizations, and communities from staging a smooth transition from one way of doing things to another that offers better performance. Inertia manifests itself as a psychological, cognitive, and organizational reluctance to pursue a new model, given established habits, routines, and procedures. That's why Swiss watchmakers missed the commercial potential of the tuning-fork and quartz technologies, even though they invented them. Yet another possibility has to do with the printed book's unique format, one that is perfect for gifts and as home décor (much to the chagrin of true bibliophiles).

So can we arrive at a general principle as to why e-books have flopped in developed markets while audio and video streaming have triumphed? The technology commentator and best-selling author Edward Tenner argues that there are several reasons people are sometimes reluctant to abandon an old technology in favor of a new one. The first involves the potential vulnerabilities of the new thing. For instance, the fax machine is now a museum piece, but for a while people continued to prefer it over emailing scanned documents out of security concerns. Another potential reason involves aesthetics and nostalgia. Although dwarfed by music CDs and streaming, vinyl record sales continue to grow within the niche market of music aficionados. And despite improvements in automatic transmissions, certain car lovers prefer stick shifts.

Perhaps the key to understanding format resilience is that technologies rise and fall as part of ecosystems, rarely on their own or by themselves. Those ecosystems need to evolve quickly, through open innovation, in order to appeal to new generations of users, transforming the landscape in the process. E-book platforms have remained fundamentally closed to external innovators, especially on the software side. As a result, the functionality of e-books remains limited. Moreover, research indicates that reading a physical book enables the reader to absorb information more efficiently than reading the same book on an e-reader or a tablet. "The implicit feel of where you are in a physical book turns out to be more important than we realized," argues Abigail Sellen, a scientist and engineer at Microsoft Research Cambridge in England. "Only when you get an e-book do you start to miss it. I don't think e-book manufacturers have thought enough about how you might visualize where you are in a book."

And according to an article published in *Scientific American*, "screens and e-readers interfere with two other important aspects of navigating texts: serendipity and a sense of control. People report that they enjoy flipping to a previous section of a paper book when a sentence surfaces a memory of something they read earlier." E-books aren't as interactive as digital magazines. In 2011 a YouTube video titled "A Magazine Is an iPad That Does Not Work" went viral. "A one-year-old girl sweeps her fingers across an iPad's touchscreen, shuffling groups of icons." She then swipes, grips, and pokes the pages of a printed magazine, becoming frustrated that nothing happens. "For my one-year-old daughter," the father observes about his born-digital child, "a magazine is an iPad that does not work. It will remain so for her whole life." The "born-digital" generation we encountered in Chapter 2 does not seem to be thrilled by e-books because they are little more than a digital version of printed books. Perhaps e-books will become more engaging if the process of creating text itself evolves. "Some writers," *Scientific American* reports, "are pairing up with computer programmers to produce ever more sophisticated interactive fiction and nonfiction in which one's choices determine what one reads, hears, and sees next."

While e-books flounder in the United States and other rich countries, they may become a godsend in developing countries—if we dare to think laterally. One of the key challenges for Africa moving forward is how to educate its rapidly growing population. As we discussed in Chapter 1, between 2020 and 2030 some 450 million African babies will be born, a third of the world's total. The mission of South African startup Snapplify, the largest platform and aggregator for digital educational content in Africa, is to bring books to areas where there are no libraries or bookstores. It presently serves a few hundred schools and 170,000 schoolchildren, so it has plenty of room for growth. San Francisco–based Worldreader, a nonprofit organization, represents another approach. They provide free access to a library of digital books through e-readers and mobile phones for schools throughout the developing world. In off-the-grid rural areas, they offer an integrated solution including solar panels, USB hubs, LED lighting, e-readers, and access to the digital library.

Africa may well become the world's leading user of e-books, much the same way that it's already at the forefront in mobile payments. One of the most counterintuitive and surprising features of this rapidly evolving world is that the "less developed" countries and regions oftentimes offer the best panoramic window into the future, while those we label as "developed" are so wedded to established ways of thinking or doing that they find it difficult to part ways with the past. "Leapfrogging" enables laggards to catch up by skipping entire periods within which incremental innovations arose in the past.

And, besides books, there are other examples of the resilience of old formats. Only a tiny proportion of total sales of wines outside of bars and restaurants take place online: a pathetic 1.8 percent in the United States, 3.3 percent in Germany and Japan, and 4.3 percent in France. The exception is China, the world's largest market by volume, where 19.3 percent of wine sales are online. Only two other countries have proportions greater than 10 percent: Australia (11.3 percent) and the United Kingdom (10.3 percent), which, given their love of wine, is perhaps unsurprising.

Why exactly are consumers reluctant to purchase wine online? This is far from an idle question. By comparison, Internet sales account for more than 50 percent of clothing and footwear purchases in many countries. On the face of it, this feels odd: clothing stores encourage you to try on different outfits and see what fits, while liquor stores only occasionally allow you to sample, from a limited selection, bottles in the store itself. Perhaps consumers, on average, know little about wine and prefer the recommendations from in-house staff. Or maybe they feel that wine purchased online will break during transport. Perhaps people are impatient and are eager to consume it right away. A more compelling reason is that most people buy wine at the last minute—say, for a special occasion or before attending a party. All of these factors undoubtedly hinder the potential of the online wine trade. But none of them help explain why China, Australia, and the United Kingdom are the exceptions to the rule.

In China, it's been difficult to build physical wine stores fast enough given the swift growth of the middle class, as we saw in Chapter 3. But what about Australia and the United Kingdom? The answer is that some wines are bottled and sold under a label (more expensive and sophisticated "terroir" wines) while others under a brand (cheaper). In France, for instance, there are 27,000 wineries and as many labels of wine, each with distinct characteristics and tastes. Terroir wine sold as a label does not lend itself as easily to the online channel as standardized wine sold under a brand name. One of the best-known wine brands is Australia's Yellow Tail. In Australia, the United Kingdom, and China many consumers see wine more in terms of a brand rather than a label because the mass market took off relatively late, in the 1980s, and new wine consumers did not have the time to explore the complexities of terroir wines. "That the UK is now one of the largest wine markets globally," writes Julie Bower in a recent research article published in the journal *Beverages*, "owes much to the success of . . . early brands and those that arrived later in the 1990s, with Australia displacing France as the source for mass-market appeal." As in the case of e-books, we see that the online option captures the imagination of consumers only under very specific circumstances. Without such circumstances, not even the most convenient or cheapest technology succeeds.

WHICH TECHNOLOGIES ARE WORTH DEVELOPING AND REINVENTING?

Given the challenges of aging populations, environmental degradation, and climate change, we might as well think carefully about which technologies are most urgent to develop before 2030. Waterless toilets and e-books for those who lack access to the conventional things would be at the top of my personal list. VR-based therapies to help people overcome chronic psychological or cognitive conditions should also receive priority. Nanotechnologies promise to liberate us from some of the materials most inimical to the environment, and 3-D printing may help us be less wasteful. But each of these technologies can be immiserating if jobs are destroyed, if they reduce our privacy, or if they encourage the proliferation of fake news.

We may also think about old technologies and how they can be deployed in new, creative ways. A tantalizing current example of "reinventing the wheel" happens to be the flywheel, an ingenious device used for millennia as part of potter's wheels to help smooth the rotational movement, making it possible to produce the finest, smoothest pottery. It was most likely invented by the ancient Sumerians in present-day Iraq. James Watt found another use for it in the 1770s, attaching a disk to the shaft of his famous steam engine so that it would rotate at a consistent speed in spite of the irregular up-and-down thrusts of the pistons.

During the 2010s a Massachusetts company developed a design based on the flywheel to help save the planet by storing excess energy that otherwise would be wasted, and to smooth out the flow of electricity in power plants for more efficient generation. Its first facility at Stephentown, New York, consists of two hundred flywheels that can store up to 20 megawatts of power, enough to meet a tenth of the state's daily electricity consumption. For this purpose, a flywheel is no longer made of stone or steel but of lightweight carbon fiber, and it is suspended inside a vacuum chamber with the help of magnets in order to reduce friction. It can thus rotate at speeds topping those of a jet engine and store energy to the extent that it retains its momentum. By applying a brake, one can transform the flywheel's kinetic energy into electricity at any desired moment. This technology also promises to improve the performance of solar panels on cloudy days and wind farms when air movements drop to a breeze or stagnate. Thus flywheel technology is finding new applications in the era of scarce energy and heightened environmental awareness, reinventing the wheel in response to new trends.

At the end of the day, technologies spread and get adopted if they resonate with something already under way in society or the economy. New technology wins if it enables growth and access, as with mobile phones and e-books in Africa or online wine sales in China and the United Kingdom. To truly change the world, to be utterly transformational, technological innovations must ride a very big demographic or economic wave, as we shall see in Chapter 7.

7.

Imagine No Possessions

RIDING WAVES, NETWORK EFFECTS, AND THE POWER OF 8.5 BILLION CONNECTIONS

Imagine no possessions
I wonder if you can
No need for greed or hunger
A brotherhood of man
Imagine all the people
Sharing all the world . . .

—JOHN LENNON

Linsey Howard does not have a nine-to-five job or own a car. She is willing to commit to odd hours and take work when opportunities arise. But she is no social misfit or underpaid temp. She is an engineer by training, but her life re-volves around digital collaborative platforms like TaskRabbit. She uses them to pick and choose tasks posted by companies from all over the world. It's called gig work. If she completes the job quickly and accurately, her pay increases. Once the task is complete, she often heads to the grocery store, like many of us. The way she gets there, however, may be less familiar: she uses a bike-share service and hails a car to help carry home all the bags. Howard is one of over 40 million such workers in the United States alone, up from barely 20 million in 2018. Some perform manual tasks such as distributing leaflets or running errands, while others, like Howard, focus on cognitive ones. In a 2018 editorial, the *Economist* imagined the future as if it were looking back on it: "Since 2026 LinkedIn, a professional-networking service, has offered a guarantee that it can find a suitable worker for any task within six hours—and, thanks to a deal with Uber, can ensure that they are on-site within one working day." By 2030, the number of things we may share—homes, cars, and jobs—may well be nearly endless.

Forecasts of the size and impact of the collaborative economy in the near future differ. The Brookings Institution estimates that it will be twenty times bigger by 2025. According to PwC, a consultancy firm, the highest rates of growth will be in crowdfunding, online staffing, peer-to-peer accommodations, ride sharing, and music and video streaming. A linear extrapolation of these trends indicates that by 2030 the collaborative economy will account for upwards of 30 percent of total work and consumption.

The power of digital collaborative platforms was first grasped by the entrepreneurs behind companies like Uber and Airbnb. On January 19, 2009, nearly 2 million people gathered on the National Mall in Washington, DC, for the epochal inauguration of President Barrack Obama. The District's hotels were clearly unprepared to provide enough accommodations for the burgeoning out-of-town crowd. Three friends and budding entrepreneurs—Brian Chesky, Joe Gebbia, and Nathan Blecharczyk—saw a unique opportunity to publicize services offered on their website, Airbnb. They envisioned everyday people offering available rooms in their homes, playing host to travelers. The three entrepreneurs would provide the mechanism for putting would-be guests in touch with would-be hosts. The iPhone had launched in 2007, and the App Store opened a year later with an initial 500 apps available. Meanwhile, Google was making it easier for everyone to get around through its Maps tool. All it took was a dose of lateral thinking to put all of these elements together in one platform.

Airbnb had been launched back in October 2007, when its first guest stayed at a row house in San Francisco's South of Market district. Today Airbnb boasts more than 4 million listings in 65,000 cities, towns, and villages in 191 countries, and the company is valued at nearly $40 billion. As Brad Stone, author of the best-selling book *The Upstarts,* put it, "If you want to build a truly great company you have got to ride a really big wave. And you've got to be able to look at market waves and technology waves in a different way than other folks and see it happening sooner." In this case, the big market wave was driven by the intersection of mobile technology and the generational shift in attitudes regarding travel and experience (see Chapter 2). As a two-sided platform, Airbnb brought together young travelers and the graying generation of homeowners.

Airbnb's value proposition lies in the benefits of intimacy as experience. "I think the key that makes Airbnb is the fact that we're a community, not just a series of commodities," Brian Chesky, co-founder and CEO, once said. "I don't travel to relax, I travel to have new and interesting experiences," says River Tatry, a twenty-three-year-old New York freelancer. "For me, it is much more worthwhile to integrate myself into a place, learn something new, make local friends to visit again, and build community." That's a fabulous example of lateral thinking that is transforming the economy and our very habits.

SHARING AND THE RETURN TO THE "OLD NORM"

Collaborative consumption and sharing assets are by no means unprecedented. In fact, for about 90 percent of recorded history, humans did not merely survive but thrived without private property, especially when it came to land. Based on the archaeological record of human communities dating back to before the agricultural revolution and the anthropological study of present-day hunter-gatherer populations in Africa, researchers argue that humans who do not own property are generally happier than those who do. "The advent of agriculture, for example, increased the collective power of humankind by several orders of magnitude," argues Yuval Noah Harari, author of *Sapiens*. "Yet it did not necessarily improve the lot of the individual. . . . Peasants usually had a worse diet than hunter-gatherers. . . . The immense rise in human power has not been matched by an equal rise in human happiness." Even some sedentary agricultural communities shunned individual property in favor of shared grazing lands. By 2030, collaborative consumption will once again trump individual property.

Today young people are turning away from owning property, preferring instead to use someone else's belongings—for a fee. They view property in a collaborative way, whereby even some of our most intimate possessions are shared with others for mutual advantage. Other age groups are also warming to the idea of renting rather than owning. Even *The Simpsons*, which has always done a good job of reflecting our evolving culture, has turned Marge Simpson into an Uber driver (and Mr. Burns has hailed an Uber). And the impact of sharing has just begun. By 2030 nearly half of our spending will be in the form of "collaborative" or "shared" consumption, which will include cars, homes, offices, gadgets, and personal items of all sorts. Owning is out; sharing is in.

"My generation is moving from a culture of 'me' to a culture of 'we,'" says Rachel Botsman, author of *What's Mine Is Yours: The Rise of Collaborative Consumption*. It's all about "sharing through the smartphone in the era of being permanently connected." In 2016, millennial entrepreneur Caren Maio argued that "in just a decade, the American Dream of homeownership has lost a good deal of its luster." Instead, "renting, long considered a stopgap solution, is quietly emerging as the new American choice." The *Financial Times* notes that "from New York and London to New Delhi and Shanghai, millennials are increasingly blurring the lines between home, work and play—sharing spaces to save money and time as well as make new friends." *Forbes* magazine has called it "NOwnership." "Whereas being a 'two-car family' (or even three- or four-car) was once a mark of status," Marr argues, "today many millennials see more status in being a one-car or even zero-car family and making use of services like Uber, Lyft, CarGo, and others."

American millennials have taken many by surprise with their reluctance not just to own a car but even to obtain a driver's license. In 2015, just 77 percent of Americans between the ages of twenty and twenty-four had bothered to get a license, compared to 92 percent in 1983, for example. At the same time, the segment of the population that's fifteen to thirty-five years old is becoming more ethnically and linguistically diverse simply because recent immigrants tend to have more children. And we know that immigrants and their children tend to aspire to get married, become homeowners, and drive their own cars. Hence, the jury is still out on what the segment of young consumers in the United States and parts of Europe will look like come 2030. It all depends on the behavior of the children of immigrants, who will make up at least two-thirds of their demographic age group.

Worldwide surveys indicate that at least two-thirds of adults (of all ages) would be willing to list their homes and cars on apps. And the proportions are higher in emerging markets, which is a good sign for the staying power of the sharing economy going forward. The sharing economy essentially puts consumption on steroids, and its added convenience and lower cost mean that it's consumer-forward. But it also poses a tremendous challenge to individuals and companies whose well-being depends on traditional industries—hotels and taxis, for example—that are being upended by the change.

Furthermore, in thinking about the future growth of the sharing economy we must pay attention to the intergenerational dynamics we covered in Chapter 2. For instance, Airbnb reports that its rental listings are growing more rapidly among the population above sixty than in other age groups. The same trend applies to ride-hailing apps like Uber and Lyft on both sides of the service: drivers and passengers. The success of the founders of these platforms is no fluke. They displayed a keen sense of lateral thinking by bringing together millennials and seniors as the two sides of a single platform.

Now let's look globally. In the Asia-Pacific, the Middle East, and Africa the proportion of millennials willing to use services or goods offered by sharing platforms is above the global average, whereas in Latin America, the United States, and Europe it is significantly below. These differences do not occur among members of the Silent Generation, the baby boomers, Gen X, or Gen Z. Clearly, millennials are different—so far.

In more ways than one, the sharing economy challenges fundamental assumptions and aspirations held for generations, even millennia. What is the "American way of life," after all, if we remove the aspiration to own stuff? Every American above the age of forty grew up at a time when the institution of property was taken for granted, at least in the so-called free world. Entire parts of the economy are dedicated to ensuring that we acquire, maintain, and benefit from property. Much of the legal system is about protecting property. Many famous writers and agitators over the course of history made a big deal about who owns what type of property. Many revolutionary ideas and manifestoes—remember Karl Marx?—promoted the abolition of private property as the way to cure all manner of social problems. Private property has long been the backbone of the social pecking order, the most important contributor to inequality, and the motivation behind many kinds of crimes, especially war. And property lies at the foundation of the market economy and economic exchange. Home mortgages are as quintessentially American as apple pie. Napoleon once said that Britain was a nation of shopkeepers. Well, America became a nation of homeowners. Property rights "are a crystallized expression of varied roles of the state, politics, law, and culture," writes Stanford sociologist Andrew Walder. "They are central in shaping patterns of social inequality and economic performance."

We used to define social class, and hence achievement and happiness, by virtue of people's possessions (or lack thereof): the landed aristocracy, shopkeepers, the commercial and industrial bourgeoisie, the middle class of homeowners, the proletariat, sharecroppers, and so on. A new social category is being ushered in by technology: the "sharing class." It's defined by lifestyle, not property. To a large extent, technology—along with changing cultural values—is behind this transformative trend. The transitive verb "uberize" has already become part of the vernacular, recognized as such with an entry in no less than the *Collins English Dictionary*: "to subject (an industry) to a business model in which services are offered on demand through direct contact between a customer and a supplier, usually via mobile technology."

If sharing homes and cars were the only big trends driven by digital platforms, the impact wouldn't be as potentially transformational. The asset-sharing economy is just one part of the broader "collaborative economy," which also includes peer-to-peer lending, crowdfunding, crowdsourcing, reselling, co-working, co-freelancing, and many other ways of cooperating online. What brings together all of the platforms that have been launched as part of the collaborative or gig economy is that "they typically have ratings-based marketplaces and in-app payment systems," comments Nathan Heller in *The New Yorker*. "They give workers the chance to earn money on their own schedules, rather than through professional accession. And they find toeholds in sclerotic industries." While many of these forms of collaboration and sharing have existed for centuries, what's new is that the companies engaged in them now "don't just represent a new way of thinking or new services," best-selling author Bernard Marr argues, "but a new way to use data effectively to provide services to people when and where they want them." Without an app and an algorithmic data-processing system behind it, Uber or Lyft would never have taken off. In fact, many of the companies that populate the sharing economy are best described as facilitators. They do not produce or deliver services themselves. These platforms reduce transaction costs, making it convenient and affordable to engage in collaboration. "I think we're just coming into the next wave of human civilization," entrepreneur Caitlin Connors says. "Humans can [now] operate on a person-to-person basis, sharing ideas and sharing business without intermediaries." The big lateral questions for 2030 are: Will the collaborative economy make the world more or less unequal? Will it make jobs as we know them disappear? Can it help address the environmental crisis?

"AND THE WORLD WILL LIVE AS ONE"

In 2014 Facebook paid $19 billion to purchase WhatsApp, a messaging app with virtually no physical assets to speak of and fewer than sixty employees. What made the company an attractive acquisition target was its expansive user base of 1.5 billion people. WhatsApp was founded in 2009 by Brian Acton and Jan Koum, two former Yahoo engineers. Koum moved to the United States from Ukraine (another "immigrapreneur" to add to the list we saw in Chapter 1), while Acton was born in Michigan. "We don't want to build a hookup app so you can find someone weird to talk to," Acton once noted. "It's not what we're about. We're about your intimate relationships." Meanwhile, Koum displayed a more ambitious attitude: "We won't stop until every single person on the planet has an affordable and reliable way to communicate with their friends and loved ones." Mark Zuckerberg, for his part, once offered the controversial explanation that people like to be connected because "it feels better to be more connected to all these people. You have a richer life."

Many types of businesses benefit from so-called network effects. In fact, the entire sharing economy depends on them. A positive network effect occurs when the value of the network to any one participant increases with the number of participants. The telephone is a classic example. The more people with a line, the more useful my own line is because I can call more people. The telephone is a one-sided network in the sense that all users can make and receive calls. By contrast, a two-sided network effect occurs when increased participation by one group raises the value of participation for a different group. The collaborative economy is all about two-sided network effects. The more people who list their rooms, apartments, or homes on Airbnb, the more guests are likely to flock to the platform, and vice versa. As the last line in John Lennon's "Imagine" goes, "And the world will live as one."

By 2030, the key question won't be if network effects dominate the economy but what type of network effects will take precedence. An important dimension will be whether network effects operate at the local, national, regional, or global level. While most people assume that all network effects are global in nature, very few actually are. For instance, local network effects are crucial in the case of ride-hailing services. As a rider, I care about how many drivers are nearby when I need a ride. Similarly, most casual-dating platforms rely on local network effects. By contrast, matchmaking apps are mostly national in scope. Certain platforms rely primarily on regional effects. For instance, Airbnb long realized that most international tourism is regional (that is, within Europe, Latin America, Africa, or Asia) rather than global. In some large countries— like the United States and China—most tourism is domestic. Thus, while Uber needs to create a critical mass of drivers and riders in each locality, Airbnb needs to reach a minimum threshold in each region. There are relatively few purely global two-sided platforms.

As Americans, we are biased toward companies like Airbnb, Uber, Lyft, We-Work, and eBay because they dominate the American market. We should start broadening our range. In China, for example, local companies reign supreme, and they are bigger than their American counterparts and expanding internationally quite quickly. These include giants such as Didi (ride hailing and bike sharing), WeChat (social media), Tujia (accommodation sharing), and

UCommune (co-working space). As of 2017, there were more sharing-economy unicorns—companies valued at $1 billion or more—in Asia than in the United States. As we saw in Chapter 3, by 2030 the situation will likely become even more tilted in Asia's favor, fundamentally because of the region's rapidly growing middle class. The sharing and collaborative economy, however, is creating entirely different stripes of consumers and workers.

PROLETARIANS OF ALL COUNTRIES, SWIPE!

Karl Marx, along with his co-author and financial supporter Friedrich Engels, called for the working class to unite in order to overthrow the established order and improve their lot. Are gig workers better or worse off than those in traditional jobs? Does the rise of the sharing class reduce or increase inequality? According to Robert Reich, who served as labor secretary in the Clinton administration, gig workers are "Uber drivers, Instacart shoppers, and Airbnb hosts. They include TaskRabbit jobbers, Upcounsel's on-demand attorneys, and Healthtap's on-line doctors. They're Mechanical Turks." They all swipe back and forth in search of opportunities. Reich argues that these "jobs" are demeaning and underpaid. "The euphemism is the 'share' economy. A more accurate term would be the 'share-the-scraps' economy."

Reich sees the sharing economy as the culmination of efforts by companies to reduce their full-time payroll, turning instead to temporary workers, temp agency workers, on-call workers, independent contractors, and freelancers. The growth of the broader gig economy has gone hand in hand with an increase in the number of workers in non-standard jobs, including those who operate as independent contractors on the supply side of the platforms. Economists Lawrence Katz and Alan Krueger (the former chair of President Obama's Council of Economic Advisers) estimate that between 2005 and 2015 the proportion of such workers grew from 10 percent of the total to nearly 16 percent.

Reich is not alone in his criticisms. Guy Standing, a British economist, coined the term "precariat" (a portmanteau of "precarious" and "proletariat") to refer to this class of workers. Writing for *Salon* in 2016, Steven Hill saw a pattern in the evolution of the sharing startups. "After launching with much fanfare and tens of millions of VC capital behind them, vowing to enact a revolution in how people work and how society organizes peer-to-peer economic transactions," he argues, "in the end many of these companies morphed into the equivalent of old-fashioned temp agencies (and others have simply imploded into black hole nothingness)." The title of Hill's best-selling book says it all: *Raw Deal: How the Uber Economy and Runaway Capitalism Are Screwing American Workers*. Rebecca Smith, deputy director of the National Employment Law Project, observes that the gig economy seems to take us back to the time when most workers were "labor brokers," as in the putting-out system, manufacturing stuff in their homes as opposed to at the factory. In her view, the gig economy platforms "are operating just like farm labor contractors, garment jobbers and day labor centers of old."

In spite of the negative effects of precarious employment, some researchers find that the sharing economy helps those at the bottom of the income distribution. Using data from Getaround, a car-sharing platform, New York University economists Samuel Fraiberger and Arun Sundararajan found that peer-to-peer rental marketplaces benefit consumers, especially lower-income ones. "This segment is more likely to switch from owning to renting, provides a higher level of peer-to-peer marketplace demand, is more likely to contribute to marketplace supply, and enjoys significantly higher levels of surplus gains." In a nutshell, they concluded that the sharing economy has the potential to help the economically disadvantaged both as consumers (the demand side) and as workers (supply).

However, there is also evidence indicating that for most people the money earned in the gig economy is supplemental income, not the main source of sustenance. Juliet Schor, a sociologist at Boston College, decided to evaluate who was actually benefiting from apps such as Airbnb, RelayRides, and TaskRabbit. In her qualitative study, she found that "providers are highly educated and many have well-paying jobs. They use platforms to augment their incomes." In her research, Schor came across "a lawyer, a political operative, management consultants, technology professionals, medical researchers, teachers, an accountant, a college teacher, and a sales representative" working on the supply side of the sharing economy.

Schor argues that there is a crowding-out effect, in that "many are engaging

in manual labor, including cleaning, moving and other tasks that are traditionally done by workers with low educational attainment." Airbnb hosts often do what clerks and housekeeping staff do after each guest checks out. At
TaskRabbit—the errands app that allows people to pay other people to clean,
drive, assemble furniture, organize rooms, fix things, and fetch groceries—
she found high-status professionals with full-time jobs doing manual work,
including a lawyer, a biotech scientist, and an accountant. Valeria, a student
who does housecleaning for TaskRabbit clients, observes that "in the beginning I sucked at cleaning. I sucked. People were leaving bad reviews. . . .
Because back at home I didn't even make my bed, you know? There was a
cleaning person in my home." The end result, Schor concludes, is an increasing degree of income inequality, both because better-educated people are
obtaining supplemental income and because the unskilled are seeing their
traditional domains invaded by the apps.

Another source of inequality stemming from the gig economy is related to
the fact that hosting on Airbnb can be a major source of income, but only to
those with enough money to own property in the first place. "It takes money
to make money," said Kiran, an Airbnb host interviewed for Schor's study.
Shira, a single young woman, makes $30,000 a year renting out an apartment—
an amount that, she says, seems "almost too good to be true." Schor found that
most people in her sample who rented on Airbnb made more money through
the service than through their primary jobs.

The desire to earn a bit of money on the side is often linked to a virtuous
cause. Many young gig economy workers "used their platform earnings to reduce debts," Schor found. "One couple, who had earned $11,000 on Airbnb,
used the money to pay off the husband's college loans." But perhaps the most
striking finding in the study is that many people saw the work they do as "tech-
nologically advanced, a new, cool thing." Some, according to Schor, thought
"they were doing something green, building social connections, helping others,
or fostering cultural exchange." Another host, wrote Nathan Heller in *The New
Yorker*, commented that "Airbnb enabled me to go back to school and become a
full-time student and work as a part-time photographer." As Sundararajan has
put it, the services offered by the gig economy are "successful because they are

tapping into people's time more efficiently. You could say that people are monetizing their own downtime."

Many gig workers are simply trying to avoid becoming a cubicle dweller like those depicted in the *Dilbert* comic strip. "I have a story I want to tell through my writing, and Uber is allowing me to do it," says Kara Oh, a sixty-seven-year-old Uber driver from Santa Barbara, California, who writes novels in the morning and drives people around in the afternoon and evening. Travis Kalanick, co-founder of Uber and erstwhile CEO, once argued that "drivers value their independence—the freedom to push a button rather than punch a clock, to use Uber and Lyft simultaneously, to drive most of the week or just a few hours." That's the main benefit that other analysts see in the gig economy. As Diane Mulcahy, a senior fellow at the Kauffman Foundation and a lecturer at Babson College, writes in her book *The Gig Economy*, "Traditional full-time jobs are insecure, increasingly scarce, and filled with employees who wish they were doing something else with their lives." Mulcahy believes that digital platforms "can offer an attractive, interesting, flexible, and even lucrative and secure alternative to the corporate cube." In her view, "there is a trend towards focusing more on time and experiences rather than material goods. The emphasis of the new American Dream is quality of life, not quantity of stuff."

There are, to be sure, others who feel that their work in the gig economy is demeaning. Katy, a law school graduate without a job commensurate with her academic credentials, explained that working on TaskRabbit "was very, very humbling." She mentions her degree in her profile, and says that people would "make comments almost pitying me for having to clean their apartment, having gone to law school, and I hated that. . . . [T]hey would be, like, 'Oh, it sucks you have to do this.' Like, 'Yes, I know it sucks. You don't have to remind me.'" Veronica, who has a master's degree in science, refused a request to fetch a coffee from Starbucks for $8. "Like no, get off your butt and get it yourself . . . I don't want to be, like a servant."

The labor market of 2030 may look very different as two-sided platforms continue to expand. It may be true that, as NYU's Sundararajan claims, they are an efficient response to the fact that some people own things desired by others, or that some people have money while others have time. As Hill reflected in *Salon*, "Eventually many traditional economy companies may adapt an app-based

labor market in ways we can't yet anticipate, . . . but that means we need to figure out a way to launch a universal, portable safety net for all U.S. workers."

A CLASS SYSTEM DEFINED BY SHARING?

"We live in a world dominated by the principle of private property," observes
Julian Brave NoiseCat, an enrolled member of the Canim Lake Bad Tsq'escen
nation in British Columbia, Canada, and an activist who seeks to advance the
rights of the native peoples of the Americas. "The fruits of billions of acres of
dispossessed and parceled indigenous land across the Americas, Africa, Asia,
Ireland and Australia enabled two English-speaking empires—first the British
and then the American—to rise to global dominance." Several other European
countries—from Denmark to Belgium and Italy and from the Netherlands to
Portugal and Spain—also participated in the bounty. After the imperialists left,
their local descendants continued to own large tracts of land and to dominate
the political system.

Like most people around the world, Americans have developed over the
years an intimate relationship to ownership. "Property," NoiseCat argues, "prop-
agates a utopian vision called the American Dream, wherein hard work, land and
a home are platforms for boundless opportunity—or at least escape—from capital domination." As we saw in Chapter 3, home and automobile ownership used
to define the American middle class. Elections and government policies were
often driven by the interests of those who owned (or aspired to own) property.

The stagnation of the old middle class in Europe and the United States and
the rise in wealth inequality—the richest 1 percent own more wealth than the
other 99 percent combined—are calling into question cherished assumptions
about the extent to which property rights should be protected, especially when
it comes to taxation. "Prior generations responded to similar crises by turning to
communism," notes NoiseCat. "But today, Marx, Lenin and Mao no longer offer
a scythe sharp enough to fell the stalks of capitalism." People are responding to
felt stresses by participating in the sharing economy, spurred by a lack of enough
resources to secure property and by a distinct preference for new, collaborative,
and communal modes of using assets such as homes and automobiles.

Ownership of a home and other expensive assets has long influenced political behavior. It is not clear, however, that they make people more likely to support conservative economic or social policies. Research has found that homeowners are more likely to vote and be politically engaged. If by 2030 most of these assets are shared rather than owned, one might predict more apathy on the part of citizens and a disinclination to be engaged politically or to turn out for elections. Given that most sharers on the demand side of these platforms tend to be young, this would tend to depress political engagement even more among people in that age group.

But there is another earth-shattering effect of the gig economy on politics. Yale political scientist Jacob Hacker argued in his book *The Great Risk Shift* that for decades now governments and corporations have been off-loading their commitments to citizens and workers, proposing instead a culture of personal responsibility. The notion of personal responsibility draws on conservative values and represents a direct attack on some of the most cherished progressive ideals that drove the adoption of social safety nets in both Europe and the United States since the Depression. As Bo Fishback, founder and CEO of Zaarly, a home services platform, once said, the gig economy has created "the ultimate opt-in employment market, where there is no excuse for people who say, 'I don't know how to get a job, I don't know how to get started.'"

The rise of the sharing class has reignited political debates about discrimination. Unlike a traditional hotel, Sundararajan notes, "someone who's hosting on Airbnb might say, 'Well, this is my space. I only want a certain kind of guest in my spare bedroom.'" The gig economy challenges conventional notions of what constitutes discrimination, yet another way in which it seems to abandon the traditional rules of the game.

If job-sharing platforms are transforming the labor market, crowdsourcing and crowdfunding are revolutionizing political campaigns. Then-senator Barack Obama's campaign for president in 2008 was the first to effectively use these new tools. His biggest success was to recruit and organize millions of volunteers through text messages and the Internet, even before the viral growth of digital social networks. Obama had about 850,000 friends on MySpace, compared to his opponent John McCain's 220,000, and 120,000 followers on

Twitter, compared to 5,000 for McCain, according to one source. One study noted that "for John F. Kennedy, it was television. And for Barack Obama, it is social media." Most importantly, his campaign raised a record $800 million from 4 million donors largely using crowdfunding techniques. The study concluded that "the Obama '08 campaign created a nationwide virtual organization that motivated 3.1 million individual contributors and mobilized a grassroots movement of more than 5 million volunteers." What made the campaign unprecedented was the comprehensive use of new techniques to achieve a variety of goals. "Clearly, the Obama campaign utilized these tools to go beyond educating the public and raising money to mobilizing the ground game, enhancing political participation, and getting out the vote." And then the 2016 election brought us "fake news" through the manipulation of pervasive social networks.

Yet another epochal political change that the rise of the sharing class might bring about is that many more workers may not retire, at least in full. Think about the lateral connection between gig work and retirement. Retirees are a distinct group when it comes to political behavior, especially voting; as we have seen, they are more likely to vote than other age groups. While many people believe that the proliferation of gig workers will exacerbate the problem of underfunded pensions, it is often forgotten that many people work beyond retirement age, especially in flexible occupations, because they enjoy it. Thus, the sharing class of gig workers may postpone retirement, or go into partial retirement, at higher rates than full-time employees. Many seniors host on Airbnb because they enjoy meeting new people.

It is also true that at a time when life expectancy continues to soar and public and employer pension systems are under stress, the gig economy may actually provide some relief. Analysts have written about "the gig economy as a backup retirement plan." Another possibility is that "employees with traditional nine-to-five jobs are using side hustles to fill gaps in their retirement savings."

The sharing class of consumers and gig workers is likely to have a different view of major political issues: discrimination, pay equity, pensions, the social safety net. Given their flexible schedules, they may also be more likely to turn out at elections than full-time employees. Their mindset of self-reliance and independence might resonate both with liberal values about the economy and with more conservative ones regarding social issues. The political landscape will indeed look very different if by 2030 more than half of the workforce in Europe, the United States, and other parts of the world consists of gig workers. But will monopolistic digital platforms with dominant market shares end up exploiting workers and consumers alike?

THE DANGERS OF TOO BIG TO BAN

In an interview with Travis Kalanick, the co-founder of Uber, an interviewer for the *Wall Street Journal* asked a seemingly innocuous question regarding Uber's response to a cease-and-desist order from the California Public Utility Commission and the San Francisco Municipal Transportation Agency four months after the company launched its ride-hailing service there.

"Did you ever cease?"

"No."

"Did you ever desist?"

"No."

"So you basically ignored them?"

"The thing is, a cease and desist is something that says, 'Hey, I think you should stop,' and we're saying, 'We don't think we should.'"

Kalanick was essentially adhering to an old principle in Silicon Valley: It's better to ask forgiveness than to get permission.

One reason the sharing economy is controversial is that it is largely unregulated. It's so new and so innovative that the existing rules don't seem to apply. In that sense, it is one of the most important ways in which the world as we know it is coming to an end.

Uber, founded in 2009, is a two-sided platform that brings together car owner-drivers and riders for mutual gain. It operates in nearly nine hundred cities and metropolitan areas in seventy-three countries. In spite of Uber's notoriety, it is important to note that there are 4,500 cities in the world with more than 100,000 residents. Thus, the company is operational in only one out of five of them. Uber seeks to create a critical mass of drivers in each location, promising them that they can be busy with a nearly endless succession of trips.

Riders like the convenience of using the phone app, the availability of cars, and the price of the service. A ratings system provides for transparency.

The only snag was that most cities have a strict licensing system for urban transportation. Taxi drivers and owners are among the most vociferous opponents of ride-hailing services. Uber's initial approach was to simply ignore the licensing requirements. Some cities tolerated the company because of its promise to offer affordable and convenient service to residents, with reduced congestion and increased tax revenue. But many cities did not, under pressure from the taxi lobby. Uber had to agree to being regulated or constrained in its expansion, and in some cases it decided to discontinue operations altogether. Marcus Wohlsen, a Silicon Valley journalist, once likened Uber to Amazon, a comparison that seems to ignore the obvious differences between the two giants. "But their stories are similar," he argues. "A startup led by a brash, charismatic CEO catches a creaky old industry unaware. It grows quickly, and its popularity explodes as its brand becomes nearly synonymous with the disruptive service it's offering." When confronted by a backlash from competitors and regulators, the two companies pressed ahead, though admittedly in different ways. What is their calculus?

Virtually every ambitious Silicon Valley startup wants to get big, fast—big because scale delivers profits, and fast to prevent other ventures from mimicking the business model. In Uber's case, the strategy was to get "too big to ban." That means enlisting the people who benefit from its services to defend the company against entrenched interests and the desire by some municipal governments to control transportation. Uber grew "in part by treating obstacles—whether competing ride-hailing companies or government regulations—as inconveniences to be bulldozed over," wrote Sheelah Kolhatkar in *The New Yorker*. Consider the example of London, one of Uber's most important success stories. It started operations in 2012 in anticipation of the Summer Olympic Games. The company presently has 40,000 active drivers in London and a whopping 3.5 million regular users. According to Kolhatkar, the company was facing multiple types of competitors as it sought to grow: "a trade dominated by a skilled guild of coachmen, able to ply for hire on the streets, with a shadow industry of occasional jobbers and private chauffeurs, making a quiet living on the side." In June 2014 the black cabbies (as licensed taxi drivers are known) staged their first demonstration against Uber. "During the afternoon, between 4,000 and 10,000 cabbies stopped work . . . turning their cars sideways on Lambeth Bridge and bringing gridlock throughout Westminster, as far as Piccadilly Circus. . . . Uber downloads jumped by 850 percent," the *Guardian* reported. "The cab protest—its crudeness, the inadvertent publicity it gave to Uber— read like the classic bungling behavior of a doomed market incumbent."

Uber's aggressive growth tactics must be seen in the context of the purely local network effects that underlie its strategy. The more drivers and riders on its platform in a particular city, the better. Its approach thus revolves around growing its base of support as quickly as possible. "Uber's transformation of the global taxi industry rests on a theorem," the *Guardian* noted. "It is that by adding huge volumes of riders and drivers to a given market—liquidity—taxis can become cheaper and drivers can earn more at the same time." As Marcus Wohlsen put it, "The more riders Uber can get in its cars and accustomed to having its push-button convenience as an option, the less incentive politicians have to stay on Uber's case." The point is that "by drastically lowering its prices, Uber is doing more than increasing its customer base. It's cultivating constituents. . . . If Uber can survive its many political battles, it stands to become a huge, and hugely valuable, global enterprise. For investors, that's a billion dollars well spent." Within days of London deciding to ban Uber in 2017, nearly 800,000 people signed a petition in the company's favor. Regulators had no choice but to allow Uber to operate until the appeal is resolved at some point in the near future. That's the type of lateral thinking that enabled Uber to grow so big. They bet that drivers and riders would come to their rescue if they were banned. They had become too big to ban.

What is truly revolutionary about the sharing economy is that it upends socioeconomic roles and relationships. Uber promises a supplementary income to low-paid workers and retired people, and self-employment to the unemployed. Drivers like the flexibility and transparency, and find the app liberating because they no longer have to depend on a dispatcher. Riders enjoy greater choice and a service that potentially reaches into underserved suburbs and inner-city neighborhoods. The company also claims that drunk-driving rates are coming down as a result of Uber's presence. Even Mothers Against Drunk Driving, the influential grassroots organization, has teamed up with the company to offer free rides on certain important dates like high school proms or game days when young people might risk driving while impaired.

Uber seized on several distinct societal trends and put everything together through lateral thinking.

In that vein, is it possible for digital platforms to help with climate change?

KILLING OR SAVING THE PLANET?
THE TRAGEDY OF THE DIGITAL COMMONS

In 2017 a reader of the *Financial Times* wrote a letter to the editor arguing that "Uber has been a textbook example" of the tragedy of the commons. He had in mind San Francisco, a city where tourists and businesspeople need convenient transportation options. However, the city has limited traffic capacity. "The result is overgrazed roads with the anticipated tragic outcome," including low wages for drivers, subpar service due to inexperienced drivers, congestion, and air pollution. In an opinion piece published in the *Guardian*, columnist Arwa Mahdawi noted that according to Airbnb, "the short-term rental market is a brilliant way to foster community, revitalize neighborhoods, help ordinary folk make ends meet, and bring about world peace." At the same time, Airbnb contributes to making housing more expensive, thus pricing out would-be homeowners as well as renters. And neighbors complain not only about rising rents but also about noise and disruption to their daily routines. Mahdawi concluded that "the so-called sharing economy is more accurately the monetize-everything-you-can economy." People's homes are no longer a sign of middle-class status. They have become a "monetization" opportunity.

Since this double-edged sword is becoming a factor everywhere, from Barcelona's neighborhoods to the streets of New York City, we must acknowledge the downsides this disruption brings, which can be both systemic and systematic.

Many years ago, Adam Smith, the enlightened Scot who is considered the founder of modern economics, argued that "it is not from the benevolence of the butcher, the brewer, or the baker that we expect our dinner, but from their regard to their own self-interest." The lateral implication was that the "invisible hand" of the free market provides the best possible arrangement for consumers and producers, with the former securing everything they need by shopping around for the best deal and the latter making a profit catering to those needs. This basic intuition holds under many circumstances, with at least two notable (and well-known) exceptions.

The first was identified by John Nash, the mathematician made famous by the film *A Beautiful Mind*, who argued that one cannot predict the outcome of the choices of multiple decision-makers if one analyzes their decisions in isolation. In the movie, this fundamental insight helps explain an event at a bar that triggered Nash's own lateral thinking. He observed several male students courting the same woman, who rejected them all; in turn, this inspired the other women in the bar to do the same, as no one wanted to be seen as the backup choice. It was a bad outcome for both the women and men involved, Nash reasoned. The example allowed him to identify a flaw in Smith's widely accepted theory that competitive behavior in a free market benefits everyone.

The second notable exception to the wonders of markets driven by self-interest is the shared-resource system known as the commons, where egoistic abuse of the common good by some individuals leads to the depletion of the resource for everyone else. The problem was first observed by the nineteenth-century British economist William Forster Lloyd, who wrote about the environmental perils of unregulated grazing on public lands. Philosophers, ecologists, anthropologists, and political scientists soon employed his perspective to study everything from air pollution and polluted watersheds to depleted fish stocks and Greenland's melting ice sheets. It was the ecologist Garrett Hardin who coined the term "tragedy of the commons" in a famous essay published in *Science* magazine in 1968, whose abstract simply read: "The population problem has no technical solution; it requires a fundamental extension in morality." Hardin was primarily concerned about population growth and what it meant for the future of Earth's limited resources. Remember that people once thought that an oversupply of babies would bring the world to an end, as we saw in Chapter 1. For him, the problem lay in an undersupply of good intentions and good institutions.

Some people react strongly, sometimes violently, against Uber and Airbnb because they see a tragedy of the commons in the making. They fear that un-regulated ride-hailing can lead to more congestion in the streets. Or that Uber drivers are more prone to accidents than taxi drivers. Or that an unprofessional class of drivers could abuse riders. And they point out the danger that an al-ready neglected public transportation system may fall deeper into disrepair as it competes with ride-hailing apps and services. For example, in New York City Uber stole customers away from taxicabs in Manhattan below 59th Street, but its presence led to a 40 percent increase in ridership in the rest of the city when compared to pre-Uber times, which has exacerbated traffic problems and reduced the appetite for investments in public transportation. Likewise, while Airbnb's services bring many benefits, the company also has been blamed for attracting excessive numbers of tourists, the degradation of neighborhoods, and rising rents that render cities unaffordable. How should we think about these benefits and problems, which appear to arise in tandem?

In defense of digital sharing platforms, let me make three lateral arguments. Sharing may help us relieve the pressure on natural resources by reducing the need to have a large stock of vehicles in operational condition, for instance. The average American only uses his or her car 6 or 7 percent of the time throughout the week. Thus, car sharing may actually be a better use of existing resources.

Second is that people seem to be willing to pay to share goods and services because it adds value to their lives. Using data on 48 million UberX sessions in the four largest cities in the United States, Steve Levitt, co-author of *Freako-nomics*, and his colleagues estimated that consumers enjoyed an implicit eco-nomic windfall thanks to Uber that was approximately 1.6 times greater than the cost of the rides themselves. That translates into an estimated $18 million per day in those four cities alone: "If Uber were to unexpectedly disappear for a day, that is how much consumers would lose."

The third argument in favor of sharing is perhaps the most important. It is simply not true that the tragedy of the commons is an inevitable outcome whenever people are given a free ride on a shared resource. The brilliant politi-cal scientist Elinor Ostrom—the first woman to win a Nobel Prize in Economic Sciences—was among many Americans who tended a "victory garden" (another type of urban agriculture) during World War II, along with her mother. This experience triggered in her mind the idea that, under certain conditions, people do cooperate for the common good. She spent a lifetime studying all sorts of situations in which people share resources, including community policing, lobster farming, forests, irrigation systems, and, yes, grazing lands. Her argument is that the tragedy of the commons can be avoided when people organize from the bottom up to avoid resource exhaustion and ecosystem collapse. Her recommendation was to define clear rules for resource sharing, establish mechanisms of conflict resolution, design a scale of graduated sanctions for violators, and promote a commitment to communal self-determination based on trust.

In a sense, Ostrom urges users to get organized and manage the common resource by themselves without waiting for the government to do so through regulation. What's become known as Ostrom's law states that "a resource arrangement that works in practice can work in theory," showing that grassroots initiatives can work when it comes to promoting the common good. Perhaps that is the best way of ensuring that the sharing economy will work for all, namely, those who participate in it and those affected by it.

"DON'T TOSS THAT LETTUCE—SHARE IT"

"About one-third of all food produced in the world goes to waste," writes Martin J. Smith. The app OLIO enables neighbors and local businesses to share food, helping to avoid that waste. The app debuted in 2015 and now has 2 million users in forty-nine countries. "Share More. Waste Less" is its motto. For example, food retailers can contribute food that is about to reach its "best by" date, especially produce. Along with food banks, which have long received unsold inventories from retailers, digital platforms can help reduce waste and the carbon footprint associated with it.

Similarly, the American startup Rent the Runway seeks to make fashion more sustainable by allowing people to rent garments instead of buy them. "Every time you rent you're saving all the water, electricity and emissions used to manufacture a new piece of clothing," the company claims. "The average woman throws away 82 pounds of clothing per year."

Avoiding unnecessary waste in food and clothes might cut global carbon emissions by as much as 10 percent. After oil, those are the two industries that contribute the most to climate change. "In a shareable world, things like car sharing, clothing swaps, childcare coops, potlucks, and cohousing make life more fun, green, and affordable," observes the online magazine *Shareable*. "When we share, not only is a better life possible, but so is a better world." *Scientific American* suggested that "sharing is caring."

Studies about the environmental benefits of sharing have not produced consistent results. One study found that the online platform Craigslist significantly decreases waste disposal after it starts to operate in a city. Car-sharing services like Zipcar have also contributed to reducing congestion and emissions. The Transportation Research Board found that in the United States, "at least five private vehicles are replaced by each shared car"; other studies put the number at thirteen. Drivers sharing information about road and traffic congestion on Waze contribute to reducing congestion and fuel use. Uber, Lyft, and the other ride-hailing services claim that they are contributing to a more efficient and cleaner environment.

Yet research by a team led by Regina Clewlow at the University of California, Davis, shows that in major U.S. cities ride-hailing platforms have resulted in "more cars, more trips, more miles" because when people have access to more convenient alternatives, they shun public transportation: "Shared mobility likely attracts Americans in major cities away from bus services and light rail (6 percent and 3 percent net reduction in use, respectively)." At the same time, ride-hailing complements other modes of transportation. For instance, commuter rail use increased by 3 percent, and walking increased by 9 percent. However, the net effect seems to be negative. "These services currently facilitate a shift away from more sustainable modes towards low-occupancy vehicles in major cities."

Similarly, Airbnb claims that travelers staying with a host use much less energy per stay than if they rented a hotel room. The company commissioned a study from Cleantech Group, a consultancy, which found that "in one year alone, Airbnb guests in North America saved the equivalent of 270 Olympic-sized pools of water while avoiding the greenhouse gas emissions equivalent to 33,000 cars on North American roads." In the European Union, the figures were even higher: water savings equivalent to 1,100 pools and emissions savings equivalent to 200,000 cars. In North America, Airbnb claims that more than 80 percent of hosts have at least one energy-efficient appliance. The study also reported that Airbnb guests are 10 to 15 percent more likely than hotel guests to use public transportation, walk, or use a bicycle—though Airbnb users are also much younger on average than hotel users. There's no independent verification of these figures, either.

It's also not clear that sharing underutilized assets is a net win for society. Yes, in many cases cars sit idle more than 90 percent of the time. But if their owners use them as a source of income by working for Uber or Lyft, the cars will last for a shorter period of time as the mileage piles up. If cars depreciate faster, they will need to be replaced earlier. Is it better to use a car 5 percent of the time over ten years or to use it 50 percent of the time over a shorter period? The answer to that question is not easy because cars also lose value over time, regardless of use, in part because they become obsolete as new models are rolled out. If by 2030 a significant proportion of all privately owned cars are on ride-hailing platforms, it is not obvious that society will be better off. For instance, if cars depreciate more quickly, we need to think concretely about how to recycle or dispose of a greater number of them, especially as new cars flood the streets. And the growth of ride-hailing may reduce reliance on public transportation. Thus ride-hailing can have negative environmental implications.

The case of accommodation sharing exhibits both similarities and differences with ride-hailing. Many people frequently leave their primary residence for a vacation or a job-related trip. Many of them have spare rooms they could rent out. From an economic perspective, it makes sense to monetize an asset that sits idle from time to time. It helps that homes do not depreciate as quickly as automobiles, and that the environmental implications are not as negative when compared with the traditional alternative, hotels.

In general, except possibly for ride-hailing, the sharing economy promises to help preserve the resources of the planet. In an international survey conducted by the Dutch bank ING, people reported that they use sharing platforms because they believe they are good for the environment and they help build communities. The more popular a sharing app, the more people believe in those environmental benefits.

SHARING AND THE FUTURE

As a card-carrying millennial, Linsey Howard is keen on doing whatever it takes to protect the environment and reduce carbon emissions. She gave up a stable job in favor of performing tasks on demand partly because she would be able to avoid commuting. She epitomizes the "jobless worker" who actually works. The collaborative economy creates a new reality by blurring concepts such as job and office, ownership and access. Sharing in a networked society means that what used to be a job is now broken down into tasks that can be performed by different people working from home or using office space that accommodates different workers at different times. Property loses some of its meaning because fractional access and use provide for flexibility and lower costs. The underlying culture is no longer one of owning but one of enjoying and experiencing, a worldview seemingly consistent with the idea of a level playing field and a stronger community. To hark back to the lyrics by John Lennon, "Imagine no possessions . . ."

These changes dovetail with massive shifts in demographics and technology, potentially creating a wholesale transformation of the social order. Can we continue to take marriage, children, the effects of aging, manufacturing jobs, home mortgages, cities, and personal computers for granted? And how about one of our most pervasive institutions—money? Let's turn to Chapter 8 to find out.

8.

More Currencies than Countries

PRINTING YOUR OWN MONEY, THE BLOCKCHAIN,

AND THE END OF MODERN BANKING

*Permit me to issue and control the money of a
nation, and I care not who makes its laws.*

—MAYER AMSCHEL ROTHSCHILD, BANKER

Most people alive today grew up in a world in which each country had distinct symbols of sovereignty—one flag, one leader, and one currency. But by 2030 some of the most important currencies in the world will be issued not by governments but by companies or even by computers. Today, though, many consider this possibility a dangerous heresy.

When he first observed the use of paper money in China at the end of the thirteenth century, Marco Polo was overwhelmed by amazement, remarking, "All these pieces of paper are issued with as much solemnity and authority as if they were of pure gold or silver." This strange paper was first put into circulation in 1260 by Kublai Khan, the founder of the Yuan dynasty and a grandson of Genghis Khan, the ruthless Mongol conqueror. Modern paper money came about centuries later, in the midst of the Anglo-French rivalry. In 1694, King William III's courtiers came up with a novel approach to fund England's seemingly endless wars with its foe across the English Channel: a new, privately owned company, the Bank of England, was given the right to take deposits of bullion from the public and to issue banknotes that could be lent again.

In some ways, having more currencies than countries would not be unprecedented: until the late nineteenth century it was not uncommon to see the commercial notes of banks or even companies circulate as currency for the purposes of extending credit or making payments. Nor were bankers shy when it came to taking advantage of new technology. As the legend goes, the Rothschild bankers used carrier pigeons to learn about Napoleon's defeat at Waterloo in 1815 before anyone else in London did, and they used that precious information to make some handsome profits in the bond market.

Scourged by their lack of control over the currencies in use within their territorial domains and by recurring banking crises, governments, beginning about 150 years ago, decided to establish national monopolies over the printing and circulation of money. By 2030, those national currency monopolies will be eroded, just as past monopolies in the airline, electricity, and telecommunications industries were. National currencies will still predominate, but digital alternatives will be available as well.

In order to visualize a future in which traditional currencies, cryptocurrencies, and other types of tokens share the stage, one must first grasp how money works. To do so, let's consider the tantalizing example of Salvador Dalí, one of the most celebrated artists of the twentieth century and a pioneering figure in Surrealism; nowadays his oil paintings sell for tens of millions of dollars. Dalí was also a savvy businessman. Once he treated a bunch of friends to a meal at an expensive restaurant in New York City. When it came time to pay, the eccentric artist adopted a lateral way of thinking and decided to run a little experiment. On the back of the check he had signed to cover the expense, he made a sketch in his inimitable style. He authenticated it with a signature and handed it to the waiter, who then passed it on to the restaurant manager. Under

Figure 9

normal circumstances, the check would have been endorsed and sent to the bank for deposit. But this wasn't a normal check. After seeing the sketch and recognizing the artist who had done it, the manager decided to frame the check and hang it on the wall for all to see (Figure 9).

Dalí was delighted and pulled the same trick several more times. Sure enough, a framed check with a Dalí sketch appeared on the walls of several restaurants. Consider how unusual this situation really was. The money offered to pay for the meals was never deposited, as the checks were transformed into artworks and took on a separate life. For Dalí, this maneuver was a stroke of genius. He could print his own money (his drawings had value), and people were willing to accept it as a form of payment. Of course, as can happen with actual money, Dalí devalued its worth by "printing" so many of them, and the drawings' value began falling below the cost of the meal. Finally the restaurant managers wised up.

The takeaway here is that anyone can print money, and that it can potentially circulate as a form of payment as long as others trust and find it convenient to use. Alternative forms of money can also be used as an investment vehicle, meaning that people might assume that money appreciates in value over time. But, as with national currencies, any money can be felled by the laws of supply and demand, as an excessive supply depreciates its worth and reduces people's willingness to use it.

▪

The world still finds itself reliant on the U.S. dollar internationally as the most important means of payment, unit of account, and reserve currency. More than half of all international debt, loans, and foreign exchange reserves are held in dollars, and about 45 percent of foreign exchange turnover and global payments use the dollar. When it comes to trade, more than 80 percent is invoiced in dollars. The supremacy of the greenback in international finance and trade, however, will be called into question as we approach 2030.

Emerging markets already account for more than half of the global economy. Moreover, China already is the largest trading nation, and it is poised to become the largest economy. But its renminbi ("the people's money" in Mandarin) is not a currency people trust—not even in China. It is not convertible, freely traded, or subject to free capital flows. If China becomes the world's leading economic power, it will be the first time in history that the world's leading economic power doesn't control the world's fiat currency. When Rome ruled the Mediterranean world, the *aureus* reigned supreme. During the heyday of Byzantium, merchants honored the *solidus* (in my view, the best name ever given to a currency). When Florence dominated commerce, the *fiorentino* was widely used. Then came the Dutch *guilder*, the Spanish and their *real de a ocho* (dubbed the "Spanish dollar" because it was widely used in the early United States), the British with the pound sterling, and, of course, the U.S. dollar. Each dominant economy or empire had a currency everybody trusted and used.

"THERE IS NO SUCH THING AS A FREE LUNCH"

As Milton Friedman, one of the most famous economists of the twentieth century, reminds us, everything has a price. Money is a peculiar and ingenious device built on trust. Government-issued currencies are sometimes backed by real assets such as gold, a strategy the British adopted during different periods of time to boost confidence and to prevent politicians from overspending and overborrowing. Of course, that required the need for actual gold, which made the British go to war twice against the Boers in South Africa, where there were significant deposits of the metal. In 1944, the United States also adopted the gold standard, to stabilize the global financial system in the last days of World War II. Later, in 1971, as deficits soared and the Federal Reserve continued to print money, President Richard Nixon brought the arrangement to an end. Since then, currency volatility, speculation, and crises have proliferated around the world.

I frequently tell my students that they can't fully understand the value of money unless they experience firsthand a country dealing with hyperinflation (the severe erosion of a currency's value coupled with the rapid rise of prices). Here's a question I ask them: Under such circumstances, would you take the bus or a taxi? Most of my students say they'd take the cheaper alternative (public transportation) when confronted with rapidly rising prices. But relative prices do not matter as much as timing when inflation runs at triple-digit rates. In other words, you're better off taking a taxi because you pay at the end of the ride, when the value of the currency has fallen, as opposed to paying up front when you board a bus. You realize that inflation has become a problem when it's relatively "cheaper" to take a taxi than a bus. Similarly, inflation benefits debtors as opposed to lenders.

Milton Friedman once said that "inflation is always and everywhere a monetary phenomenon in the sense that it is and can be produced only by a more rapid increase in the quantity of money than in output." In other words, inflation occurs when there's too much money chasing too few goods, as in the boomtowns of the American West during the gold rush or in the Great Plains during the recent shale oil boom. It follows that governments would be wise to control the supply of money if they have their citizens' economic well-being in mind. That's one way of thinking about monetary policy (that is, the policy adopted by the central bank authority of a country). For every economist who agrees with Friedman's approach, there's another who believes that this monetary orthodoxy is way too rigid in dealing with the ups and downs of the business cycle. Friedman was correct, however, in arguing that "inflation is taxation without representation," something that messes up markets, confuses decision-makers, and eventually impoverishes the population. He was in favor of a steady rate of monetary growth, and he thought that a computer would do a much better job than the Federal Reserve at managing monetary policy.

ENTER THE CRYPTOCURRENCIES

As we approach 2030, technology seems to be offering new ways of thinking about money. Unless you were a government, printing currency used to be a cumbersome, costly, and mostly illegal affair. Digital cryptocurrencies are neither cumbersome nor costly to create, and—until governments forbid them— they tend to proliferate quickly. Currently, the total value of cryptocurrencies in use reaches hundreds of billions of dollars (though this is admittedly difficult to calculate with precision). For the first time in generations, there are more currencies in circulation than countries, and this discrepancy will only broaden as more cryptocurrencies, however fleeting, are launched each year. What makes cryptocurrencies truly revolutionary is that they don't need a central government authority to be issued and circulate widely. All that's required is a computer network. Now, *that* is truly revolutionary—and potentially disruptive.

In theory, at least, cryptocurrencies also fulfill Milton Friedman's dream of "replacing the Fed with a computer." That is, instead of the governors of the Federal Reserve making decisions about interest rates and the supply of money, cryptocurrencies would be controlled by computer algorithms.

What does this exciting new world of cryptocurrencies really mean? Speculation will bring vast wealth to a few and much disappointment to most, because the value of cryptocurrencies thus far has tended to fluctuate frequently and widely. Consider how cryptocurrencies may alter citizens' relationship to their government if the government no longer has control over the value of money and the worth of assets and liabilities over time. It will certainly change the practice of finance and banking as we know it.

Cryptocurrencies are a form of electronic cash in which transactions are authenticated by senders using cryptography. Payments and balances are recorded in a kind of electronic registry that every participant can access. This record-keeping device has been given an intriguing name: the blockchain. In reality, it's a very simple idea. Imagine a mile-long brick wall. Records of various kinds can be inscribed on the bricks by people who pass by, starting with the top row. Perhaps they write their names and the date of their visit to the wall, or the names of the people they love, or the title of their favorite book. The only rule is that they must write on a brick next to one previously inscribed, ensuring that there are no gaps. Thus, as people contribute, the top row fills up, then the row below, and so forth. No record can be erased once it has been inscribed on a brick, and everyone can see each and every record. Once our imaginary wall is full, a second mile-long wall is built in parallel and the process resumes. These walls can be used for any number of purposes—for example, keeping track of who stays in each room at a hotel, how many incidental expenses each hotel guest racks up each day, and how much they pay when they check out. Or who owns each coin or banknote in circulation and when the money is used to make a payment.

Instead of keeping these kinds of records on a physical wall, we can create a digital registry of concatenated and immutable records—a blockchain. The computers with access to it verify each transaction and provide the whole system with the required transparency. Each computer has an identical copy of the entire blockchain. We can further add the safety requirement that more than half of the computers in the network must provide approval for the modification of a record of a transaction. On the face of it, the bitcoin blockchain is very secure. Consider that the likelihood of guessing a winning Powerball lottery number is 1 in 292 million. The probability of hacking a bitcoin private key, which uses 256-bit encryption, is a minuscule 1 in 2^{256}, or 1 in over 115 quattuorvigintillion—a number with seventy-six digits. That's equivalent to the odds of winning Powerball nine times in a row.

This decentralized system of transparency is exactly what Satoshi Nakamoto—a pseudonym—proposed in the famous white paper "Bitcoin: A Peer-to-Peer Electronic Cash System," posted on a cryptography mailing list on October 31, 2008. This date is significant, as it came a few weeks after Lehman Brothers collapsed. The paper proposed the revolutionary notion that "a purely peer-to-peer version of electronic cash would allow online payments to be sent directly from one party to another without going through a financial institution."

Ever since we invented money and banking, trust has been at the core of any financial activity. The boldest claim contained in the bitcoin white paper is that a cryptocurrency operationalized through the blockchain is "a system for electronic transactions without relying on trust." For Nakamoto, "the network is robust in its unstructured simplicity." It's a system in which the nodes "vote with their CPU [central processing unit] power, expressing their acceptance of valid blocks. . . . Any needed rules and incentives can be enforced with this consensus mechanism." With the stroke of a key, Nakamoto might well have brought thousands of years of financial development to an unceremonious end.

Nakamoto's purported goal was to democratize financial services, an objective shared by all cryptocurrency visionaries, aficionados, and entrepreneurs. "Our mission is to create an open financial system for the world," says Coinbase CEO Brian Armstrong. "We believe open protocols for money will create more innovation, economic freedom, and equality of opportunity, just like the Internet did for publishing information." Here we find once again the promise of a liberating technology that, proponents claim, will make the world a better place.

For every strong believer in cryptocurrency, however, there are many more who are skeptical, if not deeply hostile. "If you're 'stupid' enough to buy bitcoin," says JPMorgan Chase CEO Jamie Dimon, "you'll pay the price one day." Nouriel Roubini, whose prediction of the 2008 meltdown earned him the nickname "Dr. Doom," refers to the cryptocurrency space as a "stinking cesspool." He is on record as saying, "It is indeed laughable to think that useless cryptocurrencies or s***coins have any fundamentals of value." He believes that "their fundamental value is ZERO or actually negative . . . if you price correctly their negative externality of hogging energy and destroying the environment," referring to the fact that running the blockchain (which supports bitcoin) consumes as much electricity annually as the entire country of Austria, home to nearly 9 million people.

While bitcoin as a currency has had its ups and downs—as reflected in its value falling from a peak of nearly $20,000 at the end of 2017 to less than $2,500 a year later—the underlying digital infrastructure has endured. The reason is that the blockchain provides a simple, elegant, and efficient solution to the classic "double-spend problem." That is, how is it possible to prevent someone from using the same means of payment more than once, as when someone uses counterfeit money to pay for things? The blockchain overcomes this issue by making the digital registry open, transparent, and verifiable by the people who participate in it so that no double spend of the same bitcoin can take place. To boost confidence, cryptocurrencies promise constant and relatively slow rates of growth in their supply, always driven by a computer algorithm that is predictable and steady. Another attractive feature is that, in Nakamoto's words, "nodes can leave and rejoin the network at will, accepting the longest proof-of-work chain as proof of what happened while they were gone."

In spite of its sound technical foundation, bitcoin has largely failed to establish itself as a trustworthy and convenient means of exchange, let alone a unit of account or store of value. The reasons are complex but mostly have to do with the uncertainty as to how governments intend to regulate cryptocurrencies, and with the insatiable desire of speculators to make an easy killing. Other popular cryptocurrencies are also languishing, including XRP, Ethereum, Litecoin, Zcash, and Maker. But while no cryptocurrency has yet supplanted any physical currency, the blockchain has already begun changing the world as we know it in fundamental ways.

"THE TOKENIZATION OF EVERYTHING"

Every day, billions of transactions are made in the global market economy. With each one, there are at least two counterparties: for example, buyer and seller, insurer and insured, or borrower and lender. More broadly, humans engage in all kinds of transactions where there is a party and a counterparty, including legal agreements such as marriage, divorce, or a will that distributes property after someone dies. Technology like the blockchain may make this whole process easier and cheaper. And it won't end there. As cryptocurrency expert Joseph Buthorn argues, the blockchain could lead to the "tokenization of everything," or essentially creating a digital certificate of equities, commodities, debt, real estate, art, births, civil unions, diplomas, votes, and so on. Even data could be turned into a token, potentially disrupting the likes of Google and Facebook.

Until now, official registries were centralized and controlled by an entity or person trusted by all users or, most frequently, created by the state. While the earliest written records date back five thousand years, the printed book and, more recently, the computer changed the business of record-keeping and record-sharing. The blockchain, with its unique decentralized and immutable nature, promises to bring about even more revolutionary change.

According to a report by the European Union, digital registry technologies create "opportunities in all kinds of public services such as health and welfare payments and, at the frontier of blockchain development, are self-executing contracts paving the way for companies that run themselves without human intervention." The most pathbreaking potential of blockchains is that they "shift some control over daily interactions with technology away from central elites, redistributing it among users. In so doing, they make systems more transparent and, perhaps, more democratic." This might well reverse centuries of centralization, undo the relationship between citizens and governments, and unravel bureaucracy as we know it.

The beauty of the blockchain is that it enables all manner of lateral extensions. One possible development would combine digital currencies with smart contracts, digital record management, and decentralized autonomous organizations where decisions are made outside of the usual hierarchical structures— all supported by the blockchain. "The idea is that blockchains could track all the rights and obligations of a given contract and automatically trigger payments as the contract progresses, without anyone having to chase up payments offline," writes Mike Orcutt in the *MIT Technology Review*. Tax collection might also be made less complex by automatically deducting the government's share from every transaction recorded on the blockchain. In general, the management of supply chains would be simplified and accelerated through a combination of the mechanisms involving contract execution, record-keeping, tracking, payment collection, and restocking.

Blockchain technologies may also be used to trace the origin of certain goods, and consumers are increasingly demanding such transparency in an era flush with stories of corporate exploitation of people and resources. In the clothing industry, for instance, some companies are assigning each garment a unique digital token, which allows consumers to see into the whole supply chain, from the sourcing of materials to the distribution operation, thus helping stop the use of child labor or the use of some prohibited material.

One of my former students, Michal Benedykcinski, launched Dexio, a venture that uses blockchain technology to trace the origin of diamonds, providing assurances to customers hoping to avoid "blood diamonds"—the name attached to gemstones procured through exploitation and the dislocations of war. Another student, Ajay Anand, has focused on making sure everyone knows exactly what they're buying when they're buying an engagement ring. To do research for a paper, he traveled with other classmates to India, Bangladesh, and the Philippines to learn about child labor practices. They met with children's rights activist Kailash Satyarthi (who would win the Nobel Peace Prize in 2014). This work pushed Ajay toward thinking entrepreneurially. Inspired by an internship with the United Nations, he launched Systmapp, a company dedicated to optimizing management practices for nonprofit organizations; it's now operational in fifty countries and receives funding from the Gates Foundation. And the rings? Well, a lightbulb went off for Ajay when he decided to get engaged. He found it exceedingly difficult and time-consuming to decide which diamond ring to purchase. He was struck by the opacity in the market, with people desperately seeking information about prices and quality. He decided to use AI and machine learning to analyze market trends, launching the venture Rare Carat in October 2016. "We can predict the prices of diamonds," he claims, "more accurately than Zillow can predict the prices of homes." He presented his idea at the IBM Global Entrepreneurship competition, finished in the top fifty, and received funding. Then he used blockchain to make information in the diamond trade more transparent. Today his company has thirty employees and over $100 million in revenue.

A MATCH MADE IN CRYPTO HEAVEN

Until the digital revolution made it easier to steal software, video, music, and other types of digitized goods and services, the old system of protections— patent, trademark, and copyright—was relatively effective. That's no longer so. And as the pace of technological innovation accelerates, so does the flow of patent, trademark, and copyright applications. In 2018, *Forbes* magazine asked, "How can we make intellectual property rights 'smarter' with the blockchain?"

One of the key challenges involves the kind of sharing platforms we discussed in Chapter 7. Original music or video content not subject to a license can be shared online, with the royalties allocated and distributed through a blockchain that keeps track of what is available and how many people use it. Companies are also exploring the possibility of using the blockchain as a means to transfer ownership rights to another party and ensuring payment in exchange. Blockchain technology "can help minimize infringement as well as provide an electronic chain of custody for every piece of IP [intellectual property]." In this way, the public can judge "the strength and value of any particular work," writes Andrew Rossow in *Forbes*. According to Tracy Reilly, a professor of law at the University of Dayton, "While the digitization of copyrighted songs themselves is nothing new through platforms such as Grokster, Napster, and iTunes, what is new and very exciting for copyright owners is the vast potential by which blockchain technology may soon be able to create a workable digital footprint that would assist in better enforcement of unauthorized digital uses . . . particularly with respect to social media sites." Moreover, the blockchain can facilitate the licensing process that all artists, filmmakers, and producers go through as part of their job.

Birgit Clark, a lawyer with Baker McKenzie, argues that blockchain and IP is "a match made in crypto heaven." In her view, potential uses of the blockchain include "evidence of creatorship and provenance authentication, registering and clearing IP rights; controlling and tracking the distribution of (un)registered IP; providing evidence of genuine and/or first use in trade and/or commerce; digital rights management (e.g., online music sites); establishing and enforcing IP agreements, licenses or exclusive distribution networks through smart contracts; and transmitting payments in real-time to IP owners." The idea is to leverage a blockchain in which one can find an immutable registry of the entire history of events concerning a specific piece of property.

The current set of regulators and authenticators of intellectual property was put in place during the pre-digital age, at a time when no one could have anticipated the rapid evolution of technology. Writing in *Information Age*, Nick

Ismail argues that the blockchain can help optimize the entire innovation cycle, from brainstorming to establishing ownership and licensing. This is especially the case with complex products such as cars and computers, and also with intangible content such as software, music, and video.

"Managing IP in a globalized economy is extremely challenging," he argues. "Companies need to decide where to seek protection for ideas and then individually apply for protection in relevant geographies." The key advantage is that a digitized registry "offers the opportunity to place an initial idea on a blockchain and then update it." This new technology could become an integral part of the creative process. "Ultimately, blockchain could be more impactful on the IP industry than it has been even to the financial services industries," he notes. "The challenge will be in creating the right adoption path for the technology."

CUTTING THE RED TAPE

Other lateral applications of the blockchain would relate to the interactions between government agencies and citizens, between corporations and shareholders, between political parties and members, and between governments and voters. Most elections, for instance, are still conducted around the world using paper ballots or very rudimentary voting machines. Blockchain-enabled e-voting would eliminate the need for voting stations, making it more convenient to vote. Each citizen registered to vote would have a record on the blockchain. He or she could exercise the right to vote after authentication using a personal key. Some political parties in Denmark have used such a system for internal votes, and in Estonia companies use it to gather the votes of shareholders. Another major advantage of e-voting would be the elimination of voter intimidation. Engagement and turnout might increase, although the possibility that uneven digital accessibility could augment inequality is a concern. In fact, with blockchain technology, voter participation might be even higher among better educated and more sophisticated groups of individuals, who already have high participation rates. For national elections, the stakes would be high. "It is not enough for the result to be fair and valid," argues a study published by the European Parliament. "The whole electorate, even if they are disappointed with the result, must accept that the process was legitimate and reliable. As such, beyond providing actual security and accuracy, [e-voting] must also inspire confidence and trust."

What if we thought laterally? Consider a tantalizing opportunity: what if we used blockchain technology to force government officials to automatically act on campaign promises under certain pre-agreed conditions? For instance, after an election certain policies could be implemented through "smart contracts" or money allocated to specific budgetary categories. Or citizens could track how much the government is spending and whether it is fulfilling its promises or not. Smart contracts could be used throughout the economy, and not just in the context of government policymaking. They include a set of instructions agreed upon by the parties to a transaction that would be automatically triggered if certain conditions are met. A simple example would be a loan contract whereby a lower insurance premium on a mortgage kicks in if the market interest rate goes down. Such a contract would be, as the European Parliament put it, "self-contained, self-performed, and self-enforced," although one would need to build into it the requirement that "the law of the land always sits above the 'law' inscribed in the code."

"Algorithms that enable the creation of [blockchains] are powerful, disruptive innovations," reads the first sentence of a 2016 report by the UK government's chief scientific advisor. Blockchains "could transform the delivery of public and private services and enhance productivity through a wide range of applications." In particular, the report proposed using blockchain technology to improve government services by cutting costs, supporting compliance, and fostering accountability. It would also help collect taxes, disburse benefits, and make interactions with citizens more fluid.

DIGITAL REPUBLICS

If you would like to see what the interaction between citizens and their government will look like in 2030, visit Estonia, home to the most advanced e-government in the world, so much so that it presents itself to the world as "e-Estonia." The citizens of this tiny country of 1.3 million can apply for benefits, obtain medical prescriptions, register their businesses, vote, and access nearly three thousand other government digital services online. *Wired* magazine named Estonia "the most advanced digital society in the world." Writing for *The New Yorker*, Nathan Heller dubbed it the "Digital Republic," saying that "its government is virtual, borderless, blockchained, and secure." He refers to it as "a coordinated governmental effort to transform the country from a state to a digital society."

Estonia's model has many would-be imitators. The Catalan autonomous government sought to learn from Estonia how to set up lean and digitized state structures as part of its futile attempt to become an independent nation-state—an effort in direct contradiction with what the Estonians are actually trying to do, which is to move beyond old conceptions of the "state." Tellingly, Heller writes, the country has a "digital 'residency' program, which allows logged-in foreigners to partake of some Estonian services, such as banking, as if they were living in the country"—surely a convenience for some users and a source of revenue for Estonia, but potentially also the source of many unforeseen risks. The Estonians are in effect creating the first borderless, postmodern, virtual country. Nearly thirty thousand foreigners have so far applied for e-residency. Estonia has broken new ground thinking about lateral applications of the blockchain across the entire economy and society.

As with mobile payments and urban agriculture, some African countries, including Ghana and Kenya, are at the forefront of global efforts to bring government closer to the people through technology. According to the World Bank, "the eGhana project represented a pioneering design for ICT [information and communication technology] projects to reduce bureaucracy and bring services closer to the public that is being replicated in a number of African countries." An independent research team evaluated Kenya's efforts and concluded that the country "has created an enabling political, legal and business environment that is suitable for the implementation of . . . e-government," bringing benefits such as a "reduction of bureaucracy, round the clock accessibility of services, fast and convenient transactions, increased transparency and accountability, improved staff productivity, and easy flow of information." Ghana and Kenya continue to be at the forefront in the use of information technology, especially in the areas of health, mobile money, and public administration. The issue of the digital divide remains, however. "There exists a group of people in the rural areas who are disenfranchised as they lack skills and infrastructure to access online services offered by the government," according to the study.

Governments are capitalizing on a central feature of the blockchain. As in the business world, "the fact that data in the blockchain is immutable . . . provides transparency and accountability," the European Parliament study argues. As long as privacy and data protection are guaranteed, the blockchain could make citizens' lives easier and simplify the jobs of government employees— though perhaps making some of them redundant, as we shall see shortly. As with voting, the better-educated and those with easier access to the Internet might benefit the most, a situation that can only be overcome with renewed efforts at digital inclusion.

"A BLOCKCHAIN SOLUTION TO GUN CONTROL"

That's the title of a paper made public in November 2017 by Thomas Heston, a professor of public health at Washington State University, proposing another lateral application of the blockchain. "Blockchain technology can be utilized to improve gun control without changing existing laws," he wrote, noting that "through better gun tracking and improved screening of high-risk individuals, this technological advance in . . . technology will improve background checks on individuals and tracing of guns used in crimes." He innocently thought that "a blockchain-based digital gun safe would improve the implementation of existing gun laws, maintaining privacy and improving gun control."

The reality is that the United States lacks a centralized gun registry, which seriously limits the ability of law enforcement to prevent and investigate crimes in a country with 4.5 percent of the world's population but 42 percent of the civilian-owned guns. Gun rights defenders don't trust the federal government with such a database. "What's the natural solution to record centralization? It is record decentralization," said Luke Strgar, a computer science student at the University of California at Berkeley. "It is building a platform where the records can be maintained by the gun-owning community, so to speak." His goal is to find a solution that both sides in the gun control debate can agree upon.

No success so far, however—except that the pro-gun-rights lobby appears to be deeply concerned. Several lawmakers seemed to be so alarmed by the idea that they decided to take action. In April 2017 Arizona passed a bill banning the use of any kind of blockchain application to trace guns, the first state to do so. Nick Schroer, a Missouri state representative who sponsored a similar bill later that year, argued that "legislative members are still incredibly uneasy with the thought of a third party or a 'big brother' monitoring how many shots you take at different points of time." The promise of blockchain technology for gun control continues to be stonewalled, just like other attempts at reining in the availability of guns throughout America.

TOKENS AGAINST POVERTY

Writing in the *MIT Technology Review,* Mike Orcutt noted that "Satoshi Nakamoto invented the Bitcoin blockchain as a way for people to make financial transactions without the need for banks or governments," adding, "It's ironic that one of the world's biggest boosters of blockchains . . . is the World Bank." The World Bank is using the blockchain to allow donors to see how their money is being used to promote education. It has also launched a blockchain-based bond to raise $80 million for sustainable development initiatives. The World Bank raises $60 billion annually in the form of bonds to fund development projects, and the blockchain can reduce the number of intermediaries needed in that fund-raising process and ensure that most of the money raised actually benefits people on the ground. The technology could also help cash-strapped municipalities by streamlining their tax collection, billing, and payment procedures.

One major impediment to economic development is the lack of access by a majority of people in the world to the formal financial sector. In parts of Africa and South Asia, less than 5 percent of the population and only about half of micro and small enterprises have a bank account. The Bill and Melinda Gates

Foundation has launched the Level One Project as part of its Financial Services for the Poor program aimed at creating national digital payments systems based on the blockchain. Unlike payments made by mobile phones under existing systems, the blockchain would enable people and small firms to move money around regardless of what telecom company people subscribe to. "My dream is that all of Africa will be one big, interoperable payment platform," says Kosta Peric, the project's leader.

In Somalia, a textbook case of a "failed state," nearly 60 percent of the population is nomadic or semi-nomadic. Nonetheless, mobile payment platforms have become popular. Nine in ten Somalis age sixteen and older own a mobile phone, and seven in ten use their phone for mobile payments at least once a month. Because the country does not have a functional banking system, Somalis have no alternative to mobile payments. The downside is that the system is also used for money laundering and financing terrorism. The limited accountability and traceability of mobile phones could be improved with a blockchain-based, decentralized registry.

SAVING THE PLANET

In 2018 a 66-foot blue whale washed ashore on the Atlantic coast of Chile. Gabriela Garrido, a researcher at the Museum of Natural History Río Seco, watched in disbelief as people jumped on top of the dead mammal to take selfies and graffiti its body, in what became a viral story around the world. Alessandro Roberto, an activist for endangered species in Puerto Rico, asks, "How can we protect these species from human beings?" The Ugandan NGO Care for the Uncared is using blockchain technology to track, tag, and protect endangered species like the blue whale, the Indian tiger, the sea otter, the Asian elephant, and the giant panda. "This record would be publicly accessible in the block," says Bale Kabumba, the organization's spokesperson. "This will change the way we behave and interact with nature. This record will eventually help understand the determining factors in species extinction." Care for the Uncared is also launching a bitcoin platform to obtain donations.

In combination with the Internet of Things, made up of interconnected chips and sensors, blockchains may also help with environmental protections. One potentially important proposal is to encourage environmentally conscious behavior on the part of companies and individuals by enabling them to transform carbon credits into digital tokens that can be traded on an exchange.

The blockchain can be used to benefit the environment in other ways, too, if we think laterally. For example, the blockchain can help facilitate the process of selling excess solar power generated by homeowners without the cumbersome paperwork involved in dealing with their local utility. The European startup WePower proposes "making that power tradable and accessible to anyone" through a peer-to-peer network, writes Ben Schiller in *Fast Company*. "It's giving people more control." Nick Martyniuk, one of its co-founders, argues that "the increasingly decentralized nature of energy production will see the grid become more decentralized and the nature of the blockchain means the two developments will go hand in hand."

Energi Mine, another startup, uses the blockchain to give people "gold stars" in the form of tokens if they reduce their carbon footprint by taking public transportation, replacing their old appliances with more efficient ones, or better insulating their homes. "Because [the] tokens have a market value, they can then be redeemed to pay for energy bills, electric vehicle recharging or they can be exchanged for 'regular' (non-digital) currency," *Forbes* reported. Other startups are creating blockchains to help companies manage their carbon credits so that they can be more easily traded. Carbon credits put a price on reductions in carbon emissions, but "without a universal ledger it isn't easy to track how much carbon you've used or—if you offset it—what the impact of your reduction has been on a tangible level," says Lisa Walker, CEO of Ecosphere+. Both companies and governments will be able to keep track of how big a carbon footprint their products and services produce. Consumers would then be in a position to understand the environmental consequences of their choices. "With millions of micro-transactions scaling up to make a huge collective impact," Walker argues, the blockchain could greatly contribute to slowing climate change.

But there's a darker side to the use of information technologies to save the planet—it turns out they're major contributors to climate change themselves. Forecasts indicate that by 2030 more than 20 percent of electricity will be used to power the information and telecommunications infrastructure, *Nature* reported. "Data centers contribute around 0.3 percent to overall carbon emissions, whereas the information and communications technology (ICT) ecosystem as a whole—under a sweeping definition that encompasses personal digital devices, mobile-phone networks and televisions—accounts for more than 2 percent of global emissions. That puts ICT's carbon footprint on a par with the aviation industry's emissions from fuel." And that's not even counting the anticipated increase in cryptocurrency trading, which is extremely energy-consuming. "We are a very data-hungry society, we're using more and more and more data and all of that is using more and more energy." More than one-third of data traffic in the United States is tied to streaming on Netflix, and a similar chunk has to do with sharing high-definition photographs. The carbon footprint can only be mitigated if there's a commitment to go green. The largest American digital companies mostly operate their data centers with solar and wind power. So far, however, that's not the case in China.

WILL TOKENS KILL BANKING
(AND OTHER INDUSTRIES TOO)?

"Silicon Valley is coming," wrote Jamie Dimon in his 2015 annual letter to the shareholders of JPMorgan Chase. "There are hundreds of startups with a lot of brains and money working on various alternatives to traditional banking." Millions of jobs in the banking sector are at stake because of automation and the use of the blockchain. "As computers become smarter, we no longer need humans as intermediaries," argues Amy Webb, founder of the Future Today Institute. "Professions whose basis is in transactions will be disrupted by machines—there is no question. And it will happen fast." Experts note that of the banks, banking, and bankers of today, only one will survive the blockchain revolution. Banks are under threat because of blockchain technology in their back office, and because younger generations prefer to use apps, while bankers' jobs can be robotized, as the trend toward "robo-advising" attests. Banking can occur in the future without banks or bankers.

The impact of blockchains on the labor market will be as profound as that of the robotics we discussed in Chapter 6, precisely because it changes the rules of the game. Historically, liberal capitalism, based as it is in contract law and records, has given rise to many different kinds of occupations that act as intermediaries to handle diverse aspects of economic and financial transactions, such as trading, clearing, verification, fulfillment, settlement, and record-keeping. These occupations employ tens of millions of people worldwide. A decentralized, public, distributed blockchain that resides online, accessible to all, would push many of the intermediaries out of existence, simply by circumventing them. The financial services sector, including some well-paid jobs, might be forever altered.

Blockchain-based smart contracts, such as those mentioned earlier in this chapter, can make legions of lawyers and accountants redundant. Enrollments in U.S. law schools have plunged by 29 percent since 2010, in part due to artificial intelligence solutions for document discovery, which in part contributed to an oversupply of human lawyers, a task previously performed by young lawyers. Smart contracts might take a further bite out of the legal job market, although some experts disagree. "Lawyers worried about losing their jobs to robots, you're actually doing something that's mostly complementary to a smart contract," warns Nick Szabo, co-founder of the cryptographic assets firm Global Financial Access. "Smart contracts are mostly making possible new things that haven't been done before." In his view, "traditional law is manual, local and often uncertain," while "public blockchains are automated, global and predictable in their operations."

Accounting jobs will be severely affected by the blockchain. According to Statista, there were roughly 1.3 million people employed as accountants or auditors in the United States as of 2018. Some low-level services like account reconciliation, confirmations, receivables, and payables may be handled by the blockchain instead of people. Other tasks, such as audit, attest, and tax reporting, may be more efficiently performed with the aid of a blockchain, although accountants and auditors would still be necessary. "Blockchain is a topic that inspires equal parts fear and excitement among accounting professionals," *Accounting Today* observed, "but it does not have to be something that remains unknown."

The blockchain will change the world of 2030 because it will do away with many registries and eliminate vast amounts of paper shuffling—and jobs.

A FUTURE OF BLOCKCHAINS AND CRYPTOCURRENCIES?

It all began with turning money into encrypted tokens. As important as digital currencies will be by 2030, the potential applications of the blockchain in fields as diverse as government services, intellectual property, trade transactions, counterfeit regulation, gun control, poverty alleviation, and environmental protection, to name but a few, are tantalizing, and they are all the product of lateral thinking. I submit that cryptocurrencies will capture the imagination of large numbers of users—and perhaps regulators—only if they transform the way in which we think about money and how we use money, if they open new horizons and possibilities not only for doing business or managing our personal finances but for improving our lives. If digital currencies merely substitute for cash, then we might be disappointed. But if we can do away with the high costs of moving cash around while at the same time providing incentives for individuals to preserve resources or diminish their carbon footprint, then we might witness a tectonic shift in the world of finance—and save the planet at the same time. The trick will be to link the adoption of cryptocurrencies to some desirable behavioral change. People need to receive some immediate benefit (like ease of use or a reduced cost per transaction) in addition to the long-term benefit to everyone in society (a reduction in carbon emissions). For instance, the interest paid on my holdings of cryptocurrency should be higher if I reduce my wasteful behavior concerning food and clothes by sharing those items on a digital platform.

As I have aimed to show throughout this book, however, demographic, geopolitical, and technological forces are all in motion, whether we like it or not, and inextricably intertwined. How we deal with them will be one of the defining tests of this new world to come.

Conclusion:
Lateral Tips and Tricks to
Survive 2030

If you fight [external trends], you're probably fighting
the future. Embrace them and you have a tailwind.

—JEFF BEZOS, FOUNDER AND CEO OF AMAZON

In 2019, a team of scientists shocked the world when they announced that they had produced the first photographic evidence of a black hole, more than a hundred years after Einstein first proposed his theory of general relativity in 1915. The snapshot was actually a composite image made of myriad stills taken over a period of four days from an international network of eight radio telescopes. "We have seen what we thought was unseeable," proclaimed Sheperd Doeleman, the astrophysicist who led the effort.

Seeing the unseeable has been my mission in *2030*—the effort to visualize a metaphorical black hole, if you will, of an emerging world remade by shifting demographics, global warming, technological disruption, and geopolitical dis-array. Are we doomed?

None of us can predict the future, but we can approach it wisely. To do so, we must continuously think laterally. Here are seven principles showing how, which I'll explore in detail afterward:

1. Lose sight of the shore
2. Diversify with purpose
3. To be successful, start small
4. Anticipate dead ends
5. Approach uncertainty with optimism
6. Don't be scared of scarcity
7. Take the current

LOSE SIGHT OF THE SHORE

"You cannot swim for new horizons," William Faulkner once wrote, "until you have courage to lose sight of the shore." Fear of the unknown prevents people from seizing the opportunities embedded in the massive transformations to come in 2030 and beyond. Let me illustrate this insight with the Spanish con-quest of Mexico, one of the most perilous and improbable quests of all time. After the ruthless Hernán Cortés disembarked at Veracruz in 1519 on his way to the Aztec capital of Tenochtitlán, at the site of present-day Mexico City, he ordered his eleven ships to be scuttled. He wanted to ensure that none of his more than two hundred men attempted to return to Cuba, according to one of his soldiers. He wanted them to "rely on our own good swords and stout hearts."

The soldier-chronicler was Bernal Díaz del Castillo, born not far away from my hometown in northwestern Spain. He left for the Americas in 1514, when he was eighteen, and wrote about his many adventures throughout his life. His account reveals how Cortés, with only a sketchy understanding of the terrain, both physical and political, rallied his troops against overwhelming odds. Cortés disobeyed direct orders by Diego Velázquez de Cuéllar, the governor of

Cuba, to turn around and return to safety; Velázquez "sent two of his servants post haste . . . with orders and authority to cancel the appointment of Cortés, detain the fleet, arrest Cortés, and send him as a prisoner to Santiago," according to Díaz del Castillo's account.

But Cortés was no reckless fool. He was always toying with lateral paths of action that enabled him to cover his tracks in case a venture failed. "This matter of destroying the ships which we suggested to Cortés during our conversation," Díaz del Castillo wrote, "had already been decided on by him, but he wished it to appear as though it came from us, so that if anyone should ask him to pay for the ships, he could say that he had acted on our advice and we would all be concerned in their payment." His bold bargain paid off. He reached Tenochtitlán on November 8, 1519, nearly one year after he had set sail from Cuba. After a series of skirmishes, deceptions, and intrigues, smallpox made its fateful appearance, and the Aztec Empire collapsed in August 1521.

Population growth in Africa, immigration, automation, and cryptocurrencies strike most Americans as treacherous developments fraught with challenges and threats. Some of these concerns may not be unfounded, but fear of them hinders rather than enables adaptation to new circumstances. The lesson of Cortés is to overcome fear by looking ahead, by losing sight of the shore. Instead of assuming that immigrants compete for jobs, a dose of lateral thinking reveals their many contributions to the economy; instead of feeling pessimistic about Africa's future, we might want to partner with Africans to educate the 450 million babies to be born there before the decade is over. The forces behind automation and cryptocurrencies seem overpowering, but perhaps we can accept the reality of technological disruption, embrace innovation, and ensure that nobody is left behind.

DIVERSIFY WITH PURPOSE

In the midst of uncertainty, fear leads people to diversify—to dilute their exposure to the perceived threat. It's the old adage about not putting all your eggs in one basket. Investors, managers, and those of us who are lucky enough to have a pension fund use this tip on a daily basis to navigate the turbulent waters of an uncertain marketplace. But the principle is useful in many other circumstances, as long as one diversifies with purpose.

Consider the case of Lego, a company whose products have mesmerized generations of children and adults alike. In the 1990s this family-owned company headquartered in a quaint Danish village was reeling from the success of video games and other types of electronic toys. It decided to reinvent itself as a "lifestyle" company, venturing into Lego-branded clothing, jewelry, and watches. It also started its own video game company and a theme parks division. The efforts all failed miserably. A new chief executive appointed in 2001, Jørgen Vig Knudstorp, changed course, went "back to the brick," and reengaged with diversification, this time with purpose. It worked. Sales soared to such an extent that Lego became the largest toy company in the world, surpassing Hasbro and Mattel. It was dubbed the "Apple of toys." What did it do differently?

Diversification fails if you lose sight of your audience—and what gave you an advantage to begin with. Founded in 1932, Lego began manufacturing its signature plastic bricks in 1949 after the founder's son, Godtfred Christiansen, improved upon an existing "self-locking building brick"; the company filed for a U.S. patent for its toy in 1958. The basic idea behind it was compatibility. "Before Lego, there really was no system of toys that worked together," writes Will Reed, a math tutor, writer, and Lego enthusiast. "The versatility of this system lets the user build just about anything they can dream of: a dinosaur, car, building, even something that only exists in the world of tomorrow." The idea was highly dynamic. "Just six bricks yield more than 915 million potential combinations," wrote David Robertson in *Brick by Brick: How LEGO Rewrote the Rules of Innovation and Conquered the Global Toy Industry*. Lego redefined toys and games. "It's about problem solving. It's about collaboration. It's about acquiring skills that will help [children] to be stronger and more successful in the world," says Julia Goldin, the company's chief marketing officer. "We believe that we have a massive role to play in the lives of children in terms of their development."

Lego realized that the formula for sustainable success was to bridge the gap between generations, a key learning point for 2030. It pursued buildable action figures, board games, and family-style movies and series such as *The Lego Movie, Lego Star Wars, Lego Batman,* and *Lego Ninjago.* "Regardless of age or ability, anyone can pick up Lego pieces and let their imagination run wild," observes John Hanlon, a TV producer who launched Lego YouTube along with his brother Joshua in 2011. "Lego brings together the young and old for wholesome, non-electronic fun."

But there's a deeper way in which we must diversify with purpose in order to thrive after 2030. "Ideas are like rabbits," wrote John Steinbeck. "You get a couple and learn how to handle them, and pretty soon you have a dozen." In this vein, Lego's boldest diversification had to do with its sources of inspiration—something we all will need to address in the future. It has nearly a million adults on its Lego Ideas online community. That's how it has incorporated the digital revolution into its business—by engaging users as opposed to changing its product. Lego is relying on "the wisdom of crowds," to quote the title of James Surowiecki's best-selling book. "If you want to act in a world that is constantly disrupting," says Lars Silberbauer, Lego's director of social media and video, "you have to have [many] different perspectives on what you're doing right now." Lego has implemented a variant of crowd-sourcing to empower its customers to define the wants and needs of its core audience.

Coping with 2030 demands that we open our minds to a multitude of new ideas. It's simply misleading to believe that sticking to our long-held beliefs and ways of doing things will help us navigate the implications of the sustained increase in life expectancy, population aging, and artificial intelligence. When there are so many moving parts in the world, "time-tested" actually means "outdated." Hence the need to welcome fresh perspectives about how to, say, reinvent retirement or job descriptions in the age of the smart machine.

TO BE SUCCESSFUL, START SMALL

Another counterproductive belief when coping with large-scale change is that success must come from making big moves. When we are beset by fear, we tend to overreact. Apple—the first company to reach a market valuation of

$1 trillion—illustrates that starting from small ideas and moving incrementally through repeated iteration and lateral thinking at each step is a far better approach than attempting a major breakthrough. Apple is the firm that disrupted everything from computing and telecommunications to music and entertainment, bringing us a series of gadgets we no longer can do without. And yet its approach relies on small, incremental changes to existing products and services, always looking for new combinations, permutations, and lateral connections. In a *New Yorker* essay titled "The Tweaker," Malcolm Gladwell reflects on Walter Isaacson's biography of Steve Jobs, noting that Jobs did not invent the digital music player, the smartphone, or the tablet. Rather, he made them better, "forcing developers to do another version, and then another, about twenty iterations in all, insisting on one tiny tweak after another." Apple essentially promises its customers that their products will continuously improve over time. Each incremental improvement is driven not by a grand plan but by anticipating new market and technological shifts and by acting on customer feedback. It's like a continuous feedback loop between design and reality. Jobs knew that the best way to deal with a rapidly shifting landscape is not to plan for every move in advance but rather to be on the alert for how to improve things along the way.

The incremental approach cannot work for you unless you're open to recognizing when and where you went wrong. Stay on the lookout for the piece of feedback that doesn't fit your model of reality, then take it seriously and change course accordingly. It's called "updating your priors"—being willing to incorporate new information as you proceed.

Consider how problematic it is to stubbornly continue down the same path even when faced with evidence that what you're doing is not working. This unhelpful approach is called the "escalation of commitment," a term coined by Berkeley psychologist Barry Staw. In simple terms, it means that when faced with negative outcomes, you double down on your decision-making—either through rationalization or self-justification—even though it will only lead to more negative outcomes. The option of changing course and thus producing a desirable outcome never crosses your mind. It falls squarely in your blind spot.

A great example of the perils of the escalation of commitment without changing course is the long string of failed foreign interventions in Afghanistan.

The British, the Soviets, and the Americans each stepped up their involvement in this vast and rugged Central Asian country in spite of the warning issued by the Duke of Wellington, the military genius who defeated Napoleon at Waterloo, bringing the Frenchman's illustrious career to an end. Wellington once observed that in Afghanistan, "a small army would be annihilated and a large one starved." Every army that invaded Afghanistan ignored this piece of advice. As wars went on indefinitely with no end in sight, the invaders committed more and more troops, to no avail. No external power was able to subjugate this unwieldy country because they stubbornly stuck to a losing course of action. The generals succumbed to one of the most basic mistakes a gambler can make at the casino: thinking that by persevering one can put an end to a losing streak. Even if you lose on red ten times in a row at roulette, there's no guarantee that the wheel will fall on red the next time it spins. As 2030 approaches, don't assume that escalating will work. Massive changes call for incremental adaptation, not obstinacy.

ANTICIPATE DEAD ENDS

Lateral moves and incremental course corrections cannot occur if you find yourself in a dead end, up against the wall—a situation that tends to provoke fear. By keeping your options open, you ensure that you can adapt as the rules of the game shift. This principle goes against the conventional wisdom in much leadership thought and practice, and in myriad books providing advice for everyday life situations. For instance, the headline for a 2011 *Fast Company* article was "Why Keeping Your Options Open Is a Really, Really Bad Idea." I would argue that keeping your options open is a really, really good idea. What if you're facing overwhelming uncertainty? What if you're not sure about the implications of large-scale demographic, economic, and technological change? Isn't keeping your options open a reasonable way to proceed when you can't take anything for granted, when there are no safe assumptions you can make about the future state of the world? Wouldn't you prefer to be able to change direction if your priors about the future prove to be wrong?

The idea that having options is detrimental borrows from research by

Harvard psychology professor Dan Gilbert, who demonstrated that reversible decisions result in lower levels of satisfaction. Apparently humans are always trying to figure out if they made the right choice, which wastes their energies and leads them to wonder if they're on the right track. Keeping your options open is said to result in lower performance because your commitment to any one option isn't locked in.

Really?

Let me illustrate how "options thinking" works with an everyday-life example from my childhood. My family used to spend most of our summers at our grandparents' home. If the adults left us home alone, we would invite our cousins and the neighborhood kids over to play hide-and-seek. To make the game more thrilling, we would play in the dark. Thirty or forty kids, ranging in age from five to fifteen, would switch off all the lights and begin playing hide-and-seek. That felt scary. But there was another source of uncertainty and fear that had nothing to do with the absence of light. Rather, the older kids would change the rules of the game altogether by pursuing the younger ones around the house, scaring the hell out of them. Darkness was bad enough, but now the younger kids had to deal with true terror.

Playing hide-and-seek with limited or no visibility is a metaphor for the predicament of many people who feel frightened about being caught helpless in a rapidly changing economy, subject to threats unknown. Think about a five-year-old child panicky about being caught by the older kids; he or she gets into a room, heads for the closet, and hides there. Inevitably, the younger kid will be found and tickled mercilessly by the older kids, and the younger one will have no option to escape.

Let's say that to avoid that fate, the little kid retains McKinsey consultants for advice. What do you think they would suggest?

Well, there are a number of things that might improve the kid's situation. The first step is to choose a large room rather than a small one, and preferably a room with more than one door. The next step would be to keep the doors open and to stand at an equal distance from each of them, not to hide under a table or inside the closet. In following that chain of decisions, the little kid would be maximizing the value of his or her options, while hiding inside the closet would reduce those options to zero.

This is what keeping your options open is all about. Never make decisions that run you into a corner, with no escape route. Never do anything that precludes a lateral move. Avoid making decisions that are irreversible or costly to reverse. Invest in real options, which are similar to financial options in that they increase in value the larger uncertainty looms.

Let's listen to an actual McKinsey consultant explain the logic. "Real options can be valuable because they allow decision-makers to re-optimise over time without incurring substantial sunk costs," argues Hugh Courtney, an associate principal in the company's strategy practice. The trick consists of overcoming the "all-or-nothing, now-or-never" dilemma by recognizing that there are different shades of gray between the extremes of doing nothing and diving into the pool. "Options preserve the potential upside that greater uncertainty creates, while limiting the downside." In a way, options thinking is a more general approach that includes committing to a course of action as a special case of a wider array of options. "The best strategic decision-makers then," concludes Courtney, "should systematically address real option and full-commitment alternatives, and 'keep their options open' when it comes to deciding whether or not to 'keep their options open.'" The lesson here is that each of us should focus on preserving our options, lest the transformations ahead catch us off guard, and we end up stuck with nowhere to turn.

APPROACH UNCERTAINTY WITH OPTIMISM

"Every day is a new opportunity," legendary baseball pitcher Bob Feller once said. "You can build on yesterday's success or put its failures behind and start over again." Fear of the uncertain is such a formidable stressor that even seasoned athletes reel from "competition anxiety," especially when they are thrown off balance by an unanticipated turn of events in the field—perhaps when an opponent scores an implausible point or when an unforced mistake puts them on the defensive. Musicians and actors call it stage fright.

Like elite athletes and music virtuosos, we feel more anxious about our own future when we perceive that we've lost control over our environment. Anxiety about failing induces us to try to avoid losses rather than to lock in wins. This phenomenon is called the "loss aversion bias," as we saw in Chapter 1. Recall that this bias leads people to prefer avoiding losses over locking in equivalent gains.

The bottom line is that the more we focus on opportunities rather than downsides, the greater our chances of adapting successfully to the challenges of 2030. As Winston Churchill once put it, "The pessimist sees difficulty in every opportunity, while the optimist sees opportunity in every difficulty." Climate change, for example, feels like an intractable problem, but every problem presents an opportunity for action.

DON'T BE SCARED OF SCARCITY

By 2030, we will have to wrestle with shortages of freshwater, clean air, and hospitable land. Perhaps we can learn a lateral trick or two from older societies that had to overcome significant environmental crises of their own. Consider Rapa Nui, better known as Easter Island, often mentioned as the world's most remote inhabited place. This tiny volcanic enclave of sixty-three square miles was once home to a stunning civilization that had remarkable artistic, religious, and political achievements, including the building of the thousand-odd larger-than-life statues known as moai, the largest weighing over eighty tons and measuring nearly thirty feet in height.

Rapanui civilization went into a tailspin after depleting its resource base well before Europeans arrived in 1722. "The parallels between Easter Island and the whole modern world are chillingly obvious," writes Jared Diamond in his insightful best-selling book *Collapse*. "Polynesian Easter Island was as isolated in the Pacific Ocean as the Earth is today in space," with no possibility of escape or outside assistance. "Those are the reasons why people see the collapse of Easter Island society as a metaphor, a worst-case scenario, for what may lie ahead of us in our own future."

The conventional story, as laid out by Diamond and others, tells of fanatical competition among a dozen territorial clans on the island. "The increase in statue size with time suggests competition between rival chiefs commissioning the statues to outdo each other. . . . I cannot resist the thought that they were produced as a show of one-upmanship." Diamond's narrative begins with population growth and competitive moai carving, followed by forest clearing for intensive agriculture and statue transportation, biodiversity losses, dwindling food production, and ultimately "starvation, a population crash, and a descent into cannibalism."

Anthropologist Terry Hunt and archaeologist Carl Lipo tell a different story in their book *The Statues That Walked*. "It was not a reckless mania for moai that exhausted the island's forest and tipped the ecological scales towards catastrophe." The forests were destroyed not by humans but mainly by the rats that traveled with them in their canoes when they colonized the tiny island. The islanders did not fight each other, as indicated by the dearth of weapons found and the relative scarcity of skeletons with evidence of violence. And they engaged in lateral innovations to feed a growing population on such a barren piece of land. "Little by little the island was transformed into an endless series of gardens," some twenty-five hundred of them, enclosed by protective stone walls.

Regardless of whose narrative you find more compelling, the key point to grasp is that this stone-age civilization flourished in the first place not because they had access to plentiful resources, for they never did. Two archaeologists write that "the story of Rapa Nui is one not of ecological suicide but of persistence and resilience in which the islanders employed innovative approaches." The real enigma, then, is not why this Polynesian society collapsed, but how it managed to do so well over hundreds of years on a small and isolated island devoid of significant natural resources.

The innovation capacity of the people of Rapa Nui is best exemplified by the techniques behind the design and transportation of the massive moai without wheels or draft animals. Experimental research indicates that teams of no more than twenty people can make the statues "walk" upright for miles from the only quarry on the island along carefully constructed roads by methodically using ropes to rock the multi-ton monoliths sideways, as if they were an inverse pendulum. In all likelihood, they didn't use any wood for sleds, rollers, or sliders.

Not surprisingly, global warming presently poses the greatest threat to Rapanui culture. The moai on the platforms next to the water are at risk of being flooded by rising sea levels. "You feel an impotency in this, to not be able to protect the bones of your own ancestors," says Camilo Rapu, leader of the indigenous organization that runs Rapa Nui National Park. "It hurts immensely." But Sebastián Paoa, the head of planning, is guardedly optimistic. "They knew their environment was coming apart, but that didn't stop them from persisting here," he said. "It's the same with climate change today." Globally, the current climate crisis means that we're going to have to do with fewer resources and lower gas emissions even as global middle-class consumption and cities continue to grow.

Perhaps archaeologist Paul Bahn and botanist John Flenley put it best when they wrote that there's a dual message in Rapa Nui's history. "There's a lesson for our planet, but at the same time a hopeful example of humans' capacity to innovate and to overcome adversities. . . . The islanders managed to adapt themselves quite successfully to new circumstances." The unique takeaway from Rapa Nui, Bahn and Flenley conclude, has to do not with its decline but with the fact that "peace appears to have reigned for a millennium." According to anthropologist Dale Simpson Jr., the different territorial clans did not appear to be in competition or conflict with one another. Rather, a "continued pattern of minimum sources–maximum use suggests a form of collaboration," whereby territorial clans shared resources as needed. "I think that that goes against the collapse model that says all they were doing was competing to build bigger statues," Simpson asserts.

In their quest for survival, the Rapanui went as far as changing their culture—something we may have to do as well. They switched from "a religion based on deifying ancestors (a typical Polynesian pattern) to a single deity, the god-creator Make Make, with most rituals and ceremonies centered on fruitfulness and fertility, including human fertility." The new cultural practice included an annual competition or "ritual race for the first egg" to select the "birdman," who would rule for the following year, a rather peaceful and effective way of coping with a declining resource base. Thus, the islanders had already started to move away from the gargantuan and consuming task of moai creation well before the Europeans arrived. "It is estimated that no more stat-ues, or very few of them, were erected after 1500." The birdman competition was a governance solution to the distribution of scarce resources among terri-torial clans not unlike those proposed by Elinor Ostrom in order to overcome the tragedy of the commons. Perhaps we can conclude, with geologist David Bressan, that prehistoric Rapa Nui is an example of "a society deprived of many future possibilities"—just like ours.

As we approach 2030, our mindset should be to avoid reducing our options by innovating and by preserving our finite riches. Mundane adaptations and lateral thinking will go a long way toward arresting climate change and other global threats if we adopt more environmentally friendly behaviors.

TAKE THE CURRENT

The rules of the game keep changing. While the only possible response to change is change itself, one cannot successfully respond to any transformation—large or small—by merely trying to minimize losses or by overcoming scarcities one at a time, as they manifest themselves. The seventh and last principle is to become "surfers" and organize ourselves to catch the waves of demographic, economic, cultural, and technological change as they come our way. In Shake-speare's *Julius Caesar*, Brutus voiced this principle in very simple terms: "And we must take the current when it serves, or lose our ventures."

The importance of riding the wave of change manifests itself across many areas of the economy and of technology. We frequently wonder what the next big business or technological breakthrough might be. Yet the history of in-vention is replete with examples of ideas whose shining moment had not yet arrived because there was no trend to serve as a tailwind. In fact, many entre-preneurs succeed by retrieving from oblivion some long-forgotten insight or device, only to infuse it with a new life years, decades, or even centuries after it was first envisioned or discovered. "When you watch the technology indus-try long enough," write Ron Miller and Alex Wilhelm, "you begin to see some of the same ideas recycled. Maybe they didn't catch on the first time because they were too early." WebVan failed in the 1990s in the business of grocery home delivery two decades before a torrent of startups conquered that space; the IBM Simon smartphone, fitted with a touchscreen keypad, launched in 1992, fifteen years ahead of the iPhone; the "information rights management" concept emerged a few years before cloud computing became pervasive; Microsoft's Tablet PC predated the iPad by a decade; and PointCast came up with the idea of imposing character limits on the length of messages a decade before Twitter. "Just because an idea isn't original doesn't mean it won't succeed," conclude Miller and Wilhelm. "The world may be more ready for these concepts than when the early companies made their first attempts." Precocious companies often languish, while those that wait for the right moment succeed. "You cannot resist an idea whose time has come," cautioned Victor Hugo.

▪

It isn't yet too late to prepare for 2030. The first, indispensable step is to realize that the world as we know it will irretrievably evanesce at some point during our lifetime, most likely within ten years. This awareness must lead to challenging received wisdom instead of continuing to honor inherited assumptions and ways of thinking. Pursue lateral connections by diversifying your ideas, taking incremental steps, keeping your options open, focusing on opportunity, considering scarcity as an incentive, and riding the tailwinds.

We will not survive the challenges of 2030 unless we change our traditional mindset, which is too linear and too vertical to help us. It isn't too late to prepare yourself for the transformations ahead. Success will require striking a delicate balance around each of the seven lateral tips and tricks. And remember: there's no turning back. The world as we know it is about to change, and it won't be returning anytime soon, if ever. The rules are changing—forever.

"It's a great game—the pursuit of happiness," wrote the playwright Eugene O'Neill.

Embrace 2030, and seize the opportunities ahead.

Postscript

HOW A DISRUPTIVE EVENT LIKE COVID-19 IMPACTS
THE TRENDS DISCUSSED IN 2030

On November 17, 2019, the first case of COVID-19, an infectious disease caused by a novel strain of coronavirus, was detected in the Wuhan Province of China. By the middle of March, the pathogen had spread to over a hundred countries, and the World Health Organization declared it a global pandemic emergency. At the time of this writing (March 2020), the scale of the pandemic is not completely known, but it will certainly infect hundreds of thousands if not millions of people around the world. Already, its significant impact on consumer and financial markets has prompted governments to engage in dramatic fiscal and monetary policies to minimize the damage. It's quite possible that by the time this book is first published, in August 2020, a prolonged recession and sharp rise in unemployment will be a part of our global reality. As I said in the introduction, it's impossible to know what the future holds, but the COVID crisis offers a unique case study in how a surprising phenomenon with global consequences impacts the arguments in this book.

Most people believe that a major crisis disrupts ongoing trends, as if there is a clear "before" and "after." The coronavirus pandemic is one such crisis, but contrary to conventional wisdom it will most likely intensify and accelerate—rather than derail—the trends analyzed here. Consider the declining fertility rate discussed in Chapter 1. There are three reasons why a pandemic will accelerate that trend. First, people usually postpone major decisions (like having a baby) when faced with uncertainty. Second, having a baby is a financial commitment, and the threat of a recession will force many to reconsider whether the timing is right. We saw this during the Great Depression in the 1930s and in the aftermath of the 2008 financial crisis. Third, life-altering events like war, natural disasters, and pandemics disrupt our daily routines and priorities, and this includes our fertility decisions.

The divergence of generational experiences, discussed in Chapter 2, is another trend that will accelerate. As of this writing, the virus is considered lethal to people who are immunocompromised, which includes many people over the age of sixty and people with pre-existing medical conditions. The virus also seems to affect age groups differently, which is all the more troubling when we consider how common generational mixing is nowadays. And as we look to the future of populations and aging, with Europe and East Asia composed of an older age cohort and Africa and South Asia experiencing a baby boom, the share of the world's population moving to the latter will only accelerate if the mortality rate internationally continues at the pace we are witnessing.

The crisis will also continue the existing trend toward inequality: the working poor and the homeless, in particular, are unlikely to have access to good healthcare, and their immune systems may already be compromised due to poor diets or insalubrious living conditions. While the virus won't discriminate by income or healthcare coverage, people at the bottom of the socioeconomic pyramid are far more exposed to the consequences of infection.

There are also grave economic consequences to this crisis we must consider. For example, the pandemic comes at the worst time for many European countries, which are still recovering from the 2008 financial crisis. Italy and Spain, in particular, are among the most affected, and with their public sectors severely underfunded, they will be limited in what they can do. Europe's middle class is already stagnant compared to the middle classes of emerging markets, as we saw in Chapter 3, and this trend will only intensify during the pandemic. For countries that are already politically unstable or economically vulnerable, like Iran, the crisis will be a severe test for leadership, as pressure will mount from all sides by an already anxious public.

As a society, we are generally prepared to cope with familiar natural disasters like earthquakes or hurricanes. There are guidelines for people and companies to follow. Our infrastructure, like commercial buildings and residential housing, is built to withstand such catastrophes. Are we equipped to do the same with pandemics? The World Health Organization recorded 1,307 regional epidemic outbreaks between 2011 and 2017. Generally, the world faces a global pandemic every forty to seventy years: the Third Plague of 1855, the flu pandemic of 1918–1919, the AIDS pandemic beginning in the early 1980s, and now COVID-19 in 2020. Significant earthquakes occur in roughly the same intervals: for instance, in the San Francisco Bay area, the last two big earthquakes occurred in 1906 and 1989. Similar to our contingency plans for earthquakes, both the public and private sectors should have protocols in place to effectively manage the moment when an epidemic becomes a pandemic. The existence of such protocols should ease public hysteria and concern. They would include, of course, a healthcare system that's well staffed and equipped to handle a public health crisis and to scale its efforts accordingly.

Aside from policy decisions, personal responsibility solutions such as social distancing and "sheltering in place" to limit community spread are more important in densely populated areas like cities (which, as we saw in Chapter 5, is where most people are headed in 2030 and beyond). These will intensify several trends under way: online shopping (Amazon, feeling the demand surge, went on a hiring spree and increased overtime pay for all warehouse employees), virtual communication (from remote work to maintaining social connections, nearly everyone has turned to telecommunication services like Zoom or WhatsApp to stay in touch), and digital entertainment (producers of movies, books, and music, for example, will be forced to find their customers online rather than in bricks-and-mortar retail establishments). The sharing economy, already a disruptive force, will further accelerate under the crisis; which industries suffer consequences (like transport) and which will experience a boom (like digital platforms) will have lasting effects on how we live, work, and interact with each other and the economy for the foreseeable future. Add to that the emerging revolution in technology, which I compare in significance to the Cambrian explosion, explored in Chapter 6. For example, 3D printers are already being used to produce healthcare necessitites like ventilators and respirators—a sign that this technology will move to the forefront of society sooner rather than later.

How all these trends intensify and adapt to something like the coronavirus is unfolding before our very eyes. Most of the trends—from declining fertility, to intergenerational dynamics, to the use of technology—will accelerate due to the pandemic. But the key question we must ask ourselves is whether something like COVID-19 (or the next unforeseen crisis) will better prepare us or blind us to the collective changes already under way that, as I argue, will reach a tipping point within the next decade.

ACKNOWLEDGMENTS

No author is an island, and this book has been long in the making. I started to do research on it seven years ago. During this time, I have benefited from the stimulating intellectual environment of the Wharton School and the University of Pennsylvania, which enabled me to focus on the research that led to this book.

I was fortunate to be guided by some of the most helpful and fun-to-work-with people in the book world: Jane von Mehren of Aevitas Creative Management; at St. Martin's Press, my editor, Pronoy Sarkar, production editor Alan Bradshaw, and copy editor Sue Warga; Barbara Monteiro of Monteiro & Company; and my team of publicists at FINN Partners, Paul Sliker, Louisa Baxley, and Stacy Topalian. Francis Hoch at Chartwell Speakers Bureau also helped with getting the word out about the book and its main ideas. Their professionalism and sheer intellectual drive were a constant source of inspiration and encouragement. Jane opened up an entire new universe of possibilities for me in the publishing world. Pronoy was the best editor I could possibly have, focused as he was on the primacy of ideas and on the best way to convey them. I am also grateful to Michelle Cashman, Gabi Gantz, Laura Clark, Paul Hochman, Ervin Serrano, and the rest of the St. Martin's Press team for their commitment to this book.

I am most grateful to the thousands of students, executives, and policymakers who asked me tough questions during presentations based on the book. I also received encouraging feedback from the tens of thousands of people who have taken my Coursera and Wharton online classes. Benito Cachinero, José Manuel Campa, Carlos de la Cruz, Álvaro Cuervo, Mohamed El-Erian, Julio García Cobos, Geoffrey Garrett, Victoria Johnson, Emilio Ontiveros, Sandra Suárez, and Joseph Westphal provided me with myriad excellent leads and tips on the various topics covered in the book.

My wife, Sandra, and my daughters, Daniela and Andrea, allowed me to submerge myself in the book and to travel incessantly to distant places in search of material. I dedicate this book to the three of them.

SOURCES

SOME FACTS AND FIGURES

All websites last accessed on November 1, 2019.

On African agriculture, see African Development Bank, "Africa Agribusiness," https://www .afdb.org/en/news-and-events/africa-agribusiness-a-us-1-trillion-business-by-2030-18678.

The projections on women's wealth come from Capgemini and RBC Wealth Management, *World Wealth Report*, 2014, https://worldwealthreport.com/wp-content/uploads/sites/7 /2018/10/2014-World-Wealth-Report-English.pdf.

The projections on hunger and obesity are from UN, "Goal 2: Zero Hunger," https://www.un .org/sustainabledevelopment/hunger; UN, "Pathways to Zero Hunger," https://www.un .org/zerohunger/content/challenge-hunger-can-be-eliminated-our-lifetimes; T. Kelly et al., "Global Burden of Obesity in 2005 and Projections to 2030," *International Journal of Obesity* 32, no. 9 (2008): 1431–1437; WHO, "Obesity and Overweight," February 16, 2018, https://www.who.int/news-room/fact-sheets/detail/obesity-and-overweight##targetText

=Some%20recent%20WHO%20global%20estimates,%25%20of%20women)%20
were%20overweight. See also the sources to Chapter 5.

The data on cities are from Chapter 5; see sources for that chapter.

The data and projections on babies are from Chapter 1; see sources for that chapter.

The data and projections on the middle class are from Chapter 3; see sources for that chapter.

INTRODUCTION: THE CLOCK IS TICKING

All websites last accessed on September 22, 2019.

The statistics mentioned in this introduction are referenced in subsequent chapters.

The words by Judge Taylor in Harper Lee's *To Kill a Mockingbird* are in chapter 17.

The Indian Mars mission budget is discussed in Ipsita Agarwal, "These Scientists Sent a Rocket to Mars for Less than It Cost to Make 'The Martian,'" *Wired*, March 17, 2017. See also Jonathan Amos, "Why India's Mars Mission Is So Cheap—and Thrilling," BBC, September 24, 2014, https://www.bbc.com/news/science-environment-29341850.

On the Indian finding of water on the Moon and NASA's confirmation, see Helen Pidd, "India's First Lunar Mission Finds Water on Moon," *Guardian*, September 24, 2009; Jesse Shanahan, "NASA Confirms the Existence of Water on the Moon," *Forbes*, August 22, 2018.

De Bono's quote is from Shane Snow, "How to Apply Lateral Thinking to Your Creative Work," 2014, https://99u.adobe.com/articles/31987/how-to-apply-lateral-thinking-to-your-creative-work.

The title of George Day and Paul J. H. Schoemaker's book is *Peripheral Vision: Detecting the Weak Signals That Will Make or Break Your Company* (Boston: Harvard Business School Press, 2006).

Proust's quote is from his book *The Captive*, which is the fifth volume of *Remembrance of Things Past*, published in 1923. The full text is available at http://gutenberg.net.au/ebooks03/0300501h.html.

CHAPTER 1: FOLLOW THE BABIES

All websites last accessed on May 12, 2019.

The Edwin Cannan quote is from V. C. Sinha and Easo Zacharia, *Elements of Demography* (New Delhi: Allied Publishers, 1984), 233.

Paul R. Ehrlich and Anne Ehrlich's book, *The Population Bomb*, was published in 1968 by Sierra Club/Ballantine Books. For some reason, she was uncredited as an author. A concise guide to different theories of population can be found at http://www.economicsdiscussion.net/theory-of-population/top-3-theories-of-population-with-diagram/18461. A good introduction to demographic theories and trends appears in chapter 4 of *Global Turning Points*, by Mauro F. Guillén and Emilio Ontiveros, 2nd ed. (Cambridge: Cambridge University Press, 2016). The data and forecasts on population, fertility, and life expectancy are compiled and updated regularly by the United Nations Population Division, http://www.un.org/en/development/desa/population. The data for the first chart in this chapter were calculated using the medium population projection.

The Malthus quote comes from *An Essay on the Principle of Population*, originally published in 1798, http://www.esp.org/books/malthus/population/malthus.pdf, 44. On the declining appetite for sex in the United States, see Jean M. Twenge, Ryne A. Sherman, and Brooke E. Wells, "Declines in Sexual Frequency Among American Adults, 1989–2014," *Archives of Sexual Behavior* 46, no. 8 (2017): 2389–2401.

On blackouts and their effect on fertility, see A. Burlando, "Power Outages, Power Externalities, and Baby Booms," *Demography* 51, no. 4 (2014): 1477–1500; and Amar Shanghavi, "Blackout Babies: The Impact of Power Cuts on Fertility," *CentrePiece* (London School of Economics), Autumn 2013.

The survey on and personal examples of why Americans are not having as many babies as in the past are discussed in Claire Cain Miller, "Americans Are Having Fewer Babies. They Told Us Why," *New York Times*, July 5, 2018. The estimates of how much it costs to raise a child in the United States are summarized in Abha Bhattarai, "It's More Expensive than Ever to Raise a Child in the U.S.," *Washington Post*, January 10, 2017.

Gary Becker's demographic theories are aptly summarized by Matthias Doepke, "Gary Becker on the Quantity and Quality of Children," *Journal of Demographic Economics* 81 (2015): 59–66. The quote comes from Gary Becker, *A Treatise on the Family* (Cambridge, MA: Harvard University Press, 1991), 144.

The data on Chinese fertility in rural and urban areas before and after the adoption of the one-child policy come from Junsen Zhang, "The Evolution of China's One-Child Policy and Its Effects on Family Outcomes," *Journal of Economic Perspectives* 31, no. 1 (2017): 141–160. The myths surrounding the one-child policy are discussed in Martin King Whyte, Wang Feng, and Yong Cai, "Challenging Myths About China's One-Child Policy," *China Journal* 74 (2015): 144–159, and by Amartya Sen, "Women's Progress Outdid China's One-Child Policy," *New York Times*, November 2, 2015.

The savings surplus in China due to the one-child policy is assessed in Shang-Jin Wei and Xiaobo Zhang, "The Competitive Savings Motive: Evidence from Rising Sex Ratios and Savings Rates in China," NBER Working Paper no. 15093, 2009; Taha Choukhmane, Nicolas Coeurdacier, and Keyu Jin, "The One-Child Policy and Household Savings," September 18, 2014, https://economics.yale.edu/sites/default/files/tahamaclunch100214_2.pdf.

The data on digital dating services come from Statista, *eServices Report 2017* (Hamburg: Statista, 2017). The experiment on the Chinese dating platform was conducted by David Ong and Jue Wang, "Income Attraction: An Online Dating Field Experiment," *Journal of Economic Behavior and Organization* 111 (2015): 13–22.

The Siberian shortage of men and the study by Caroline Humphrey were reported in Mira Katbamna, "Half a Good Man Is Better than None at All," *Guardian*, October 26, 2009. See also Kate Bolick, "All the Single Ladies," *Atlantic*, November 2011.

The stories of Samuel Owiti Awino, Celestina Mumba, Felix Afolabi, and other African farmers are recounted on the African Agricultural Technology Foundation website, https://www.aatf-africa.org/fieldstories.

On Africa's fifty-four soverign states, see Center for Systemic Peace, Global Report 2017, www.systemicpeace.org/vlibrary/GlobalReport2017.pdf.

On cassava farming in Africa, see Emiko Terazono, "African Farming: Cassava Now the Centre of Attention," *Financial Times*, January 21, 2014. The story of Naomi Wanjiru Nganga is recounted in Harry McGee, "How the Mobile Phone Changed Kenya," *Irish Times*, May 14, 2016. E-health initiatives in Kenya are described in Martin Njoroge, Dejan Zurovac, Esther A. A. Ogara, Jane Chuma, and Doris Kirigia, "Assessing the Feasibility of eHealth and mHealth: A Systematic Review and Analysis of Initiatives Implemented in Kenya," *BMC Research Notes* 10 (2017): 90–101.

The data, analysis, and quotes on the characteristics of immigrants are from *UN Migration Report 2015* (New York: United Nations, 2015); OECD, *Is Migration Good for the Economy?* (Paris: OECD, 2014); Giovanni Peri, "Immigrants, Productivity, and Labor Markets," *Journal of Economic Perspectives* 30, no. 4 (2016): 3–30; David H. Autor, "Why Are There Still So Many Jobs?," *Journal of Economic Perspectives* 29, no. 3: 3–30; and National Academies of Sciences, Engineering and Medicine, *The Economic and Fiscal Consequences of Immigration* (Washington, DC: National Academies Press, 2017).

For statistics on foreign-born workers in the United States, see Nicole Prchal Svajlenka, "Immigrant Workers Are Important to Filling Growing Occupations," Center for American Progress, May 11, 2017, https://www.americanprogress.org/issues/immigration/news/2017/05 /11/431974/immigrant-workers-important-filling-growing-occupations. The research by Britta Glennon is described in Stuart Anderson, "Restrictions on H-1B Visas Found to Push Jobs Out of the U.S.," *Forbes*, October 2, 2019.

The data and analysis on immigrant-founded ventures and companies come from Stuart Anderson, *American Made 2.0: How Immigrant Entrepreneurs Continue to Contribute to the U.S. Economy* (Washington, DC: National Venture Capital Association, 2015); Stuart Anderson, *Immigrant Founders and Key Personnel in America's 50 Top Venture-Funded Companies* (Arlington, VA: National Foundation for American Policy, 2011); and Stuart Anderson, *Immigrants and Billion Dollar Startups* (Arlington, VA: National Foundation for American Policy, 2016).

The data on foreign-born workers in the U.S. healthcare sector come from George Mason University Institute for Immigration Research, "Immigrants in Healthcare," June 2016; Anupam B. Jena, "U.S. Immigration Policy and American Medical Research: The Scientific Contributions of Foreign Medical Graduates," *Annals of Internal Medicine* 167, no. 8 (2017): 584–586.

On the loss aversion bias, see Daniel Kahneman and Amos Tversky, "Choices, Values, and Frames," *American Psychologist* 39, no. 4 (1984): 341–350; Daniel Kahneman and Amos Tversky, "Advances in Prospect Theory: Cumulative Representation of Uncertainty," *Journal of Risk and Uncertainty* 5, no. 4 (1992): 297–323; Thea Wiig, "Can Framing Change Individual Attitudes Towards Migration?," master's thesis, University of Bergen, 2017, https://pdfs.semanticscholar.org/f48f/2aac7860277f9fb97e234f0d28963b5d618d.pdf; Mehtap Akgüç et al., "Risk Attitudes and Migration," *China Economic Review* 37, no. C (2016): 166–176; William A. V. Clark and William Lisowski, "Prospect Theory and the Decision to Move or Stay," *Proceedings of the National Academy of Sciences* 114, no. 36 (2017): E7432–E7440; Mathias Czaika, "Migration and Economic Prospects," *Journal of Ethnic and Migration Studies* 41, no. 1 (2015): 58–82; James Surowiecki, "Losers!," *New Yorker*, May 30, 2016.

On the impact of immigration on Social Security, see *The 2018 Report of the Board of Trustees of the Federal Old-Age and Survivors Insurance and Federal Disability Insurance Trust Funds* (Washington, DC: Social Security Administration, 2018), https://www.ssa.gov/OACT /TR/2018/tr2018.pdf; Andrew Cline, "Social Security and Medicare Are Slowly Dying, but No One in Washington Will Lift a Finger," *USA Today*, June 13, 2018; Alexia Fernández Campbell, "Why Baby Boomers Need Immigrants to Fund Their Retirement," *Vox*, October 23, 2018, https://www.vox.com/2018/8/1/17561014/immigration-social-security; Nina Roberts, "Undocumented Immigrants Quietly Pay Billions into Social Security and Receive No Benefits," Marketplace, January 28, 2019, https://www.marketplace.org/2019/01/28 /undocumented-immigrants-quietly-pay-billions-social-security-and-receive-no.

The concept of "brain circulation" was developed in AnnaLee Saxenian, "From Brain Drain to Brain Circulation: Transnational Communities and Regional Upgrading in India and China," *Studies in Comparative International Development* 40 (2005): 35–61. The World

Bank study on transnational entrepreneurs was published as *Diaspora Networks and the International Migration of Skills* (Washington, DC: World Bank, 2006). On Miin Wu, see AnnaLee Saxenian, "Brain Circulation: How High-Skill Immigration Makes Everyone Better Off," Brookings Institution, 2002, https://www.brookings.edu/articles/brain-circulation -how-high-skill-immigration-makes-everyone-better-off. On James Joo-Jin Kim, see Tim Hyland, "Kim: 'There Is Much to Be Done,'" *Wharton Magazine*, Summer 2010, http:// whartonmagazine.com/issues/summer-2010/kim-there-is-much-to-be-done/#sthash .bepdPPNK.dpbs.

The Conference Board of Canada study can be found at https://www.conferenceboard.ca /press/newsrelease/2018/05/15/imagining-canada-s-economy-without-immigration ?AspxAutoDetectCookieSupport=1.

CHAPTER 2: GRAY IS THE NEW BLACK

All websites accessed on July 9, 2019.

Throughout the chapter, data on the number of people in different age groups are from United Nations, World Population Prospects, 2019 Revision, https://population.un.org/wpp.

The quote from Morgan Stanley is from John Gapper, "How Millennials Became the World's Most Powerful Consumers," *Financial Times*, June 6, 2018. The media headlines about millennials are compiled in Carly Stern, "'I Wanted to Make a Memorial of All Our Destruction,'" *Daily Mail*, August 17, 2017.

Healthcare spending in the United States by age group is analyzed in Tate Ryan-Mosley, "U.S. Health-Care Costs Are Soaring, but Don't Blame Old People," *MIT Technology Review*, September–October 2019, 57.

On the wealth of the senior population, see AARP and Oxford Economics, *The Longevity Economy: How People over 50 Are Driving Economic and Social Value in the US*, September 2016, https://www.aarp.org/content/dam/aarp/home-and-family/personal-technology/2016/09 /2016-Longevity-Economy-AARP.pdf.

Neil Howe's quotes and the wealth data from the Federal Reserve are in Neil Howe, "The Graying of Wealth," *Forbes*, March 16, 2018. The quote by John Dos Passos can be found at https://www.brainyquote.com/quotes/john_dos_passos_402864. Linda Bernstein's article "What to Say When They Blame It on the Boomers" appeared in *Forbes*, November 15, 2016.

The theories of generations quoted in the text come from Karl Mannheim, "The Problem of Generations," in *Essays on the Sociology of Knowledge*, edited by Paul Kecskemeti (London: Routledge & Kegan Paul, 1952), 276–322; Pierre Bourdieu, *Outline of a Theory of Practice* (Cambridge: Cambridge University Press, 1977).

The quote from Peggy Noonan is from https://www.brainyquote.com/quotes/peggy_noonan _159262.

Stefano Hatfield's article appeared as "Why Is Advertising Not Aimed at the Over-50s?," *Guardian*, December 3, 2014. The AARP's article "Selling Older Consumers Short" can be found at https://www.aarp.org/money/budgeting-saving/info-2014/advertising-to-baby -boomers.html.

On seniors as a consumer group, see Paul Irving, "Aging Populations: A Blessing for Business," *Forbes*, February 23, 2018; "The Grey Market," *Economist*, April 7, 2016; Elizabeth Wilson, "Find Hidden Opportunities in the Senior Market," *Entrepreneur*, April 16, 2019. The Wilson article includes the quote from Maria Henke, while Chanel's comes from Ben Cooper, "Analysis: Why Retailers Should Be Engaging the Aging," *Retail Week*, July 28, 2017.

The quotes by Jeff Beer, Sarah Rabia, and Nadia Tuma are from Jeff Beer, "Why Marketing to Seniors Is So Terrible," *Fast Company*, June 6, 2019.

The quotes about washing machines are from Nellie Day, "Elder Friendly Guide to Top-Loading Washing Machines," Elder Gadget, December 1, 2019, http://eldergadget.com/eldergadget -guide-to-top-loading-washing-machines.

The data on quality of life of seniors are from "The United States of Aging Survey," https:// www.aarp.org/content/dam/aarp/livable-communities/old-learn/research/the-united -states-of-aging-survey-2012-aarp.pdf.

The International Council on Active Aging locator of age-friendly gyms is at https://www .icaa.cc/facilitylocator/facilitylocator.php.

The data from eMarketer on seniors' online shopping can be found at https://www-statista -com.proxy.library.upenn.edu/statistics/868862/online-shopping-buying-related -activities-internet-users. The data on discretionary spending are from Fung Global Retail and Technology, *The Silver Wave: Understanding the Aging Consumer*, 2016, https://www .fbicgroup.com/sites/default/files/Silver%20Wave%20The%20Aging%20Consumer%20 Report%20by%20Fung%20Global%20Retail%20Tech%20May%2023%202016_0.pdf.

The section on Philips is based on the information at the Philips Museum, https://www .philips.nl/en/a-w/philips-museum.html, as well as other online sources.

The Jennifer Jolly quotes are from her article "Best New Tech to Help Aging Parents," *USA Today*, May 11, 2014.

On Internet use and depression, see Shelia R. Cotton, George Ford, Sherry Ford, and Timothy M. Hale, "Internet Use and Depression Among Retired Older Adults in the United States," *Journals of Gerontology, Series B*, 69, no. 5 (September 2014): 763–771. The quotes by Annena McCleskey are from Robin Erb, "Teaching Seniors to Use Internet Cuts Depression Risk," *USA Today*, April 22, 2014.

The section on Rendever is based on Gökay Abacı, "Reconnecting the Elderly with the Joys of Everyday Life Through Virtual Technology," *Medium*, August 8, 2018, https://medium.com /@MassChallengeHT/reconnecting-the-elderly-with-the-joys-of-everyday-life-through -virtual-reality-277bf957483e. On exoskeletons, see Jonas Pulver, "An Ageing Japan Looks to Mechanical Exoskeletons for the Elderly," *World Weekly*, February 4, 2016.

The study on price-to-earnings ratios in the U.S. equity markets is Zheng Liu and Mark M. Spiegel, "Boomer Retirement: Headwinds for U.S. Equity Markets?," FRBSF Economic Letter 2011-26, Federal Reserve Bank of San Francisco, August 22, 2011, http://www.frbsf.org /publications/economics/letter/2011/el2011-26.html.

The quotes by Lau, Kotansky, Flax, and Tischler are from Penny Crosman, "6 Fintechs Targeting Seniors and Their Families," *American Banker*, June 20, 2018.

On seniors as entrepreneurs, see Lauren Smiley, "Late-Stage Startup," *MIT Technology Review*, September–October 2019; Roger St. Pierre, "How Older Entrepreneurs Can Turn Age to Their Advantage," *Entrepreneur*, May 26, 2017.

On financial abuse of seniors, see Sara Zeff Geber, "Hot Tech Solutions to Keep Older Adults Safe from Financial Abuse," *Forbes*, April 23, 2019; Victoria Sackett, "New Law Targets Elder Financial Abuse," AARP, May 24, 2018, https://www.aarp.org/politics-society/government -elections/info-2018/congress-passes-safe-act.html. On EverSafe, see Financial Solutions Lab, "EverSafe," http://finlab.finhealthnetwork.com/challenges/2017/eversafe.

The quotes from Collinson and Weinstock are from Kenneth Terrell, "Why Working After Retirement Works," AARP, August 13, 2018, https://www.aarp.org/work/working-at-50 -plus/info-2018/why-work-after-retirement.html.

On the intergenerational teams at BMW, see Helen Dennis, "The HR Challenges of an Ageing Workforce," *HR Magazine*, February 16, 2016; Robert M. McCann, "Aging and Organizational Communication," *Oxford Research Encyclopedias: Communication*, August 2017, doi: 10.1093/acrefore/9780190228613.013.472.

The different views about millennials appear in Jean Twenge, *Generation Me: Why Today's Young Americans Are More Confident, Assertive, Entitled—and More Miserable than Ever Before* (New York: Free Press, 2006); *PR Newswire*, October 20, 2016; William Strauss and Neil Howe, *Millennials Rising: The Next Great Generation* (New York: Vintage Original, 2000); David Burstein, *Fast Future: How the Millennial Generation Is Shaping Our World* (Boston: Beacon Press, 2013); Eric Hoover, "The Millennial Muddle," *Chronicle of Higher Education*, October 11, 2009; Jia Tolentino, "Where Millennials Come From," *New Yorker*, November 27, 2017; Council of Economic Advisers, *15 Economic Facts About Millennials*, October 2014, https://obamawhitehouse.archives.gov/sites/default/files/docs/millennials _report.pdf; World Values Survey, http://www.worldvaluessurvey.org/WVSContents.jsp ?CMSID=Findings; Kathleen Shaputis, *The Crowded Nest Syndrome* (New York: Clutter Fairy, 2004).

On millennials and savings, see Josh Zumbrun, "Younger Generation Faces a Savings Deficit," *Wall Street Journal*, November 9, 2014; Bank of America, *2018 Better Money Habits Millennial Report*, https://bettermoneyhabits.bankofamerica.com/content/dam/bmh/pdf/ar6vnln9 -boa-bmh-millennial-report-winter-2018-final2.pdf.

On Generation Z, see Varkey Foundation, "Generation Z," January 2017, https://www .varkeyfoundation.org/what-we-do/policy-research/generation-z-global-citizenship -survey.

On Chinese seniors, see Chong Koh Ping, "China's Elderly: Old and Left Behind," *Straits Times*, October 28, 2017; Jieyu Liu, "Ageing, Migration, and Familial Support in Rural China," *Geoforum* 51 (January 2014): 305–312.

On the nursing home dorm, see Tiffany R. Jansen, "The Nursing Home That's Also a Dorm," Citylab, October 2, 2015, https://www.citylab.com/equity/2015/10/the-nursing-home -thats-also-a-dorm/408424.

The quote by Levine comes from Bridey Heing, *Critical Perspectives on Millennials* (New York: Enslow, 2018), 23.

The Wired-Pfizer project on aging can be found at "The Future of Getting Old: Rethinking Old Age," *Wired*, April 2018, https://www.wired.com/brandlab/2018/04/the-future-of -getting-old.

CHAPTER 3: KEEPING UP WITH THE SINGHS AND THE WANGS

All websites were last accessed on August 29, 2019.

Margaret Halsey's views on the middle class are from her book *The Folks at Home* (New York: Simon & Schuster, 1952).

The story of the Tata Nano is recounted in "Ratan Tata Hands Over First Three Nano Cars to Customers," *Economic Times*, July 17, 2009; Saurabh Sharma, "How a Scooter on a Rainy Day Turned into Ratan Tata's Dream Project Nano," *Business Today*, April 14, 2017; Kamalika Ghosh, "It's Time to Say Ta-Ta to the World's Cheapest Car," *Quartz*, July 13, 2018. On the success of the Weber-Stephen barbecue in India, see Dave Sutton, "8 Common Mistakes When Expanding into Emerging Markets," TopRight, April 20, 2017, https:// www.toprightpartners.com/insights/8-common-mistakes-expanding-emerging-markets;

Natasha Geiling, "The Evolution of American Barbecue," *Smithsonian.com*, July 18, 2013; Shrabonti Bagchi and Anshul Dhamija, "Licence to Grill: India Takes to the Barbecue," *Times of India*, November 18, 2011.

The data on the purchasing power of the middle class around the world come from Homi Kharas, "The Unprecedented Expansion of the Global Middle Class," Brookings Institution, February 2017, https://www.brookings.edu/wp-content/uploads/2017/02/global_20170228 _global-middle-class.pdf. The comparison of sales during Singles Day, Black Friday, and Cyber Monday can be found in Niall McCarthy, "Singles' Day Sets Another Sales Record," Statista, November 12, 2018, https://www.statista.com/chart/16063/gmv-for-alibaba-on -singles-day.

The Charles Dickens quote is from a letter to William C. Macready dated October 1855, http://www.victorianweb.org/authors/dickens/ld/bezrucka1.html. The George Orwell quote is from the last paragraph of *The Road to Wigan Pier*, http://gutenberg.net.au /ebooks02/0200391.txt. The Clive Bell quote is from Clive Crook, "The Middle Class," *Bloomberg*, March 2, 2017, https://www.bloomberg.com/quicktake/middle-class. The J. K. Rowling quote is from https://www.stylist.co.uk/people/life-according-to-jk-rowling -harry-potter-books/18793. On Homer Simpson's economic status, see "Homer Simpson: An Economic Analysis," posted by Vox on YouTube on September 16, 2018, https://youtu.be/ 9D420SOmL6U.

The Margaret Halsey quote is from *The Folks at Home* (New York: Simon & Schuster, 1952), and the Gertrude Stein quote is from *Three Lives* (New York: Pocket Books, 2003), 250.

The idea of conformity was tested by Damon J. Phillips and Ezra W. Zukerman in "Middle-Status Conformity: Theoretical Restatement and Empirical Demonstration in Two Markets," *American Journal of Sociology* 107, no. 2 (September 2001).

The study on breaking the law is P. Piff et al., "Higher Social Class Predicts Increased Unethical Behavior," *Proceedings of the National Academy of Sciences of the United States of America*, 109, no. 11 (2012): 4086–4091.

The story of Zhou Yuanyan appeared in David Pilling, "Asia: The Rise of the Middle Class," *Financial Times*, January 4, 2011, and the story of John Monday is in Norimitsu Onishi, "Nigeria Goes to the Mall," *New York Times*, January 5, 2016.

The Deloitte study, "Africa: A 21st Century View," can be found at https://www2.deloitte.com /content/dam/Deloitte/ng/Documents/consumer-business/the-deloitte-consumer-review -africa-a-21st-century-view.pdf, and the Brand Africa rankings at http://www.brandafrica .net/Rankings.aspx.

Data on patenting can be found in World Intellectual Property Organization, "World Intellectual Property Indicators 2017," 12, http://www.wipo.int/edocs/pubdocs/en/wipo_pub _941_2017.pdf.

The story of the Hooker Furniture Corporation is recounted in Jason Margolis, "North Carolina's Fight to Keep Its Foothold on Furniture," *The World*, May 2, 2018, https://www.pri.org /stories/2018-05-02/north-carolina-s-fight-keep-its-foothold-furniture. Other data come from Hooker Furniture, "Creating Opportunities: 2018 Annual Report," http://investors .hookerfurniture.com/static-files/3551b785-4637-4d55-a5b7-8221c1b15164.

The Pew Study, "The American Middle Class Is Losing Ground," can be found at http://www .pewsocialtrends.org/2015/12/09/the-american-middle-class-is-losing-ground.

The sales data for Spotify can be found at the company's IPO filing, https://www.sec.gov /Archives/edgar/data/1639920/000119312518063434/d494294df1.htm. The data on Netflix are from Louis Brennan, "How Netflix Expanded to 190 Countries in 7 Years," *Harvard Business Review*, October 12, 2018; Manish Singh, "Netflix Will Roll Out a Lower-Priced Subscription Plan in India," TechCrunch, July 17, 2019, https://techcrunch.com/2019/07 /17/netflix-lower-price-india-plan; and P. R. Sanjai, Lucas Shaw, and Sheryl Tian Tong Lee, "Netflix's Next Big Market Is Already Crowded with Cheaper Rivals," *Economic Times*, July 20, 2019, https://economictimes.indiatimes.com/industry/media/entertainment /media/netflixs-next-big-market-is-already-crowded-with-cheaper-rivals/articleshow /70287704.cms.

The examples of the flip-flops of American firms around the world are from "10 Successful American Businesses That Have Failed Overseas," International Business Degree Guide, September 12, 2013, https://www.internationalbusinessguide.org/10-successful-american -businesses-that-have-failed-overseas.

The stories and quotes about the indulgent behavior of young Chinese consumers are from Yiling Pan, "Why Chinese Millennials Are Willing to Max Out Their Cards for Luxury Goods," originally published on January 2, 2019, in *Jing Daily*, and available in English from https://www.scmp.com/magazines/style/people-events/article/2178689/can-chinas-debt -ridden-millennial-and-gen-z-shoppers; and from Stella Yifan Xie, Shan Li, and Julie Wernau, "Young Chinese Spend Like Americans—and Take on Worrisome Debt," *Wall Street Journal*, August 29, 2019.

The China/U.S. recycling woes are covered in Cassandra Profita, "Recycling Chaos in U.S. as China Bans 'Foreign Waste,'" *Morning Edition*, NPR, December 9, 2017, https://www.npr .org/2017/12/09/568797388/recycling-chaos-in-u-s-as-china-bans-foreign-waste; Sara Kiley Watson, "China Has Refused to Recycle the West's Plastics. What Now?," NPR, June 28, 2018, https://www.npr.org/sections/goatsandsoda/2018/06/28/623972937/china -has-refused-to-recycle-the-wests-plastics-what-now; and Amy L. Brooks, Shunli Wang, and Jenna R. Jambeck, "The Chinese Import Ban and Its Impact on Global Plastic Waste Trade," *ScienceAdvances* 4, no. 6 (2018), http://advances.sciencemag.org/content/4/6 /eaat0131.

The Reddit posts can be found at https://www.reddit.com/r/jobs/comments/6e6p3n/is_it _really_that_hard_to_find_a_job_as_a. The OECD study is *Under Pressure: The Squeezed Middle Class* (Paris: OECD Publishing, 2019). Quotes are from 26, 57, and 69.

Patrick Coleman's piece appeared as "America's Middle-Class Parents Are Working Harder for Less," Fatherly, May 15, 2019, https://www.fatherly.com/love-money/american-middle -class-parents-cant-afford-kids.

The Buffalo recovery is discussed in David Russell Schilling, "Buffalo: The Best Designed & Planned City in the United States," Industry Tap, January 25, 2015, http://www.industrytap .com/buffalo-best-designed-planned-city-united-states/26019; Courtney Kenefick, "Buffalo, New York, Is Staging a Comeback," *Surface*, June 26, 2017, https://www.surfacemag .com/articles/architecture-buffalo-newyork-urban-renewal; David A. Stebbins, "Buffalo's Comeback," Urbanland (blog), Urban Land Institute, October 17, 2014, https://urbanland .uli.org/development-business/buffalos-comeback; and Jesse McKinley, "Cuomo's 'Buffalo Billion': Is New York Getting Its Money's Worth?," *New York Times*, July 2, 2018. The Brookings study by Alan Berube and Cecile Murray, "Renewing America's Economic Promise Through Older Industrial Cities," April 2018, can be found at https://www.brookings.edu /wp-content/uploads/2018/04/2018-04_brookings-metro_older-industrial-cities_full -report-berube_murray_-final-version_af4-18.pdf#page=16.

Daniel Raff's article appeared as "Wage Determination Theory and the Five-Dollar Day at Ford," *Journal of Economic History* 48, no. 2 (June 1988): 387–399. John Dos Passos, *The Big Money* (New York: New American Library, 1979), was originally published in 1936; the quote is on page 73. The material from *The Henry Ford* can be found at https://www .thehenryford.org/explore/blog/fords-five-dollar-day. On the $15 wage at Amazon, see Louise Matsakis, "Why Amazon Really Raised Its Minimum Wage to $15," *Wired*, October 2, 2018. Nathan Heller's "Who Really Stands to Win from Universal Basic Income?" appeared in *The New Yorker*, July 9–16, 2018.

The results of the Johnson administration pilot on a negative income tax are summarized by Jodie T. Allen in "Negative Income Tax," *Encyclopedia of Economics*, http://www.econlib.org /library/Enc1/NegativeIncomeTax.html.

The quotes and studies on universal basic income come from Catherine Clifford, "Why Everyone Is Talking About Free Cash Handouts—an Explainer on Universal Basic Income," CNBC, June 27, 2019, https://www.cnbc.com/2019/06/27/free-cash-handouts-what-is -universal-basic-income-or-ubi.html. The National Bureau for Economic Research study on Alaska is Damon Jones and Ioana Elena Marinescu, "The Labor Market Impacts of Universal and Permanent Cash Transfers: Evidence from the Alaska Permanent Fund," NBER Working Paper No. w24312, February 2018. The more pessimistic study is Hilary W. Hoynes and Jesse Rothstein, "Universal Basic Income in the U.S. and Advanced Countries," NBER Working Paper No. 25538, February 2019. The study of the social effects of the Alaska dividend is Mouhcine Chettabi, "What Do We Know about the Effects of the Alaska Permanent Fund Dividend?," Institute of Social and Economic Research, University of Alaska Anchorage, May 20, 2019, https://pubs.iseralaska.org/media/a25fa4fc-7264-4643-ba46-1280f329f33a /2019_05_20-EffectsOfAKPFD.pdf.

CHAPTER 4: SECOND SEX NO MORE?

All websites were last accessed on September 6, 2019.

Margaret Atwood's speech at *Variety*'s Power of Women luncheon in 2018 can be found at https://variety.com/2018/tv/features/margaret-atwood-power-of-women-handmaids-tale -1202751729.

The data on women's social and economic status used in this chapter include Sarah Jane Glynn, "Breadwinning Mothers Are Increasingly the U.S. Norm," Center for American Progress, 2016, https://www.americanprogress.org/issues/women/reports/2016/12/19/295203 /breadwinning-mothers-are-increasingly-the-u-s-norm; Capgemini and RBC Wealth Management, *World Wealth Report*, 2014, https://worldwealthreport.com/wp-content/uploads /sites/7/2018/10/2014-World-Wealth-Report-English.pdf; Equal Measures 2030, "Harnessing the Power of Data for Gender Equality: Introducing the EM2030 SDG Gender Index," 2019, https://data.em2030.org/2019-global-report; Alexandre Tanzi, "U.S. Women Outpacing Men In Higher Education," Bloomberg, August 6, 2018, https://www.bloomberg .com/news/articles/2018-08-06/u-s-women-outpacing-men-in-higher-education-demo graphic-trends.

The Harvard-Yale Study by Neil G. Bennett, David E. Bloom, and Patricia H. Craig appeared as "The Divergence of Black and White Marriage Patterns," *American Journal of Sociology* 95, no. 3 (November 1989): 692–722. The article that set off the storm was written by Lisa Marie Petersen, "They're Falling in Love Again, Say Marriage Counselors," *Advocate* (Stamford, CT), February 14, 1986, A1 and A12. The *Newsweek* cover feature "The Marriage Crunch" appeared in the June 2, 1986, issue. A critical review of the controversy was written by Andrew Cherlin, "A Review: The Strange Career of the 'Harvard-Yale' Study," *Public Opinion Quarterly* 54, no. 1 (1990): 117–124.

The statistics on consumption, saving, and investing by gender are from "Sales Share of the Luxury Goods Market," https://www.statista.com/statistics/246146/sales-of-the-luxury -goods-market-worldwide-by-gender; S. A. Grossbard and A. Marvao Pereira, "Will Women Save More than Men? A Theoretical Model of Savings and Marriage," Working Paper No. 3146, Ifo Institute for Economic Research, Munich, 2010; Gary Charness and Uri Gneezy, "Strong Evidence for Gender Differences in Risk Taking," *Journal of Economic Behavior and Organization* 83, no. 1 (2012): 50–58.

The divergent experiences of women like Groff and Scanlon are from Quoctrung Bui and Claire Cain Miller, "The Age That Women Have Babies," *New York Times*, August 4, 2018. The anonymous single mother is featured in Mike Dang, "A Conversation with a Single Mom Living on $40,000 a Year," Billfold, April 22, 2013, https://www.thebillfold.com/2013/04/a -conversation-with-a-single-mom-living-on-40000-a-year. The information on divorces comes from Pamela J. Smock, Wendy D. Manning, and Sanjiv Gupta, "The Effect of Marriage and Divorce on Women's Economic Well-Being," *American Sociological Review* 64, no. 6 (December 1999): 794–812; Jay L. Zagorsky, "Marriage and Divorce's Impact on Wealth," *Journal of Sociology* 41, no. 4 (2005): 406–424.

The stories and data about teenage mothers are from CDC, "About Teen Pregnancy," https:// www.cdc.gov/teenpregnancy/about/index.htm; Jamie Rush as told to Debra Immergut, "My Life as a Teen Mom," *Parents*, https://www.parents.com/parenting/dynamics/single -parenting/my-life-as-a-teenage-mom; Kevin Ryan and Tina Kelley, "Out of the Shelter: How One Homeless Teenage Mother Built a Life of Her Own," *Atlantic*, November 16, 2012; Paul Heroux, "Two Stories of Homeless, Teenage Mothers," *Huffington Post*, July 9, 2016, https://www.huffingtonpost.com/paul-heroux/homeless-teenage-mothers_b_7758958 .html; Poverty USA, "Facts: The Population of Poverty USA," https://povertyusa.org/facts.

On childless women and men, see U.S. Census Bureau, "Childlessness Rises for Women in Their Early 30s," May 3, 2017, https://www.census.gov/newsroom/blogs/random-samplings /2017/05/childlessness_rises.html; Lindsay M. Monte and Brian Knop, "Men's Fertility and Fatherhood: 2014," Current Population Reports, P70-162, June 2019, https://www.census .gov/content/dam/Census/library/publications/2019/demo/P70-162.pdf; Claire Cain Miller, "They Didn't Have Children, and Most Said They Don't Have Regrets," *New York Times*, July 23, 2018; Sian Cain, "Women Are Happier Without Children or a Spouse, Says Happiness Expert," *Guardian*, May 25, 2019; Jennifer Glass, Robin W. Simon, and Matthew A. Anderson, "Parenthood and Happiness," *American Journal of Sociology* 122, no. 3 (November 2016): 886–929.

On underage wives and mothers, see Girls Not Brides, "Child Marriage Around the World," https://www.girlsnotbrides.org/where-does-it-happen; Office of the High Commissioner on Human Rights, "Ending Forced Marriage Worldwide," November 21, 2013, https://www .ohchr.org/EN/NewsEvents/Pages/EnforcedMarriages.aspx; United Nations Population Fund, "Female Genital Mutilation," https://www.unfpa.org/female-genital-mutilation.

On women and entrepreneurship, see Ester Boserup, *Woman's Role in Economic Development* (London: Earthscan, 1970); UNIFEM, *Annual Report 2009–2010* (New York: United Nations Development Fund for Women, 2010), with Clark's quote appearing on page 3; Global Entrepreneurship Monitor, https://www.gemconsortium.org. The stories of Kisyombe,

Sambo, Fahmy, Wu, Dionne, Roa, Kasuri, Kkubana, and Zamora are recounted in Mauro F. Guillén, ed., *Women Entrepreneurs: Inspiring Stories from Emerging Economies and Developing Countries* (New York: Routledge, 2013). The World Bank Study on the legal status of women is *Women, Business, and the Law* (Washington, DC: World Bank, 2010).

The discussion and quotes about work and family balance are based on "5 Women, 5 Work-Life Balance Tales," *Forbes*, May 29, 2013; "If I Think about My Money Problems Too Much, I'll Miss My Babies Growing Up," *HuffPost*, December 6, 2017, https://www.huffpost.com /entry/helen-bechtol-working-poor_n_4748631?utm_hp_ref=%40working_poor; Katie Johnston, "The Working Poor Who Fight to Live on $10 an Hour," *Boston Globe*, August 17, 2014; Adrienne Green, "The Job of Staying Home," *Atlantic*, September 30, 2016; M. Bertrand, C. Goldin, and L. F. Katz, "Dynamics of the Gender Gap for Young Professionals in the Financial and Corporate Sectors," *American Economic Journal*, July 2010, 228–255; Emma Johnson, "You Cannot Afford to Be a SAHM," June 20, 2019, https://www .wealthysinglemommy.com/you-cannot-afford-to-be-a-sahm-mom; Motoko Rich, "Japan's Working Mothers," *New York Times*, February 2, 2019; Wendy J. Casper et al., "The Jingle-Jangle of Work-Nonwork Balance," *Journal of Applied Psychology* 103, no. 2 (2018): 182–214; Nancy Rothbard, Katherine W. Phillips, and Tracy L. Dumas, "Managing Multiple Roles: Family Policies and Individuals' Desires for Segmentation," *Organization Science* 16, no. 3 (2005): 243–248; Gøsta Esping-Andersen, *Social Foundations of Postindustrial Economies* (Oxford: Oxford University Press, 1999). The story of Ancharya is from Mauro F. Guillén, ed., *Women Entrepreneurs: Inspiring Stories from Emerging Economies and Developing Countries* (New York: Routledge, 2013).

The section on changing rates of mortality by gender due to work is based on United Nations, World Population Prospects, 2019 Revision, https://population.un.org/wpp; Bertrand Desjardins, "Why Is Life Expectancy Longer for Women than It Is for Men?," *Scientific American*, August 30, 2004; Rochelle Sharpe, "Women's Longevity Falling in Some Parts of the U.S., Stress May Be Factor," Connecticut Health I-Team, November 12, 2012, http://c-hit .org/2012/11/12/womens-longevity-falling-in-some-parts-of-u-s-stress-may-be-factor; Irma T. Elo et al., "Trends in Non-Hispanic White Mortality in the United States by Metropolitan-Nonmetropolitan Status and Region, 1990–2016," *Population and Development Review*, 2019, 1–35; Arun S. Hendi, "Trends in Education-Specific Life Expectancy, Data Quality, and Shifting Education Distributions: A Note on Recent Research," *Demography* 54, no. 3 (2017): 1203–1213; Monica Potts, "What's Killing Poor White Women?," *American Prospect*, September 3, 2013.

On the glass ceiling, see Justin Wolfers, "Fewer Women Run Big Companies than Men Named John," *New York Times*, March 2, 2015. The data on the proportions of women in business and in politics are from OECD, "Gender Equality," https://www.oecd.org/gender; ILO, *Women in Business and Management: Gaining Momentum* (Geneva: ILO, 2015), https://www .ilo.org/wcmsp5/groups/public/—dgreports/—dcomm/—publ/documents/publication /wcms_316450.pdf. The quote from Laura Liswood can be found at https://www.goodreads .com/quotes/159719-there-s-no-such-thing-as-a-glass-ceiling-for-women.

On Thatcher and Merkel, see Judith Baxter, "How to Beat the Female Leadership Stereotypes," *Guardian*, December 9, 2013; Daniel Fromson, "The Margaret Thatcher Soft-Serve Myth," *New Yorker*, April 9, 2013; "Nicknames of Margaret Thatcher," Searching in History (blog), https://searchinginhistory.blogspot.com/2014/04/nicknames-of-margaret-thatcher.html; Helen Walters, "Ban the Word Bossy. Sheryl Sandberg Lights Up TEDWomen 2013," *TED Blog*, December 5, 2013, https://blog.ted.com/sheryl_sandberg_tedwomen2013; "Americans No Longer Prefer Male Boss to Female Boss," Gallup News, November 16, 2017, https:// news.gallup.com/poll/222425/americans-no-longer-prefer-male-boss-female-boss.aspx.

Rosabeth M. Kanter's theory was first laid out in her article "Some Effects of Proportions on Group Life: Skewed Sex Ratios and Responses to Token Women," *American Journal of Sociology* 82, no. 5 (March 1977): 965–990.

The advice in magazines for Chinese women is summarized by Roseann Lake, "China: A Wife Less Ordinary," *The Economist 1843*, April–May 2018, https://www.1843magazine.com /features/a-wife-less-ordinary. Saudi women's automobile preferences are discussed in Margherita Stancati, "What Saudi Women Drivers Want: Muscle Cars," *Wall Street Journal*, July 18, 2018.

Recent research documenting the impact of more women in positions of power on levels of corruption and violence include Chandan Kumar Jha and Sudipta Sarangi, "Women and Corruption: What Positions Must They Hold to Make a Difference?," *Journal of Economic Behavior and Organization* 151 (July 2018): 219–233; C. E. DiRienzo, "The Effect of Women in Government on Country-Level Peace," *Global Change, Peace and Security* 31, no. 1 (2019): 1–18; Naomi Hossein, Celestine Nyamu Musembi, and Jessica Hughes, "Corruption, Accountability and Gender," United Nations Development Programme, 2010, https://www .undp.org/content/dam/aplaws/publication/en/publications/womens-empowerment /corruption-accountability-and-gender-understanding-the-connection/Corruption -accountability-and-gender.pdf.

On the impact of climate change on women and children, see WHO, *Gender, Climate Change, and Health* (Geneva: WHO, 2014), https://www.who.int/globalchange/GenderClimate ChangeHealthfinal.pdf.

CHAPTER 5: CITIES DROWN FIRST

All websites last accessed on September 12, 2019.

The statistics on cities, urban areas, and climate change are from United Nations, "World Urbanization Prospects 2018," https://population.un.org/wup; Rohinton Emmanuel, "How to Make a Big Difference to Global Warming—Make Cities Cooler," The Conversation, February 9, 2015, http://theconversation.com/how-to-make-a-big-difference-to -global-warming-make-cities-cooler-37250; Laura Parker, "Sea Level Rise Will Flood Hundreds of Cities in the Near Future," *National Geographic*, July 12, 2017, https://news .nationalgeographic.com/2017/07/sea-level-rise-flood-global-warming-science; Jonathan Watts, "The Three-Degree World: The Cities That Will be Drowned by Global Warming," *Guardian*, November 3, 2017; John Englander, "Top 10 Sinking Cities in the World," January 7, 2018, http://www.johnenglander.net/sea-level-rise-blog/top-10-sinking-cities-in -the-world.

The Wouters quote is from Larry O'Hanlon, "Heat Stress Escalates in Cities Under Global Warming," American Geophysical Union, September 8, 2017, https://phys.org/news/2017 -09-stress-escalates-cities-global.html.

The United Nations documents about climate change are at https://www.un.org/en/sections /issues-depth/climate-change. Its impact on archeology is discussed by Nick Paumgarten, "An Archeological Space Oddity," *New Yorker*, July 8–15, 2019.

The Dickens quote is from a letter to William C. Macready dated October 1855, http://www .victorianweb.org/authors/dickens/ld/bezrucka1.html.

The data on rich and poor in cities come from *World Ultra Wealth Report 2018*, WealthX, 2018, https://www.wealthx.com/report/world-ultra-wealth-report-2018; Michael Savage,

"Richest 1% on Target to Own Two-Thirds of All Wealth by 2030," *Guardian*, April 7, 2018; Economic Analysis Division, Census and Statistics Department, *Hong Kong Poverty Situation Report 2016* (Hong Kong: Government of the Hong Kong Special Administrative Region, 2017), https://www.povertyrelief.gov.hk/eng/pdf/Hong_Kong_Poverty _Situation_Report_2016(2017.11.17).pdf.

On poverty in the United States, see Allan Mallach, *The Divided City: Poverty and Prosperity in Urban America* (Washington, DC: Island Press, 2018); Barbara Raab, "Poverty in America: Telling the Story," Talk Poverty, May 21, 2014, https://talkpoverty.org/2014/05/21/raab; Poverty USA, "Facts: The Population of Poverty USA," https://povertyusa.org/facts; Leon Dash, "Rosa Lee's Story," *Washington Post*, September 18–25, 1994, https://www .washingtonpost.com/wp-srv/local/longterm/library/rosalee/backgrnd.htm.

The Gatsby quote is in chapter 9 of F. Scott Fitzgerald, *The Great Gatsby*, online edition, https://ebooks.adelaide.edu.au/f/fitzgerald/f_scott/gatsby/contents.html. The Thorstein Veblen quote is from chapter 4 of *The Theory of the Leisure Class*, online edition, http://www .gutenberg.org/files/833/833-h/833-h.htm#link2HCH0004.

On obesity, see Sarah Catherine Walpole et al., "The Weight of Nations: An Estimation of Adult Human Biomass," *BMC Public Health* 12, article no. 439 (2012); WHO, "Obesity," https:// www.who.int/topics/obesity/en; OECD, *Obesity Update 2017*, https://www.oecd.org/els /health-systems/Obesity-Update-2017.pdf; National Institute of Diabetes and Digestive and Kidney Diseases, "Overweight and Obesity Statistics," August 2017, https://www.niddk.nih .gov/health-information/health-statistics/overweight-obesity; "Why the Pacific Islands Are the Most Obese Nations in the World," Healthcare Global, April 21, 2015, https://www .healthcareglobal.com/hospitals/why-pacific-islands-are-most-obese-nations-world.

Statistics on social media usage are from "Digital in 2019," We Are Social, https://wearesocial .com/global-digital-report-2019.

The ideas about small changes that lead to big results are from Daniel F. Chambliss, "The Mundanity of Excellence: An Ethnographic Report on Stratification and Olympic Swimmers," *Sociological Theory* 7, no. 1 (1989): 70–86; Richard H. Thaler and Cass R. Sunstein, *Nudge: Improving Decisions About Health, Wealth, and Happiness* (New Haven, CT: Yale University Press, 2008); Olivier Poirier-Leroy, "Mary T. Meagher: Success Is Ordinary," Your Swim Book, https://www.yourswimlog.com/mary-t-meagher-success-is-ordinary.

The section on water is based on "Water: Scarcity, Excess, and the Geopolitics of Allocation," Lauder Institute, Wharton School, University of Pennsylvania, 2016, https://lauder .wharton.upenn.edu/life-at-lauder/santander-globalization-trendlab-2016; Willa Paterson, et al., "Water Footprint of Cities," *Sustainability* 7 (2015): 8461–8490; UN–Water Decade Programme on Advocacy and Communication, "Water and Cities: Facts and Figures," 2010, https://www.un.org/waterforlifedecade/swm_cities_zaragoza_2010/pdf/facts_and _figures_long_final_eng.pdf; *Water Security and the Global Water Agenda: A UN-Water Analytical Brief* (Hamilton, Ontario: United Nations University Institute for Water, Environment and Health, 2013); *Towards Green Growth* (Paris: OECD, 2011); *Report on Women and Water* (New Delhi: National Commission for Women, 2018), http://ncw.nic.in/pdfReports /WomenandWater.pdf; Bethany Caruso, "Women Carry More than Their Fair Share of the World's Water," Grist, July 22, 2017, https://grist.org/article/women-carry-more-than-their -fair-share-of-the-worlds-water; Kassia Binkowski, "Clean Water for a Thirsty World: Cynthia Koenig, Founder of Wello," The Good Trade, 2019, https://www.thegoodtrade.com /features/interview-series-cynthia-koenig-wello; Mary Howard, "An Idea That Holds

Water," *Trinity Reporter,* Spring 2017, https://commons.trincoll.edu/reporter-spring2017 /features/an-idea-that-holds-water; "Cynthia Koenig, Wello Water," Asia Society, April 23, 2014, https://asiasociety.org/texas/events/cynthia-koenig-wello-water.

On agriculture in cities, see Christopher D. Gore, "How African Cities Lead: Urban Policy Innovation and Agriculture in Kampala and Nairobi," *World Development* 108 (2018): 169–180; Ravindra Krishnamurthy, "Vertical Farming: Feeding the Cities of the Future?," *Permaculture News,* October 29, 2015, https://permaculturenews.org/2015/10/29 /vertical-farming-feeding-the-cities-of-the-future; Breana Noble, "Indoor Farms Give Vacant Detroit Buildings New Life," *Detroit News,* August 15, 2016; "Nigerian Entrepreneur: 'We're Farming in a Shipping Container,'" BBC, February 2, 2018, https://www.bbc .com/news/av/business-42919553/nigerian-entrepreneur-we-re-farming-in-a-shipping -container.

On the revival of Bilbao, see Herbert Muschamp, "The Miracle in Bilbao," *New York Times Magazine,* September 7, 1997; Ibon Areso, "Bilbao's Strategic Evolution," *Mas Context* 30 (2017), http://www.mascontext.com/issues/30-31-bilbao/bilbaos-strategic-evolution-the -metamorphosis-of-the-industrial-city; "The Internationalization of Spanish Companies: Ferrovial, the Rise of a Multinational," MIT, February 28, 2008, https://techtv.mit.edu /videos/16339-the-internationalization-of-spanish-companies-ferrovial-the-rise-of-a -multinational (the comment by Rafael del Pino appears at 5:09 in the video).

On the revival of Pittsburgh and other U.S. cities, see Eillie Anzilotti, "American Cities Are Reviving—But Leaving the Poor Behind," *Fast Company,* July 5, 2018; David Rotman, "From Rust Belt to Robot Belt," *MIT Technology Review,* June 18, 2018; Allan Mallach, *The Divided City: Poverty and Prosperity in Urban America* (Washington, DC: Island Press, 2018). The quote from Richard Florida's *The New Urban Crisis* (New York: Basic Books, 2017) is on page 4.

On Chattanooga, see David Eichenthal and Tracy Windeknecht, "Chattanooga, Tennessee," Metropolitan Policy Program, Brookings Institution, 2008, https://www.brookings.edu /wp-content/uploads/2016/06/200809_Chattanooga.pdf; Jason Koebler, "The City That Was Saved by the Internet," *Vice,* October 27, 2016, https://www.vice.com/en_us/article /ezpk77/chattanooga-gigabit-fiber-network; Bento J. Lobo, "The Realized Value of Fiber Infrastructure in Hamilton Country, Tennessee," Department of Finance, University of Tennessee, Chattanooga, June 18, 2015, http://ftpcontent2.worldnow.com/wrcb/pdf /091515EPBFiberStudy.pdf; Daniel T. Lewis, "A History of the Chattanooga Choo-Choo Terminal," http://lewisdt.net/index.php?option=com_content&view=article&id=77%3Aa -history-of-the-chattanooga-choo-choo-terminal-station-a-trolley&catid=39%3Ahistory -&Itemid=1.

On the culture of vibrant cities and the skills of its residents, see Saskia Sassen, *The Global City* (Princeton, NJ: Princeton University Press, 2001); Richard Florida, "Bohemia and Economic Geography," *Journal of Economic Geography* 2 (2002): 55–71; Richard Florida, "America's Leading Creative Class Cities in 2015," CityLab, April 20, 2015, https://www.citylab .com/life/2015/04/americas-leading-creative-class-cities-in-2015/390852; Richard Florida, "A New Typology of Global Cities," CityLab, October 4, 2016, https://www.citylab.com /life/2016/10/the-seven-types-of-global-cities-brookings/502994; David J. Deming, "The Growing Importance of Social Skills in the Labor Market," NBER Working Paper No. 21473, June 2017, https://www.nber.org/papers/w21473; World Values Survey, http:// www.worldvaluessurvey.org/WVSContents.jsp?CMSID=Findings.

CHAPTER 6: MORE CELLPHONES THAN TOILETS

All websites last accessed on September 21, 2019.

On the toilet, see "A Brief History of the Flush Toilet," British Association of Urological Surgeons, https://www.baus.org.uk/museum/164/the_flush_toilet; Nate Barksdale, "Who Invented the Flush Toilet?," History Channel, last updated August 22, 2018, https://www.history.com/news/who-invented-the-flush-toilet; Lina Zeldovich, "Reinventing the Toilet," Mosaic, June 19, 2017, https://mosaicscience.com/story/poo-toilet-waste-energy-madagascar-loowatt-future; Phoebe Parke, "More Africans Have Access to Cell Phone Service than Piped Water," CNN, January 19, 2016, https://www.cnn.com/2016/01/19/africa/africa-afrobarometer-infrastructure-report/index.html; United Nations University, "Greater Access to Cell Phones than Toilets in India: UN," press release, April 14, 2010, https://unu.edu/media-relations/releases/greater-access-to-cell-phones-than-toilets-in-india.html; Pramit Bhattacharya, "88% of Households in India Have a Mobile Phone," LiveMint, December 5, 2016, https://www.livemint.com/Politics/kZ7j1NQf5614UvO6WURXfO/88-of-households-in-India-have-a-mobile-phone.html.

On the history of the wristwatch, see Alexis McCrossen, *Marking Modern Times: A History of Clocks, Watches, and Other Timekeepers in American Life* (Chicago: University of Chicago Press, 2013); Michael L. Tushman and Daniel Radov, "Rebirth of the Swiss Watch Industry, 1980–1992 (A)," Harvard Business School Case 400-087, June 2000.

Schumpeter's quotes on entrepreneurship and disruption are from *Capitalism, Socialism, and Democracy* (New York: Harper & Brothers, 1942), 83.

On artificial intelligence, see Laura Geggel, "Elon Musk Says 'Humans Are Underrated,'" LiveScience, April 17, 2018, https://www.livescience.com/62331-elon-musk-humans-underrated.html; William Fifield, "Pablo Picasso: A Composite Interview," *Paris Review* 32 (Summer-Fall 1964).

On technology, robotics, and jobs, see Association for Advancing Automation, "Record Number of Robots Shipped in North America in 2018," February 28, 2019, https://www.a3automate.org/record-number-of-robots-shipped-in-north-america-in-2018; Executive Office of the President, "Artificial Intelligence, Automation, and the Economy," December 2016, https://obamawhitehouse.archives.gov/sites/whitehouse.gov/files/documents/Artificial-Intelligence-Automation-Economy.pdf; Maximiliano Dvorkin, "Jobs Involving Routine Tasks Aren't Growing," Federal Reserve Bank of St. Louis, January 4, 2016, https://www.stlouisfed.org/on-the-economy/2016/january/jobs-involving-routine-tasks-arent-growing; Michael J. Hicks and Srikant Devaraj, "Myth and Reality of Manufacturing in America," Center for Business and Economic Research, Ball State University, 2017; Mark Muro, "Manufacturing Jobs Aren't Coming Back," *MIT Technology Review*, November 18, 2016; "Automation and Anxiety," *Economist*, June 23, 2016, https://www.economist.com/news/special-report/21700758-will-smarter-machines-cause-mass-unemployment-automation-and-anxiety; Eliza Strickland, "Autonomous Robot Surgeon Bests Humans in World First," IEEE Spectrum, May 4, 2016, https://spectrum.ieee.org/the-human-os/robotics/medical-robots/autonomous-robot-surgeon-bests-human-surgeons-in-world-first; Laura Sydell, "Sometimes We Feel More Comfortable Talking to a Robot," NPR, February 24, 2018, https://www.npr.org/sections/alltechconsidered/2018/02/24/583682556/sometimes-we-feel-more-comfortable-talking-to-a-robot; Eyal Press, "The Wounds of a Drone Warrior," *New York Times*, June 13, 2018; E. Awad et al., "The Moral Machine Experiment," *Nature* 563 (November 2018): 59–64; Mauro F. Guillén and Srikar Reddy, "We Know Ethics Should Inform AI. But Which Ethics?," World Economic Forum, July 26, 2018, https://www.weforum.org/agenda/2018/07/we-know-ethics-should-inform-ai-but -which-ethics-robotics.

On 3D printing, see Tim Moore, "This Startup Is Building Houses with the World's Biggest Freeform 3D Printer," Hypepotamous, April 9, 2019, https://hypepotamus.com/companies /branch-technology; Dave Flessner, "3D Printer to Move into Branch Technology's River-side Drive Warehouse," *Times Free Press*, July 8, 2018, https://www.timesfreepress.com /news/business/aroundregion/story/2018/jul/08/branch-technology-expands-beyond -incubator3d/474370; Davide Sher, "Branch Technologies' C-FAB 3D Process Can Build Better Walls . . . on Mars," 3D Printing Media Network, February 26, 2018, https:// www.3dprintingmedia.network/branch-technologies-c-fab-3d-process-can-take-us-mars.

On projections for the Internet of Things, see Michelle Manafy, "Exploring the Internet of Things in 5 Charts," Digital Content Next, October 13, 2015, https://digitalcontentnext.org /blog/2015/10/13/exploring-the-internet-of-things-in-5-charts.

On virtual reality, see Daniel Freeman and Jason Freeman, "How Virtual Reality Could Transform Mental Health Treatment," *Psychology Today*, May 13, 2016, https://www .psychologytoday.com/us/blog/know-your-mind/201605/how-virtual-reality-could -transform-mental-health-treatment; S. M. Jung and W. H. Choi, "Effects of Virtual Reality Intervention on Upper Limb Motor Function and Activity of Daily Living in Patients with Lesions in Different Regions of the Brain," *Journal of Physical Therapy Science* 29, no. 12 (December 2017): 2103–2106; Juanita Leatham, "How VR Is Helping Children with Au-tism Navigate the World Around Them," VR Fitness Insider, June 22, 2018, https://www .vrfitnessinsider.com/how-vr-is-helping-children-with-autism-navigate-the-world-around -them.

On nanotechnologies, see "The Price of Fast Fashion" (editorial), *Nature Climate Change* 8, no. 1 (2018); Jelena Bozic, "Nano Insulation Materials for Energy Efficient Buildings," *Contemporary Materials* 6, no. 2 (2015): 149–159; Amy Yates, "Potential Breakthrough in Cancer-Fighting Nanomedicine," National Foundation for Cancer Research, June 19, 2018, https://www.nfcr.org/blog/potential-breakthrough-cancer-fighting-nanomedicine; "MIT Programmable Material Adapts to Temperature Just Like Human Skin," Design Boom, February 13, 2017, https://www.designboom.com/technology/mit-programmable-material -adapts-to-tempterature-02-13-2017; Michael Alba, "The Promise and Peril of Programma-ble Matter," Engineering.com, May 24, 2017, https://www.engineering.com/DesignerEdge /DesignerEdgeArticles/ArticleID/14967/The-Promise-and-Peril-of-Programmable -Matter.aspx.

On printed versus e-books, see Edward Tenner, "Why People Stick with Outdated Technol-ogy," *Scientific American*, November 24, 2015; Craig Mod, "Digital Books Stagnate in Closed, Dull Systems, While Printed Books Are Shareable, Lovely and Enduring. What Comes Next?," *Aeon*, October 1, 2015, https://aeon.co/essays/stagnant-and-dull-can-digital -books-ever-replace-print; Gregory Bufithis, "Books vs. E-Books," July 4, 2016, http:// www.gregorybufithis.com/2016/07/04/books-vs-e-books-lets-not-lose-sight-of-the -main-goal-diverse-reading-and-increased-literacy; Ferris Jabr, "The Reading Brain in the Digital Age: The Science of Paper Versus Screens," *Scientific American*, April 11, 2013; Pew Research Center, "Book Reading 2016," https://www.pewinternet.org/2016/09/01/book -reading-2016. The video of the one-year-old girl is at "A Magazine Is an iPad That Does Not

Work.m4v, posted by UserExperienceWOrks, October 6, 2011, https://www.youtube.com /watch?v=aXV-yaFmQNk. The statistics are from Amy Watson, "Book Formats in the U.S.," Statista, January 11, 2019, https://www.statista.com/topics/3938/book-formats-in -the-us.

On e-book platforms and children's education, see "Revolutionising eBook Access in South African Schools," Montegray Capital, February 2015, https://www.montegray.com/our-e -learning-solution-revolutionises-ebook-access-in-south-african-schools; "Worldreader," Center for Education Innovations, https://educationinnovations.org/program/worldreader.

On structural inertia and leap-frogging, see Michael Hannan, "Structural Inertia and Organi- zational Change," *American Sociological Review* 49, no. 2 (1984): 149–164; United Nations Conference on Trade and Development, *Technology and Innovation Report 2018* (Geneva: UN, 2018), https://unctad.org/en/PublicationsLibrary/tir2018_en.pdf.

Online wines sales are from Euromonitor. On the UK, see Julia Bower, "The Evolution of the UK Wine Market: From Niche to Mass-Market Appeal," *Beverages*, November 2018, https:// www.mdpi.com/2306-5710/4/4/87/pdf.

On the flywheel, see Ben Harder, "Reinventing the (Fly)Wheel," *Washington Post,* April 18, 2011.

CHAPTER 7: IMAGINE NO POSSESSIONS

All websites last accessed on September 21, 2019.

On the gig economy, see Eileen Appelbaum, Arne Kalleberg, and Hye Jin Rho, "Nonstandard Work Arrangements and Older Americans, 2005–2017," Economic Policy Institute, Febru- ary 28, 2019, https://www.epi.org/publication/nonstandard-work-arrangements-and-older -americans-2005-2017; "Run, TaskRabbit, Run: July 2030," *Economist*, July 7, 2018; Niam Yaraghi and Shamika Ravi, "The Current and Future State of the Sharing Economy," Brook- ings Institution, Impact Series No. 032017, March 2017; PwC, "The Sharing Economy," 2015, https://www.pwc.fr/fr/assets/files/pdf/2015/05/pwc_etude_sharing_economy.pdf; Brad Stone, *The Upstarts: How Uber, Airbnb, and the Killer Companies of the New Silicon Valley Are Changing the World* (New York: Little, Brown, 2017), Kindle ed., 32; Shirin Ghaffary, "The Experience Economy Will be a 'Massive Business,' According to Airbnb CEO Brian Chesky," Vox, May 30, 2018, https://www.recode.net/2018/5/30/17385910/airbnb-ceo -brian-chesky-code-conference-interview; Kari Paul, "Millennials Are Trying to Redefine What It Means to Be an American Tourist Abroad," MarketWatch, October 5, 2017, https:// www.marketwatch.com/story/what-we-can-all-learn-from-millennials-about-travel-2017 -10-04.

Yuval Noah Harari's quotes are from "Were We Happier in the Stone Age?," *Guardian*, Sep- tember 5, 2014.

On the political and social aspects of property, see Andrew G. Walder, "Transitions from State Socialism: A Property Rights Perspective," in *The Sociology of Economic Life*, ed. Mark Gra- novetter and Richard Swedberg (Boulder, CO: Westview, 2011), 510; Nathan Heller, "Is the Gig Economy Working?," *New Yorker*, May 15, 2017.

On WhatsApp, see Jillian D'Onfro, "Facebook Bought WhatsApp One Year Ago Today. Here Are 11 Quotes from Its Billionaire Cofounders," *Business Insider*, February 19, 2015, https:// www.businessinsider.com/brian-acton-jan-koum-quotes-whatsapp-2015-2#koum-on -their-no-nonsense-style-neither-of-us-has-an-ability-to-bull—10. The Zuckerberg quote is from Jillian D'Onfro, "11 Mark Zuckerberg Quotes That Show How He Built the Company That Took Over the World," *Business Insider*, January 1, 2014, https://www.businessinsider .com/best-mark-zuckerberg-quotes-2013-12?.

On the ranking and location of unicorns, see CB Insights, "The Global Unicorn Club," https://www.cbinsights.com/research-unicorn-companies.

On the culture of sharing, see Rachel Botsman, *What's Mine Is Yours: The Rise of Collaborative Consumption* (New York: HarperCollins, 2010); Caren Maio, "Forget the American Dream: For Millennials, Renting Is the American Choice," Inman, August 30, 2016, https://www.inman.com/2016/08/30/forget-the-american-dream-for-millennials-renting-is-the-american-choice/#; Enel, "Millennials: Generation (Car) Sharing," August 29, 2018, https://www.enel.com/stories/a/2018/08/millennials-sharing-economy; Blake Morgan, "NOwnership, No Problem," *Forbes*, January 2, 2019; Anjli Raval, "What Millennial Homes Will Look Like in the Future," *Financial Times*, July 30, 2018; Bernard Marr, "The Sharing Economy—What It Is, Examples, and How Big Data, Platforms and Algorithms Fuel It," *Forbes*, October 21, 2016; "Uberize," Collins Dictionary, https://www.collinsdictionary.com/us/dictionary/english/uberize; Executive Office of the President, "Artificial Intelligence, Automation, and the Economy," December 2016, https://obamawhitehouse.archives.gov/sites/whitehouse.gov/files/documents/Artificial-Intelligence-Automation-Economy.pdf; Nielsen, "Global Survey of Share Communities," 2014, https://www.nielsen.com/apac/en/press-releases/2014/global-consumers-embrace-the-share-economy/.

On the tragedy of the commons and the sharing economy, see Tad Borek, "Uber Exemplifies the Tragedy of the Commons," *Financial Times*, December 6, 2017; Arwa Mahdawi, "How to Monetise Your Home," *Guardian*, October 28, 2018; Garrett Hardin, "The Tragedy of the Commons," *Science* 162, no. 3859 (December 13, 1968): 1243–1248; Peter Cohen et al., "Using Big Data to Estimate Consumer Surplus: The Case of Uber," NBER Working Paper No. 22627, 2016, https://www.nber.org/papers/w22627; David Sloan Wilson, "The Tragedy of the Commons: How Elinor Ostrom Solved One of Life's Greatest Dilemmas," Evonomics, October 29, 2016, https://evonomics.com/tragedy-of-the-commons-elinor-ostrom.

The Adam Smith quote is from *Wealth of Nations*, chapter 2 (1776), https://www.gutenberg.org/files/3300/3300-h/3300-h.htm.

On Uber, see Andy Kessler, "Travis Kalanick: The Transportation Trustbuster," *Wall Street Journal*, January 25, 2013; Marcus Wohlsen, "Uber's Brilliant Strategy to Make Itself Too Big to Ban," *Wired*, July 8, 2014; Sheelah Kolhatkar, "At Uber, a New CEO Shifts Gears," *New Yorker*, March 30, 2018; Sam Knight, "How Uber Conquered London," *Guardian*, April 27, 2016; Christopher N. Morrison et al., "Ridesharing and Motor Vehicle Crashes in 4 US Cities: An Interrupted Time-Series Analysis," *American Journal of Epidemiology* 187, no. 2 (2018): 224–232.

On gig economy jobs, see Matt Williams, "The Evolution of American Labor: A Defense of the Gig Economy," Department of Anthropology, University of Notre Dame, April 2005, https://anthropology.nd.edu/assets/200504/williamsmatthew.pdf; Robert Reich, "The Share-the-Scraps Economy," February 2, 2015, http://robertreich.org/post/109894095095; Lawrence F. Katz and Alan B. Krueger, "The Rise and Nature of Alternative Work Arrangements in the United States, 1995–2015," https://krueger.princeton.edu/sites/default/files/akrueger/files/katz_krueger_cws_-_march_29_20165.pdf; Guy Standing, *The Precariat: The New Dangerous Class* (London: Bloomsbury, 2011); Steven Hill, "Good Riddance, Gig Economy," *Salon*, March 27, 2016; Samuel P. Fraiberger and Arun Sundararajan, "Peer-to-Peer Rental Markets in the Sharing Economy," Heartland Institute, October 6, 2015, https://www.heartland.org/publications-resources/publications/peer-to-peer-rental-markets-in

-the-sharing-economy; Juliet B. Schor, "Does the Sharing Economy Increase Inequality Within the Eighty Percent?," *Cambridge Journal of Regions, Economy, and Society* 10, no. 2 (July 2017): 263–297; Emma Plumb, "Author Insights: Diane Mulcahy on the Gig Economy," 1 Million for Work Flexibility, February 2, 2017, https://www.workflexibility.org /diane-mulcahy-gig-economy. The quotes from gig economy workers are in Schor's article.

On sharing and the class system, see Julian Brave NoiseCat, "The Western Idea of Private Property Is Flawed. Indigenous People Have It Right," *Guardian*, March 27, 2017; Jacob S. Hacker, *The Great Risk Shift* (New York: Oxford University Press, 2019). The Fishback quotes come from Hill, "Good Riddance, Gig Economy."

On the use of social media in political campaigns, see Lynda Lee Kaid, "Changing and Staying the Same: Communication in Campaign 2008," *Journalism Studies* 10 (2009): 417–423; Derrick L. Cogburn, "From Networked Nominee to Networked Nation: Examining the Impact of Web 2.0 and Social Media on Political Participation and Civic Engagement in the 2008 Obama Campaign," *Journal of Political Marketing* 10 (2011): 189–213.

On the environmental benefits of sharing, see "Sharing Is Caring," *Scientific American*, October 10, 2013; "How Green is the Sharing Economy?," Knowledge@Wharton, December 11, 2015, http://knowledge.wharton.upenn.edu/article/how-green-is-the-sharing-economy; Laura Bliss, "The Ride-Hailing Effect: More Cars, More Trips, More Miles," CityLab, October 12, 2017, https://www.citylab.com/transportation/2017/10/the-ride-hailing-effect-more-cars -more-trips-more-miles/542592; Benjamin Snyder, "Exclusive: Airbnb Says It's Saving Our World with Each Rented Room," *Fortune*, July 31, 2014; Andrew Simon, "Using Airbnb Is Greener than Staying in Hotels," Grist, July 31, 2014, https://grist.org/business -technology/using-airbnb-is-greener-than-staying-in-hotels; Martin J. Smith, "Don't Toss That Lettuce—Share It," Stanford Graduate School of Business, October 23, 2017, https:// www.gsb.stanford.edu/insights/dont-toss-lettuce-share-it; "The *Real* Sustainable Fashion Movement," Rent the Runway, https://www.renttherunway.com/sustainable-fashion?action _type=footer_link.

CHAPTER 8: MORE CURRENCIES THAN COUNTRIES

All websites last accessed on September 22, 2019.

The section on money and currencies is based on Walter Bagehot, *Lombard Street: A Description of the Money Market* (London: Henry S. King, 1873); "The Invention of Money," *New Yorker*, August 5–12, 2019; Dante Bayona, "The Fed and the 'Salvador Dalí Effect,'" Mises Institute, August 19, 2014, https://mises.org/library/fed-and-%E2%80%9Csalvador-dali -effect%E2%80%9D; Barry Eichengreen, "Number One Country, Number one Currency?," *World Economy* 36, no. 4 (2013): 363–374; Milton Friedman, *Inflation: Causes and Consequences* (New York: Asia Publishing House, 1963), 39; Milton Friedman, *There Is No Such Thing as a Free Lunch* (Chicago: Open Court, 1975); Deroy Murdock, "The Friedmans, Up Close: An Interview with Rose and Milton Friedman," *National Review*, May 11, 2001.

On the preeminence of the dollar in the global economy, see Emine Boz, Gina Gopinath, and Mikkel Plagborg-Moller, "Global Trade and the Dollar," March 31, 2018, https://scholar .harvard.edu/files/gopinath/files/global_trade_dollar_20180331.pdf; Gita Gopinath, "Dollar Dominance in Trade," Exim Bank of India, December 21, 2017, https://www.eximbankindia .in/blog/blog-content.aspx?BlogID=9&BlogTitle=Dollar%20Dominance%20in%20 Trade:%20Facts%20and%20Implications.

The Rothschilds are discussed in Michael A. Hirchubel, *Vile Acts of Evil: Banking in America* (CreateSpace Independent Publishing, 2009), 1:28.

On bitcoin, see Satoshi Nakamoto, "Bitcoin: A Peer-to-Peer Electronic Cash System" (2008), https://bitcoin.org/bitcoin.pdf; Brian Armstrong, "What Is Coinbase's Strategy?," *Medium*, June 6, 2017, https://medium.com/@barmstrong/what-is-coinbases-strategy-1c5413f6e09d; Evelyn Chang and Kayla Tausche, "Jamie Dimon Says If You're 'Stupid' Enough to Buy Bitcoin, You'll Pay the Price One Day," CNBC, October 13, 2017, https://www.cnbc.com/2017/10/13/jamie-dimon-says-people-who-buy-bitcoin-are-stupid.html; Ryan Browne, "Roubini Doubles Down on Criticisms of Crypto," CNBC, October 12, 2018, https://www.cnbc.com/2018/10/12/dr-doom-economist-nouriel-roubini-calls-crypto-stinking-cesspool.html.

On the blockchain, see European Parliament, *How Blockchain Technology Could Change Our Lives* (Strasbourg: European Parliament, 2017); Mike Orcutt, "Hate Lawyers? Can't Afford One? Blockchain Smart Contracts Are Here to Help," *MIT Technology Review*, January 11, 2019; Michael Del Castillo, "Relax Lawyers, Nick Szabo Says Smart Contracts Won't Kill Jobs," CoinDesk, last updated August 11, 2017, https://www.coindesk.com/nick-szabo-lawyers-jobs-safe-in-smart-contract-era; Jacob Pramuk, "Trump to Slap 25% Tariffs on Up to $50 Billion of Chinese Goods; China Retaliates," CNBC, June 15, 2018, https://www.cnbc.com/2018/06/15/trump-administration-to-slap-a-25-percent-tariff-on-50-billion-of-chinese-goods-threatens-more.html; Andrew Rossow, "How Can We Make Intellectual Property Rights 'Smarter' with the Blockchain?," *Forbes*, July 24, 2018; Birgit Clark, "Blockchain and IP Law: A Match Made in Crypto Heaven," *WIPO Magazine*, February 2018, https://www.wipo.int/wipo_magazine/en/2018/01/article_0005.html; Nick Ismail, "What Is Blockchain's Role in the Future of Intellectual Property?," *Information Age*, July 12, 2018; UK Government Chief Scientific Adviser, *Distributed Ledger Technology: Beyond Block Chain* (London: Government Office for Science, 2016); Nathan Heller, "Estonia, the Digital Republic," *New Yorker*, December 18–25, 2017; Matt Reynolds, "Welcome to E-stonia," *Wired*, October 26, 2016; World Bank, "eGhana Additional Financing," http://projects.worldbank.org/P093610/eghana?lang=en; Esther Nderitu Imbamba and Nancy Kimile, "A Review of Status of e-Government Implementation in Kenya," *Regional Journal of Information and Knowledge* 2, no. 2 (2017): 14–28; Sissi Cao, "Blockchain Could Improve Gun Control—But Lawmakers Hate the Idea," *Observer*, February 22, 2018; "Blockchain Could Be Key to Cracking Gun Debate," ScienceBlog, May 12, 2018, https://scienceblog.com/500871/blockchain-could-be-key-to-cracking-gun-debate; Thomas F. Heston, "A Blockchain Solution to Gun Control," PeerJ.com, November 13, 2017, https://peerj.com/preprints/3407.pdf; Matt Egan, "30% of Bank Jobs Are Under Threat," CNN Money, April 4, 2016, https://money.cnn.com/2016/04/04/investing/bank-jobs-dying-automation-citigroup/index.html; Mike Orcutt, "The World Bank Is a Verified Blockchain Booster," *MIT Technology Review*, September 13, 2018; Mike Orcutt, "The World Bank Is Betting Big on Blockchain-Based Bonds," *MIT Technology Review*, August 10, 2018; Elizabeth Woyke, "How Blockchain Can Bring Financial Services to the Poor," *MIT Technology Review*, April 18, 2017, https://www.technologyreview.com/s/604144/how-blockchain-can-lift-up-the-worlds-poor/; World Bank, "Somalia Economic Update: Rapid Growth in Mobile Money," press release, September 13, 2018, https://www.worldbank.org/en/news/press-release/2018/09/13/somalia-economic-update-rapid-growth-in-mobile-money; "Endangered Species Protection Finds Blockchain and Bitcoin Love," Bitcoin Warrior, February 22, 2018, https://bitcoinwarrior.net/2018/02/endangered-species-protection-finds-blockchain-and-bitcoin-love; Moe Levin, "Top Five Blockchain Projects That Will Save the Environment," *Medium*, March 26, 2018, https://medium.com/@kingsland/top-five-blockchain-projects-that-will-save-the

-environment-28a2d4366ec0; Kate Harrison, "Blockchain May Be the Key to a Sustainable Energy Future," *Forbes*, February 14, 2018; Lisa Walker, "This New Carbon Currency Could Make US More Climate Friendly," World Economic Forum, September 19, 2017, https://www.weforum.org/agenda/2017/09/carbon-currency-blockchain-poseidon-ecosphere; Nicola Jones, "How to Stop Data Centres from Gobbling Up the World's Electricity," *Nature*, September 12, 2018; Sean Stein Smith, "Tackling Blockchain in the Accounting Profession," *Accounting Today*, March 13, 2018.

The quotes by Jamie Dimon and Amy Webb are from Egan, "30% of Bank Jobs Are Under Threat."

CONCLUSION: LATERAL TIPS AND TRICKS TO SURVIVE 2030

All websites last accessed on September 22, 2019.

The Bezos quote about tailwinds comes from his 1997 letter to Amazon's shareholders, https://www.sec.gov/Archives/edgar/data/1018724/000119312517120198/d373368dex991.htm.

The first snapshot of a black hole was covered in, among others, Dennis Overbye, "Darkness Visible, Finally: Astronomers Capture First Ever Image of a Black Hole," *New York Times*, April 10, 2019.

The Faulkner quote is sometimes attributed to Christopher Columbus: https://www.quotery.com/quotes/one-doesnt-discover-new-lands.

The chronicle of the conquest of Mexico is by Bernal Díaz del Castillo, *The True History of the Conquest of New Spain* (New York: Penguin, 1963), first published in 1632, https://archive.org/stream/tesisnoqueprese00garcgoog/tesisnoqueprese00garcgoog_djvu.txt. Quotes are in chapters 58 and 22.

The section on Lego is based on David C. Robertson, *Brick by Brick: How LEGO Rewrote the Rules of Innovation and Conquered the Global Toy Industry* (New York: Crown Business, 2013); Mary Blackiston, "How Lego Went from Nearly Bankrupt to the Most Powerful Brand in the World," Success Agency, February 27, 2018, https://www.successagency.com/growth/2018/02/27/lego-bankrupt-powerful-brand; Lucy Handley, "How Marketing Built Lego into the World's Favorite Toy Brand," CNBC, April 27, 2018, https://www.cnbc.com/2018/04/27/lego-marketing-strategy-made-it-world-favorite-toy-brand.html; Johnny Davis, "How Lego Clicked: The Super Brand That Reinvented Itself," *Guardian*, June 4, 2017; Jeff Beer, "The Secret to Lego's Social Media Success Is in the Creative Power of Crowds," *Fast Company*, June 20, 2017; Jonathan Ringen, "How Lego Became the Apple of Toys," *Fast Company*, August 1, 2015; David Kindy, "How Lego Patents Helped Build a Toy Empire, Brick by Brick," *Smithsonian Magazine*, February 7, 2019.

Steinbeck's quote on ideas and rabbits comes from a 1947 interview: https://smallbusiness.com/monday-morning-motivation/john-steinbeck-quote-ideas-are-like-rabbits.

On Steve Jobs, see Malcolm Gladwell, "The Tweaker," *New Yorker*, November 14, 2011.

On the escalation of commitment, see Barry M. Staw, "The Escalation of Commitment: An Update and Appraisal," in *Organizational Decision Making*, ed. Zur Shapira (New York: Cambridge University Press, 1997), 191–215. The Wellington quote can be found in *The Nineteenth Century: A Monthly Review*, volume 17 (London: Kegan Paul, Trench, 1885), 905.

On options thinking, see Heidi Grant Halvorson, "Why Keeping Your Options Open Is a Really, Really Bad Idea," *Fast Company*, May 27, 2011; Hugh Courtney, "Keeping Your Options Open," *World Economic Affairs*, Winter 1999, https://www.mcgill.ca/economics/files/economics/keeping_your_options_open.pdf.

On "competition anxiety," see Nathan Davidson, "The 20 Greatest Sports Psychology Quotes of All Time," Thriveworks, August 8, 2017, https://thriveworks.com/blog/greatest-sports-psychology-quotes-of-all-time; Simon M. Rice et al., "Determinants of Anxiety in Elite Athletes: A Systematic Review and Meta-analysis." *British Journal of Sports Medicine* 53, no. 11 (2019): 722–730.

On Rapa Nui, see Jared Diamond, *Collapse* (New York: Viking, 2005); Terry Hunt and Carl Lipo, *The Statues That Walked: Unraveling the Mystery of Easter Island* (Berkeley, CA: Counterpoint, 2012), with the quotes appearing on pages 53, 92, 155, and 180; Paul Bahn and John Flenley, *Isla de Pascua, Isla de Tierra*, 4th ed. (Viña del Mar, Chile: Rapanui Press, 2018), with quotes from pages 15, 204, 235, and 257; Nicholas Casey and Josh Haner, "Easter Island Is Eroding," *New York Times*, March 15, 2018; Megan Gannon, "People of Easter Island Weren't Driven to Warfare and Cannibalism. They Actually Got Along," LiveScience, August 13, 2018, https://www.livescience.com/amp/63321-easter-island-collapse-myth.html; David Bressan, "Climate, Overpopulation and Environment—The Rapa Nui Debate," *Scientific American*, October 31, 2011.

On the revival of old technological ideas, see Ron Miller and Alex Wilhelm, "With Tech, What's Old Is New Again," TechCrunch, April 6, 2015, https://techcrunch.com/2015/04/06/with-tech-whats-old-is-new-again.

On Eugene O'Neill's quote, see his *Recklessness: It's a Great Game—The Pursuit of Happiness* (Amazon Digital Services, 2014).

INDEX